SportsDykes

Stories from On and Off the Field

Edited by Susan Fox Rogers

St. Martin's Press · New York

SPORTSDYKES

Design by Sara Stemen
Illustrations by Kris Kovick

Library of Congress Cataloging-in-Publication Data

Rogers, Susan Fox.
    Sportsdykes : stories from on and off the field / Susan Fox Rogers.
      p.   cm.
    ISBN 0-312-11072-3
      1. Lesbians and sports.   I. Title.
  II. Title: Sports dykes.
  GV708.8R64 1994
  796'.08'6643—dc20   94–90
                                      CIP

First Edition: May 1994

10 9 8 7 6 5 4 3 2 1

SPORTSDYKES

Design by Sara Stemen
Illustrations by Kris Kovick

Library of Congress Cataloging-in-Publication Data

Rogers, Susan Fox.
    Sportsdykes : stories from on and off the field /
    Susan Fox Rogers.
       p.   cm.
    ISBN 0-312-11072-3
       1. Lesbians and sports.   I. Title.
    II. Title: Sports dykes.
    GV708.8R64 1994
    796'.08'6643—dc20   94–90
                                        CIP

First Edition: May 1994

10 9 8 7 6 5 4 3 2 1

For Rebecca, who isn't a lesbian
and
Tamela, who isn't a jock

CONTENTS

ACKNOWLEDGMENTS

As with any anthology there are many people to thank: first, my editor Michael Denneny for his work as coach and referee—beyond editorial duty—and his assistants Keith Kahla and John Clark for covering all of the bases so efficiently. John Preston for his anthology advice. John Fout, Maura Shaw, and Michèle Dominy at the journal for the time to put this together. My 1993 L&T writing group. Tamela Sloan who was my best reader and decision maker, who also xeroxed and held my hand. All of the women I spoke with who gave me numbers of "X, who is a real jock," and Roxxie for publishing such a funny 'zine, *GirlJock,* which served as inspiration. And this wouldn't be a complete lesbian anthology if I didn't thank Honey Bear and Moose Cat (whose sports are hockey, soccer, and hunting) for their companionship.

ACKNOWLEDGMENTS

As with any anthology there are many people to thank: first, my editor Michael Denneny for his work as coach and referee—beyond editorial duty—and his assistants Keith Kahla and John Clark for covering all of the bases so efficiently. John Preston for his anthology advice. John Fout, Maura Shaw, and Michèle Dominy at the journal for the time to put this together. My 1993 L&T writing group. Tamela Sloan who was my best reader and decision maker, who also xeroxed and held my hand. All of the women I spoke with who gave me numbers of "X, who is a real jock," and Roxxie for publishing such a funny 'zine, *GirlJock,* which served as inspiration. And this wouldn't be a complete lesbian anthology if I didn't thank Honey Bear and Moose Cat (whose sports are hockey, soccer, and hunting) for their companionship.

INTRODUCTION

I begin this introduction with a confession: I am not a jock. From seventeen years of rock climbing I've grown a few muscles, so I've got the look of a jock, but I'm not the real thing. And I go to the gym every day but that also doesn't make me a jock, only a jock wannabe. I read and care about sports (or rather women and sports) but that doesn't make me a jock, only a jock intellectual. I am really a jock manqué, which probably makes me half a jock, but I know in my soul of souls that I am not, and never can become, a girl jock.

Girl jocks, sports dykes: if I am not one of them, who are these women?

A real girl jock has a certain feel, a *je ne sais quoi* of jockness that may be indefinable. Part of this involves a way of moving both on and off the field—you can spot a jock walking down the street, or in a bar—that exudes confidence, strength, or a don't-mess-with-me attitude. Jocks can also manage to wear basketball shoes at any occasion, and can tell a dirty joke on call. I have never been able to tell any kind of joke successfully—I forget a detail, or miss the punch line like a baseball player overrunning second base.

For those of you who, like me, doubt their jock status, this collection begins with a quiz created by Nancy Boutilier. You need not find yourself in the "Champ" category in order to read further, for in fact many of the contributors to this anthology are, along with me, just slightly better than a "Good Sport." And that is all it takes to play this game.

Though I am not a jock, I was given every possibility of becoming one, since I grew up in State College, Pennsylvania, an athletic town run by Penn State's football team. (Ironically, this is also the same university where Rene Portland, a celebrated and oft-quoted homophobe, coaches women's basketball.) Beginning in junior high school, people were obsessed with sports, competing and winning: and we always won. The junior and high school teams were dominated by the blond popular girls who dated boys on the football team. Certainly there were dykes-to-be on the field hockey team or shooting hoops, but they were more than invisible in this popularity contest.

I happily checked out of the whole scene, and discovered my own world in rock climbing. There's a freedom and play in the physical act of climbing—working your body in imaginative ways up a blank wall of rock. Rock climbing in the seventies meant living on the edge, being a social rebel. For this yet-unconscious lesbian there was a naturalness, even a comfort in being an outsider. I lived differently, did something untraditional with my body that most people, my parents included, did not, and did not want to understand. It was OK if I went off and climbed, as long as I always returned and once home didn't tell too many stories of unprotected climbs, long falls, or last-minute belay ledge bivies.

Climbing gave me a sense of power and purpose during those turbulent years. The emotional, spiritual, as well as physical strength that I got from climbing is echoed in various ways in the pieces in the second section of this collection. From Harriet Schwartz, who, in the context of the intimacy and camaraderie of women's basketball, was able to come out, to herself and the world, and found sanity and order only in the structure of the court and the game, to Pat Griffin's inspiring tale of coming back to sports and competing in Gay Games III after having cancer, these stories reveal the connection between physical movement, whatever the sport, and women's sense of strength and power.

I came out in New York City in the early eighties. It was a somewhat delayed process, perhaps due to bad therapy, perhaps because I was so immersed in climbing and really wasn't interested in being sexual or emotionally intimate. Like most newborn dykes I searched for the lesbian community. My choices seemed to be the bar, or the softball field—the two loci of women's gatherings. So I headed first to the softball field, and later to an all-women's karate dojo. I would go and watch the women playing softball in Central Park and with enormous pride would spot them, those women who were supposed to be like me. My powers of detection were still pretty crude, so I felt as if I had accomplished some wonderful piece of gay detection in singling them out, even though they were unmistakable dykes, the real dykes that no one could miss. Sports dykes are often our butches, or our women who don't pass, and I was grateful to these women for looking like what I imagined a lesbian was supposed to look like.

Yet I didn't feel I could join these women athletes, not because I didn't feel myself lesbian enough—I wasn't enough of a jock. They were not exactly the lesbian equivalent of the blonds from my high school days, but it was clear that they were the in-crowd, and that there was a double privacy of language: I had to be able to speak sports and lesbian, a vocabulary I was just becoming familiar with. And, by some means, I also had to know how to play flawless ball. These women would never be caught training, but rather seemed to materialize on the field as perfect catchers and hitters. So though I idealized my new lesbian world—we were kind, fair, accepting, supportive (a few hard lessons followed)—I knew that they would want their second basewoman to be able to catch and throw. It didn't seem an unreasonable request, but I was most definitely excluded.

Though I couldn't be a part of this group, of all of the lesbians I had located I felt the most affinity with these women. This is perhaps because even though I have never been able to catch or throw, my history parallels that of many lesbians and probably of all jocks. I grew up as a tomboy, spent my afternoons in Fairmount Park playing tackle football, and that curiously named game, "smear the queer." That made me different from the girls in my class, and was the first sign that I didn't completely fit in with the gender options and order that the world offered me.

So the early jock life is familiar, and will be so to many lesbians, jocks or not. These early experiences are described with insight and humor in the "Tomboy Days" section of this collection with short stories by Lesléa Newman, Merril Mushroom, and Nancy Boutilier.

Though I feel a kinship with fellow tomboys, once girls become women, and then serious about their sport, their lives become a mystery to me. Team sports—elite, competitive, and professional—are a different world. Sports are not just fun and games, but a job, a means to something else—most often an education. I have been watching from the sidelines for several years now, curious about lesbians in the "real" sports world.

College, and elite or professional, teams often try to ignore, even stifle the lesbian invasion to keep it quiet, and the women within closeted, even during a time when most closet doors are flying open. Homophobia runs deep in the sports community and as a testimony of how deep it is, how slowly things are changing, the third section, "Politics," offers a perspective from 1979, ten years after Stonewall, and two years after Title IX. Author Betty Hicks analyzes why there is such a vocal, insistent resistance to women in sports and concludes that "lesbian athletes may be the ultimate articulation of women's liberation," an idea that is echoed in Mariah Burton Nelson's piece on her own experiences with homophobia in the professional basketball world. Hicks ends her piece with the thoughts of one lesbian athlete who notes that nothing has changed since 1939—the myths persist that women who play sports are mannish, and mannish women are lesbians. That logic, which poses such a threat to our gender system, is picked up in Victoria Brownworth's investigative piece written twelve years later as she explores the inside of the "competitive closet." What keeps so many of these women closeted is a fear of losing scholarships, sponsors, and of tarnishing their all-American images. For we look to our athletes as role models. Sports are American culture: it is our pastime, pride, or religion. And America is not yet ready to be proud of gay people, athletic or not.

Yet in this world of sports, in our lives as lesbians, we are always looking for role models, famous people to show us the way, guide us in our journeys through life, love, and physical play. We are reminded how few the images are as writer Jaye Zimet takes us channel-surfing in search of lesbian athletes. One option is to fantasize: Zimet inserts herself into the play, while cartoonist Joan Hilty, while watching the women's Olympic volleyball team, searches and imagines she sees lesbian players among all of the strong women athletes. Again and again the one woman we turn to is Martina Navratilova, tennis champion and superb athlete—not a superb woman athlete or a superb lesbian athlete. In a three-part essay, Rachel Lurie looks at her changing attitude toward, and perspective on, Martina, while also chronicling Martina's evolution as a spokesperson and champion for gay rights.

For those lesbians whose sports are play, whose careers do not depend on their athletics, they can celebrate openly their sexuality, can form all-women's teams, can unabashedly acknowledge the connection between sexuality and sport. For being physical in a sport—sweating, moving intimately with other women—can be erotic, as the pieces in the "Sex and Other Games" section reveal. Author Robbi Sommers's game is sports erotics and she makes no apologies about sweating as she reveals the steamy side of working out. What really happens on a gay team—that question: do teammates really all sleep with each other—is explored by *GirlJock* editor Roxxie. Kris Kovick's fantasy piece—at the center of which is a question most true girl jocks might have trouble answering— ends with a hilarious, surprising sexual twist.

In getting lesbian writers and jocks to write about their experiences in sports, I wanted to come to understand the various experiences, what it means to be a lesbian who plays (or has played) sports, physically, socially, emotionally, and sexually. The pieces gathered here reflect my curiosities, and reveal, once again, the diversity of lesbian perspectives and experiences. This is not a portrait of the sportsdyke, but rather a collage of sportsdykes and the collage is at times lopsided. The styles and approaches are various: there are fiction and investigative pieces, interviews and personal narratives. Not all sports are represented and not all perspectives have been heard. What is offered here is a slice of lesbian culture.

Gathering all of these pieces was difficult. Many of my friends teased me: how hard is it to find girl jocks? Yet though there are many girl jocks, they are doing sports, and are not interested in sitting down and writing about them. Writers write, they don't do sports, and even those who do sports or write about them were not always cooperative: I was told by one lesbian reporter that she covered real sports, men's sports. So the women who have contributed here are a unique blend of lesbian writer/athlete, or athlete/writer and I thank them all for sitting down and writing.

THE LESBIAN LOCKER ROOM LAW

NO MATTER WHERE YOUR ASSIGNED LOCKER IS
LOCATED, 90% OF THE PEOPLE IN THE ROOM
WITH YOU AT ANY GIVEN TIME WILL BE
USING LOCKERS IN CLOSE PROXIMITY TO YOURS.

HOW GIRLJOCK ARE YOU?

Nancy Boutilier

How Girljock are you? Here's a way to get in touch with your Inner Athlete. We've devised this little test for personal assessment and self-reflection. Because Girljock is a state of mind, it doesn't matter whether or not you've ever actually been in any of the scenarios described. What matters is how you see yourself responding to these situations if they were to arise.

So, to find out where you stand on the Girljock Scale, circle the letter that best reflects your Inner Athlete.

1. If you lost a tooth in a field hockey game, you would
   a) invest in a mouth guard
   b) get a gold cap engraved with your girlfriend's initials
   c) learn to whistle through the gap in your smile
   d) it couldn't happen since you take your teeth out before play begins

2. In your code of ethics, pulling hair is
   a) a nasty foul
   b) just part of the game
   c) a strategy for winning
   d) a come-on

3. To relax during the game, you chew
   a) gum
   b) tobacco
   c) flesh (your own)
   d) flesh (someone else's)

4. Which nickname comes closest to yours?
   a) Sunblossom
   b) Feather
   c) Mommy Sir

   d) Hairball
   e) Meat

5. Safe sex means
   a) a latex barrier
   b) you've showered after practice
   c) you're a hundred miles from the nearest nuclear reactor
   d) you're a hundred miles from your girlfriend
   e) no sharp objects

6. The last time a teammate put the moves on you, you
   a) said you were straight
   b) quit the team
   c) invented a girlfriend
   d) sidelined her with a killer hip check

7. You complain of pain when you
   a) break a nail
   b) have cramps
   c) are fouled
   d) break a bone
   e) what's pain?

8. Your role is best described as
   a) mascot
   b) bench warmer
   c) cheerleader
   d) all-star

9. A training meal is
   a) complex carbohydrates
   b) decaf and oatcakes
   c) Pop Tarts and Diet Coke
   d) your girlfriend

10. When your line drive hits the pitcher in the eye, you
    a) run to your teammates for support
    b) call "Time Out" and run to the mound
    c) sprint to first base and apologize to the first base coach
    d) run around the bases, laughing

11. For a floor burn, you
    a) use makeup
    b) ignore it
    c) pick the scab
    d) tattoo around it

12. In romance, you assume she's yours when
    a) she comes to your games
    b) she comes to your practices
    c) she comes

13. An easy workout is
    a) an oxymoron
    b) a sprint to the fridge for beer
    c) rhythmic stretching
    d) a swim to Alcatraz and back followed by a run to Fresno

14. When your nose is clogged, you
    a) take yourself out of the game to go to the restroom
    b) tastefully blow your nose while pretending to wipe the sweat from your face with your jersey
    c) wait till nobody's looking and shotgun*
    d) wait till everyone's looking and shotgun*
    *clearing one nostril by sealing the other and blowing forcefully

15. When a referee misses a call, you
    a) never notice because you don't know the rules
    b) tell your teammate loudly so that the ref hears you
    c) pout
    d) tell the ref to open her eyes
    e) shoot to kill

16. Aerobic exercise is
    a) doing the dishes
    b) walking your dog
    c) picking your scabs
    d) smoking

17. When choosing sides
    a) you are last chosen
    b) each team tries to give you to the other
    c) you want to be on Shirts
    d) you want to be on Skins
    e) you do all the picking

18. In a food fight, you
    a) encourage everyone to be more mature
    b) run away
    c) dive for the ice cream
    d) throw unripe fruit with your throwing arm
    e) chew first, then spit

19. Your game jewelry includes
    a) long, dangling earrings
    b) a knee brace
    c) nipple rings
    d) handcuffs

20. Your hair is best described as
    a) big hair
    b) dreadlocks
    c) Lesbian Haircut #3
    d) what hair?

21. Your favorite cologne is
    a) Passion
    b) Brut
    c) sweat
    d) Old Spice
    e) vaginal fluid

22. When on the bench, you
    a) feel a sense of relief
    b) cheer enthusiastically for your teammates
    c) hate it
    d) poison the water

23. When you score a goal, you
    a) faint in shock
    b) squeal with delight
    c) act as if it was nothing
    d) swear because you were aiming a little further to the left
    e) give the goalie the finger and smile

24. When your inner child cries, you
    a) cry with her
    b) go to therapy
    c) slap it silly
    d) what inner child?

25. When your opponent throws a dirty elbow, you
    a) apologize for getting in the way
    b) give her a dirty look
    c) call her a dirty name
    d) call her a dirty name and ask for her phone number

Scoring: 0 points for every question you do not understand; 5 points for every A response; 10 points for every B response; 15 for every C; 20 for every D; and 25 points for every E.

If you score under 100, you can consider yourself a **Good Sport,** but perhaps you should be reading *Better Homes and Gardens.* Being a Good Sport is a lot like being a Gemini, only different.

If your score falls between 100 and 199, you are an **Encounter Athlete.** You join the game, not to compete, but to join in the cosmic exchange of energy. You may even recall that matter can be neither created nor destroyed, and so you are simply engaging in the natural process of motion.

If you score anywhere from 200 to 299, you are a **Challenger,** a candidate for Ms. Congeniality. Winning isn't everything, but getting her number is something. You don't aim high, but you often hit your target. Others enjoy being on your team.

A score between 300 and 399 means you are a **Competitor.** What you lack in raw talent, you make up for with your hustle and perseverence. An asset to any team, and a scrapper in every sense of the word. The word *quit* isn't in your vocabulary.

Scoring between 400 and 499 suggests that you don't compete, you win. You are an **MVP** (most valuable player). And you win big, or else you don't play at all.

Over 500 and you're a **Champ.** You should consider joining the American Gladiators or challenging Martina to a little one-on-one. You have trouble separating foreplay from aftplay—it's all play to you. Your motto is: Just do it out of earshot.

Note: This quiz was first presented orally at Red Dora's Bearded Lady, a cafe in San Francisco. The next incarnation appeared in GirlJock *magazine.* GirlJock *has been called a humor magazine for the lesbian athlete with a political consciousness. Some of us see it not only as a way of life, but also as a way of sport.*

SportsDykes

TOMBOY DAYS

TOMBOY DAYS

THE TOURNAMENT

Merril Mushroom

I was hugging myself with joy, heart singing with excitement, as I ran up the front steps and into my house. I looked around the living room, checked the kitchen, delighted to find no one else in sight. Quickly I closed myself into the sanctuary of the bathroom, there to savor my triumphant pleasure in private for a few delicious moments more and to rehearse the way I'd tell my family, practicing the words I'd use to announce the news—that I had won in the individual semifinals, and I would be in the finals! After years of mediocrity, I was a winner at last!

This was the dream of a lifetime come true for me, and I felt full to bursting with the satisfaction of my achievement. From the moment of my first awareness of the magic of winning (which came at an indeterminate but early age), one of my primary desires in life was to be a winner myself; was to be, myself, one of those proud, athletic girls, one who excelled in sports, who was the focus of all eyes after the contest, who received the applause of the crowd. I enjoyed sports. I loved to play the game. I thrived on the physical and mental exercise, the feeling of moving my body. I loved team play as well as individual contests, and I craved to be included in the tight camaraderie of the group of girls who were the best athletes at school.

Alas, this was not to be my lot. Always I had aspired to be proficient at physical contests, to be good at sports. I tried, but I lacked the ability. I just did not have the innate talent some other children had. I was big, but I was not very strong for my size. I was slow. I was not graceful. I was nearsighted. I was agile enough, but not exceptionally so; and I was, at the very best, passably adequate at some events, but never consistently outstanding at any.

However, in spite of my general mediocrity, I did manage to excel at a few games. When reach and dexterity counted more than strength and speed, I was in my element. I was able to hold my own in badminton, Ping-Pong, pick-up-sticks, and jacks.

Actually, I showed a good bit of ability at jacks—enough to be able to dream of possibly becoming a winner. And so I practiced, learned the skills necessary to be proficient, and, gradually, I developed my game until I became one of those girls who hogged all the jacks, one of those who other girls hated to play with because her turn was never over, because she was so good. I could play on and on and on, through one throw after another, fancy after fancy, controlling the fall of the jacks, the bounce of the ball, rarely missing my scoop.

Even so, I was not as good as the girls who regularly played tournament jacks. Every summer from the age of seven, I had competed in my local playground's Jacks Meet toward District semifinals and Citywide finals, and every summer I was defeated early in the game. But as time went on, my game improved. This was my second year to make the semifinals, and, this time, after years of being eliminated, today I had won my matches one after another, until I had won them all! I had made the finals! At last I would have my time in the limelight. At last I would experience, as had countless other athletes before me, the satisfaction of the payoff for all these years of hard work and perseverance. And it was none too soon—I was eleven years and seven months of age, and this would be my last year in the junior division. Seniors could be tournament spotters, but they did not play competitive jacks in the recreation department leagues. It was now or never for me!

The semifinals had been held at a park an hour's drive from home. The girls from my park met at the playground early that morning. There, we crammed our excited, giggling selves into a recreation department bus. I was disoriented by having to rise at an earlier hour than usual, and by the time we arrived, I was excited, distracted. My senses were overstimulated by the unfamiliar surroundings, by the different placement of courts and sand and bathrooms, by the different vegetation. The very air felt strange upon my skin, the sounds different, smells different, people I didn't know. We girls from home clung together in a knot, seeking solace in the closeness of each other, as we waited for the tournament to begin.

And begin it finally did, and then the day seemed to rush by so quickly—the events, the eliminations, the winning. I bravely faced each opponent, aware of all eyes on us as I waited my turn,

blocking out everything except the game. I knew that I was playing my best and that my opponents could not match my skill.
And then, before I knew it, the tournament was over; and we
were back on the bus going home; and this time I had made the
finals!

Now, sitting in the bathroom, I rerehearsed what I'd tell my
folks: They'd ask how it went. I'd respond casually, "Oh, okay,"
then add, almost as an afterthought, "I made the finals." I'd be
very cool about it all. At least I'd try to be cool. But even now
I couldn't keep that bubble of excitement in my belly from
swelling until I was sure it would burst forth in a long, loud
hoot.

The morning of the finals was cloudy. I prayed that it wouldn't
rain. My neighborhood park would be hosting the event, so I
would have the advantage of playing on my own turf, on familiar floors. I knew that I played best on the outdoor concrete
and asphalt basketball court. If it rained, we'd have to play in-
doors, under the shelter. Part of that floor was wood; and I
couldn't get as good a bounce to my ball on the wood as on
the harder surface of the outdoor court. The rest of the floor
was poured concrete, rough, finger-tearing stuff—a floor that
could take the skin off a girl's knuckles down to the bone. No,
we *had* to play outdoors! I did every childhood ritual against
rain that I knew of, hoping to stave it off for as long as possible.

I had practiced my worst fancies one last time before I left
home that morning, easily flipping those elephant jacks—ten of
them—over to the backs of my hands, then ringing them into
my palms again without a single piece of metal detaching from
the whole of the clump. Immediately, I'd tossed the ten jacks
onto the floor so that they practically lined themselves up by
twos, waiting to be scooped into my ready hand. I skipped to
the first required fancy, one that I had only recently completely
mastered, one that had been especially difficult for me—"cherry
in the basket," also affectionately nicknamed "baskets." I made
it to ninesie before missing, a personal best for me. Then I went
on to "poison," using one hand only, holding all the jacks in the
same hand I used to pick them up and hoping each time I tossed
the ball, that the jacks would not fly out along with it like they
were *supposed* to do in the "dutchman" fancies. Finally, I

worked on "double poisons," where the ball was tossed, the jacks picked up, and the ball caught from out of the air on the fly *before* it bounced.

After practice, I ate a good breakfast, then put on my whites while Mom packed my lunch. I ran the three blocks to the playground and arrived in time to see the buses from the other parks arrive and the lines of girls disembark. I saw their expressions of trepidation and the way they clung to each other as they looked around. I recalled the way I had felt on strange turf during the semifinals, and I was happy to be on my home ground now for this competition.

At last the park director blew her whistle. It was time to start. The air was thick with excitement. We were matched against our first opponents, and, together with a spotter, moved to our assigned places on the courts. The spotters were senior division girls who would mark our plays and make sure we followed all the rules. They would also settle disputes about near-misses and moving jacks. We had five required fancies to do, and these were changed as we moved up through the levels. The girl who finished each fancy first after the required ones could choose the next fancy. We'd play as far as we could get, turn about, until each girl had missed three times. Then we'd report to the director for our next competition assignment. I won my first rounds easily, and almost before I knew it, we were breaking for lunch, sitting on the playground and digging into our paper sacks of sandwiches, fruit, and cookies, while we chattered about the events of the tournament, congratulating the winners and consoling the girls who had already been eliminated.

That afternoon my name continued up the ladder until there was only one line left blank—the one at the top—and I had only one more competition to win in order to see *my* name filled in there. I was to play Sharon Bishop, a girl from Northshore Park, a girl I'd lost to year after year every time I played against her, a girl who was snotty and unfriendly and stuck-up. She had won the championship last year and the year before that, and she had told everyone that three was her lucky number, and she would win this year also. She was three months older than I was, and this would be her last summer to play tournament jacks, too. I knew she wouldn't mess around.

But before the round began, the clouds, which had been gathering all afternoon, finally massed to the spilling point; and spill they did, first in large drops and then in smaller but increasingly thicker and faster streams. We girls scrambled up and raced to the shelter where rainy day activities took place. Our spotter was talking with the director. Finally she came back and motioned Sharon and me over to a large area on the concrete part of the floor. *Uh-oh,* I thought. I knew this floor well. There was a place in it where tiny shells were imbedded in the concrete—almost invisible little shells but sharp and prominent enough to shred the last joint on a girl's pinky finger should she scoop a careless forehand over it.

I glanced sideways at Sharon Bishop. She was strutting through the shelter, aware that all the girls crowding in to watch the playoff or finish their own games for their ranking knew who she was, aware of her fame as a two-time winner. I wondered if I should warn her about the floor. It could certainly swing the competition in my favor if she was unaware of the potential hazard before us. But I couldn't do that. Not only would it be poor sportsmanship on my part to withhold this sort of information, but Sharon might actually end up hurting herself.

Taking a deep breath, I addressed my opponent. "Um, Sharon?" The look she turned on me was enough to curdle fresh milk, as though I might presume to address *her,* perhaps, but she did not owe me the courtesy of a response. Undaunted, I continued, "Um, to be perfectly fair, I, um, need to tell you that the floor we're playing on has some really bad places. . . ." My voice trailed off, as Sharon's sneer grew wider and wider.

"Don't think you're so great just because we're playing on *your* turf," she spat. I could tell that she would have none of my advice, so I shrugged and found myself a spot where the floor was the least abrasive and where my ball would not hit any pocks that might cause it to bounce unevenly.

We sat down. Sharon was one of the few girls who could sit flat on her butt with both knees bent and both legs turned back behind her—a real killer position. This gave her the advantage of being able to play to her front with a maximum of reach and balance. I couldn't sit this way at all. I couldn't even sit the way most of the other girls sat, mermaid-style, with both knees bent in the same direction and one leg turned backward, the other bent in front with foot against thigh. My tendons stretched the other way, and I preferred to sit with both legs spread wide and turned out with the sides of both knees on the floor. This formed boundaries inside which to gauge my throw, but it had the disadvantage of creating a hazardous area for the ball to bounce against leg or jacks.

Sharon and I both played well, moving rapidly through the easy fancies and into the more difficult ones. I was aware of the girls crowded around watching us, the admiring eyes, the sighs of appreciation at skillful, difficult plays, the groans when either of us missed.

We had two misses each and were on our last round when Sharon got into the shells. She was leading, but not by much. We both were in "baby on the back fence," a particularly difficult fancy where we had to place all ten jacks on the back of our left hand by appropriate numbers, then flip them over and catch them without letting any fall to the floor. She had missed on fivesies, I'd missed on threesies, and this would be the deciding round.

Sharon tossed the jacks, and I could tell by the way they spread when they hit the floor that they were on the shells. She tossed the ball, picked up the first five jacks in a clump with her fingertips, and expertly deposited them on the back of her left hand. The last five jacks were spread out, and Sharon tossed the ball and scooped them together, scraping the top knuckles of both her pinky and ring fingers along the shells. I must say that she was cool. If I didn't know the floor as well as I did, I would not have guessed that she had just grated the entire skin off the last two joints of her ring and pinky fingers clear down to the nerve endings. She bit her lip slightly, and a flash of pain showed in her eyes, but she immediately covered up, acting as if nothing had happened. I looked at her hand and saw the exposed pink flesh that lay beneath her flayed skin. I saw the blood slowly well into the scrape, and I knew that she was hurt bad.

She missed on sixies, and then it was my turn, my last chance to beat her and claim the championship. I selected my spot, tossed the jacks. Taking a deep breath, spreading my left fingers out just far enough to contain the jacks without allowing them to drop through, I bounced and caught the ball, carefully placing three, three, three, and one jack, on the back of my hand. Expertly, I flipped them into my palm, catching them all. Again I tossed the jacks, completed foursies, fivesies, and, miraculously, sixies. I missed on sevens, but it didn't matter. I had won! I had beaten Sharon Bishop for the all-county recreation department jacks championship! I was a winner at last!

LESS UGLY

Lesléa Newman

Chocolate pudding had just been passed out and the Minnows at the next table were busy flinging it at each other when Sam stood up and Marlene stopped breathing. Marlene was in love with Sam, with his stringy blond hair and wire-rimmed glasses, with his long slender fingers and the way he'd wrap them around the neck of his Martin guitar, with his twangy voice which Marlene insisted was fifty times better than Bob Dylan's any day. But Sam didn't know Marlene was alive, he being a senior counselor and all, and she, like me, being a lowly Trout, which wasn't as bad as being a Minnow. But still it would be two years until we were Dolphins, and some of the Dolphins went out with counselors on the sly even though they weren't supposed to, especially since three years ago a girl got pregnant under a canoe and her parents sued Camp Wildwood for almost a million dollars. At least that's what Tina Jacobs said and she was a wealth of such vital information. She's the one who informed me that anything over a mouthful's a waste anyway the first time she saw me in a bathing suit. But Marlene said she was just jealous because Tina was as flat as the postcards our counselors handed out every Friday so we could write to our parents and tell them what a great time we were having or something to that effect if we wanted to help ourselves to a make-your-own-sundae at nine o'clock in the canteen.

Anyway, like I said, Sam stood up, cleared his throat and held up a plastic baggy full of cigarette butts. The usual roar of the dining room fell to a hushed din as Sam dramatically turned the baggy upside down and dumped its contents onto the wooden floor. "I don't smoke," he said, and for one second the room was silent except for Marlene's sigh of utter ecstasy. Then Sam sat down and the general chaos of two hundred campers and counselors started up again.

"Oh Marlene." I lowered my glasses to the tip of my nose and looked over their tortoise-shell rims at her in mock dismay. She was still staring at Sam, her eyes huge and all liquidy, like two pools of chocolate pudding about to ooze down her face. Sam was now biting into an organic Macintosh apple he had fished out of his Save-A-Tree canvas backpack and Marlene pushed her pudding aside. "What?" she asked, turning to me. "I can dream, can't I?"

"Sure," I said, sliding my glasses back up my nose, the-better-to-see-you-with, my-dear. I was doing plenty of dreaming myself that summer, but not about Sam or Larry or Wayne or Roger or even Claude, the swimming counselor who had given his whistle to Tina Jacobs to wear around her neck. No, I had it bad, and I mean B-A-D for Barney.

Barney. First of all she had straight brown hair all the way down to the bottom of her shorts. Sometimes she wore it loose and sometimes she wore it in one braid down her back, swinging like the rope to the dinner bell we all took turns pulling on to see who could make it ring the loudest. Second of all, she had light blue eyes, the color of a husky dog's. And third of all, her skin was the color of a marshmallow toasted to perfection over a Saturday night campfire when I was lucky enough to be sitting on a log right next to her, so who cared if some stupid Flying Fish got half his some'more stuck in my hair? Barney was absolute perfection in her white shorts that frayed at the bottom just right, and her blue T-shirt that matched her eyes, and her cotton socks, one hugging the tight muscles of her calf, the other rolled down twice to meet the rim of her black high-top sneaker. God, I wanted to be just like her. But how could I be? Try as I might, my hair would frizz up thirty seconds after I unrolled it from the coffee can I set it around every night. Not to mention the fact that unless I drenched myself in Coppertone my skin turned an early shade of ketchup after two minutes in the sun. And then of course there were my ugly, ugly, ugly, ugly glasses which hopefully would be replaced by contact lenses next summer, if not before.

Anyway, Barney didn't seem to worry about what she looked like. I mean, after all she was perfect, so there was nothing much to worry about anyway, but still, she didn't spend too much time hanging out with the other girl counselors who were always painting their nails and pouring peroxide into their hair to streak it. Barney didn't have time for that stuff. She was too busy tossing around a frisbee or oiling her mitt or fixing the volleyball net.

That's another reason I liked her so much. She was like one of the guys. So much so, they let her play in the annual Wildwood versus White Birch Counselor Softball Game, which was *the* event of the summer.

The Saturday of the game, me and Marlene walked down to the softball field right after lunch to get a good seat. We plopped down on the grass right behind and a little to the left of home plate, as far from Tina Jacobs and her crowd as possible. Our team was warming up; Barney had all her hair tucked up inside a NY Yankees baseball cap and Sam had a black elastic band attached to the ear pieces of his glasses, anchoring them to his head. Soon two yellow school buses full of White Birch campers and counselors arrived. After the campers got settled and the counselors warmed up, it was time to start the game.

Barney of course was spectacular. She played first base and every time the ball came her way she'd just lift her hand up in the air as easy as you please, just like she was waving hello to me, and the ball would smack into her glove and the ump would yell, "Out!" jerking his thumb over his shoulder. Once Barney caught a ball at first base and quick as a flash threw it to Sam, who tagged the runner out at second, and Marlene and I jumped up hugging each other tight and screaming so loud we practically busted each other's eardrums.

Then all of a sudden it was the bottom of the last inning. The score was tied eleven–eleven, bases loaded, two outs and it was Barney's turn to bat. Oh please God, please God, don't let her strike out, I prayed, closing my eyes for the briefest of seconds.

Barney dusted off home plate, shifted her hips from side to side, and swung her bat up to her shoulder. The pitcher let the ball fly. Barney watched it, but didn't move.

"Strike one."

Oh Barney, Barney, Barney, don't fail me now. Sam was standing behind the third base line, giving Barney encouragement. "That's it, Barney. Don't swing at anything. You pick it now. You're a hitter. You're a hitter." The Wildwoodians were screaming, "We want a pitcher, not a glass of water," as the ball beelined to Barney, who again didn't move.

"Strike two."

I clutched Marlene's arms with both hands, almost cutting off her circulation between her elbow and her wrist. What was Barney doing? She had to swing at this one. The pitcher pitched, the ball zoomed at Barney, she swung and smack! that ball was gone— over the pitcher's head, over second base, and way past the outfielder, who leaped up in the air with his glove extended anyway, before turning around and making a dash for it.

Meanwhile, Barney tossed her bat aside and loped around the bases as gracefully as the deer we had seen last week on an overnight in the backwoods. The outfielder finally caught up with the ball and threw it to second. By this time, everyone had come home except for Barney, who was rounding third. The second baseman threw the ball wildly at the catcher. It made a wide arc in the sky, then hung suspended in the air for a second, completely blocking the sun like an eclipse before hurling itself downward, straight for me.

"Heads up, heads up," someone yelled at the same time I said to Marlene, "That ball's gonna hit me in the face." And sure enough, one second later that softball, which was anything but soft, caught me right between the eyes and cracked my glasses in two, clean as a twig someone snapped in half before tossing it into the campfire. And thus I was glasses-free and just a tiny bit less ugly for the rest of that summer, so who cared that the only thing I could see clearly from then on until I went home was Barney's face, two inches from mine, her hair spilling out of her cap and brushing against my cheek, her blue eyes filled with delicious concern as she asked me over and over, "Are you all right? Are you all right?"

HOTSHOT

Nancy Boutilier

A five-foot-eight-inch fifth grader is probably going to be one of the best basketball players in her school no matter if she's girl or boy. But I happen to be a girl, and pretty good at sticking the "J" too, so don't go challenging me to one-on-one, unless, of course, you don't mind losing. And I'm not gonna play you easy on account of what Mom calls "ego"—especially no "male ego" that some boys got. I don't play easy for any reason or anyone. It's that simple.

Most of life is simple. Too many people want to make stuff way more difficult than it is. Like the time school pictures came back and I was holding a pencil behind Tony Kramer's head so it looked like the pencil grew right out of his ear. Well, Mrs. Kramer goes and calls my teacher and then my mom and we all have to sit down and discuss it. They all try to tell me what a horrible thing I did, messing up the picture and all. And I kept trying to tell them how funny it was—and even Tony thought so too—but no one else was laughing. So I end up feeling bad about something I thought was fun—and I would never have done it to someone like Laurie Strandy or Darius Silvers because I know it would have made them feel bad. But Tony—I knew he could take it.

Oh, well, I guess I'm supposed to be learning the when's and where's of having fun. And what I like most is fun on the basketball court. Shooting, dribbling, rebounding—I can outrun and outjump anyone in the fifth or sixth grade—anyone!

Most of the teachers gave up on trying to make me stay on the girls' side of the hardtop. But old Miss Monzelli, who I call Miss Von Smelly when she can't hear me, sometimes still screeches from behind those pointy glasses with the fake little diamonds for me to get onto the hopscotch side of the blacktop. She says I can't play with the boys because it ain't ladylike. She says I might get hurt. She also says that saying *ain't* ain't ladylike neither, so I do it just to remind her who's boss. We'll see who's going to get hurt.

Truth is, no boy ever hurt me more than I hurt him. Besides, I've had stitches four different times, and not once have I even cried at the blood or the needles. Broke a bundle of bones, too— three fingers, my wrist, both collarbones, and my left ankle—seven all together.

That's how I learned that basketball is in me—it's in my bones. Every time I've been sidelined, I don't mind missing out on a football game, or the roller coaster at the carnival, but not being able to play hoops sets my skin crawling. I know it's in my blood too because my Dad is six-foot-four and played in college. He still plays at the Y, and I get to shoot around at halftime of his games. All the referees there like me. Sure, they have to show off, spinning the ball on their fingers or throwing it to me behind the back, but they all like me. I figure they are jealous of the guys like Dad who get to strut their stuff while they only get to run up and down the court blowing whistles and ticking everyone off.

But at halftime, the refs rebound for me and call me Hotshot.

I'm telling you all this so you can see how some things are born in a girl, even though most people seem to think they're reserved only for boys. And don't go calling me Tomboy unless you can give account of what it means. I'm a girl who can throw a football further and with a better spiral than anyone at Maple Street School, except for Greg Merrit, who is my best friend, and Mr. Leon, the gym teacher. I don't mind that Greg can throw further than me because he's real good and that's just that. I can respect that. Besides, I'm a better free throw shooter than he is, so really, we're even. But don't go saying that I throw like a boy any quicker than you'd say that Greg throws like a girl, which he does, because he throws like me, and I'm a girl. There's nothing Tomboy about it. I'm a girl and I can play a wizard game of Horse, I'm unbeatable at 'Round the World, I hold my own in 21 and you'll want me on your side if we're playing five-on-a-side pickup. I told you, it's that simple.

And I'm not good just because I'm tall. My dad told me not to be worried about being a six-foot girl because he says if any girl is going to dunk in high school it's going to be me. Mom says I slouch too much. I don't think I slouch at all. I just lean kind of forward when I walk and bounce on my toes so I can feel my hightops hugging my ankles. Air Hotshot! I hit the ground and my treads spring me right back up on my toes. I can see that it scares the boys a bit when I stride out onto the court bouncing like I'm the best thing since the hook shot in my black leather Cons. I'll take hightops over high heels any day!

Anyhow, what I'm trying to tell you about is my problem with Miss Monzelli. She's my Social Studies teacher who seems to think she got hired by the school solely to mess with my life. She tries to make me play only with the other girls at recess, and I told her I don't have anything against girls, but I like playing basketball, and it's the boys who play basketball. She says I'm not learning to be a lady if I don't play with girls and held me after school to point out that if I dress like the boys and talk like the boys, I'll find myself in trouble. It seemed to me that the only trouble I was in was with her, but I didn't think I'd score points by telling her so. Instead, I asked her if it was bad for me to be like the boys, why wasn't it bad for the boys to be like boys. After all, I didn't see her making no fuss about what they were wearing or playing.

Miss Monzelli got all red in the face so that her cheeks and neck matched the fire-engine-red lipstick she wears. She chewed me out for being fresh, and then insisted that the boys are supposed to act like boys because they are boys. It didn't make sense to me, so I didn't listen to most of what she was saying until I caught on that she had phoned my mom to say that I was supposed to wear dresses to school unless we were scheduled for gym class. Well, we only have gym twice a week, so Miss Von Smelly was saying that I had to wear a dress every Monday, Wednesday, and Friday! Now, I don't even like wearing dresses when I go to see my grandmother in the city, but that's the deal. And even then I don't like it, but my grandmother does. Gram is worth pleasing for the way she lets me climb on through the attic to the roof. Gram keeps a treasure chest for me in the closet and takes me to the zoo. Her oatmeal cookies are the best on this planet, and I get to lick the batter from the bowl. She even sewed me a pair of pajamas with tiger stripes and a long tail stuffed with nylon stockings. For Gram I will wear a dress.

Mom gave up with me and dresses when I was in the third grade. That's when we agreed that I wouldn't fight over wearing a dress for Sunday mass or for visits to Gram. If I didn't put up a stink on those occasions, I wouldn't have to wear dresses the rest of the whole year. At Gram's house and God's house, it makes Mom happy if I wear a dress, but no way am I wearing no dress for no old Miss Von Smelly—not even if she could bake oatmeal cookies like Gram's. Mom's only other rule was "No hightop sneakers when wearing a dress!" I don't much mind that rule, because hightops just don't look right when you got a skirt flapping around your thighs.

Mom lets me wear low-cut sneakers with my knee socks, so I can still run around, because I wear shorts underneath. I just don't like the idea that when I sprint, jump, fall or wrestle the whole world has a front-row seat to my underwear. And if I wear a dress to school, I have to put up with all Miss Von Smelly's stupid comments to us girls to sit with our knees locked together so our legs get all sore and cramped from trying to keep ourselves all shut up tight under our desks, as if it isn't easier to just tell the boys they got no business looking up our skirts in the first place.

I've never seen Miss Von Smelly in pants, and I feel like telling her how much happier she'd be if she didn't have to pay so much worrytime making sure her underwear ain't on display when she bends over, or reaches up high, or just stands in the wind. She wears all these silly shoes that make her look like a Barbie doll when she walks—stiff-kneed and pointy-toed, scuttering along.

I don't understand Miss Monzelli any better than she understands me, but I don't go telling her that she should be wearing hightop sneakers and jeans, so where does she get off calling my mom to say that I have to dress like her? That's all I want to know.

So anyway, I go home, and at dinner, Mom tells Dad about Miss Monzelli's phone call, and I just about choke on a tomato when Dad says "If that's what the teacher says, I suppose Angela will just have to put up with the rule."

"But Dad, Miss Monzelli is such a witch. She's just making me wear dresses because she knows how much I hate it! She's out to get me!"

"Now, Tiger," Dad calls me "Tiger" when we horse around or when he wants me to think that he's on my side, but he's really not. "I'm sure Miss Monzelli is not out to get you. She is your teacher, and she knows what is best for you and for the school."

"I'm not wearing dresses three times a week!"

"Honey," Mom calls me that when I start getting stubborn, and I can tell it's going to be two against one, three against one if you count Miss Monzelli. "I've let you take responsibility for your

wardrobe this year, but maybe it's time that we take another look
at what is appropriate attire for a young lady in your school. What
do the other girls wear?"

"Mom," I could hear the whine in my voice, which meant that
I knew reasoning wouldn't really work, "the other girls in my
school play hopscotch at recess, and go to the corner store for
Doritos and Coke after school. They don't play basketball or football or even climb on the jungle gym."

"Well, you could come home and change into your play clothes
after school if you wanted to. . . ."

"Aww, come on, Mom, I'd never get in the game if I came home
while the kids were choosing up teams. Dad . . ." I looked hopefully to my father for support, but he was staying out of this argument for as long as possible.

"Angela," my father said with a mix of sympathy and hesitation
in his voice, "your teacher seems to think . . ."

"Dad, my teacher is a witch who waddles around in high heels
and can't even hold a football in one hand. She picks it up at
arm's length with two hands, like it's a piece of corn on the cob,
too hot to bring within three feet of her body."

"Now, that's no way to talk about your teacher."

"Then there's no way she should talk about me as if I have no
right to dress as I please."

Both my parents seemed to be defending Miss Monzelli only
because she was my teacher, but I could tell that words were not
going to convince them of what a jerk Miss Monzelli was being.
So I sat quiet, hoping they would just forget about it, and life
would go on as usual as I trotted off to school in my hightops and
jeans the next morning. Besides, I didn't even own enough dresses
to get through a week without repeating, unless I wore the satin
dress I had from being the flower girl at my cousin's wedding.
That dress puffed out so that I looked like a piece of Double Bubble Chewing Gum wrapped up and twisted in bows at both ends.
No way was I stepping out of the house in that thing!

My other two dresses had both been made by Gram. My favorite was yellow with purple and white stripes down the side and
a big number 32 on the front. Gram made it special to look like
Magic Johnson's Lakers uniform. For a dress, it's pretty neat, but
it's still a dress. None of the other dresses I own fit me because
I've been growing too fast for my clothes to keep up with me. The

only reason the gum-wrapper dress fits is because an older cousin was supposed to be the flower girl, but she got some mono-disease right before the wedding, and I had to take her place. The dress was too big in the first place.

So Mom and Dad go on as if this conversation is over. I dig into my fish stick as if there's something special about fish sticks, which there definitely is not. I hear my fork scratching my plate, Mom's bracelets knocking against each other, and Dad's jaw cracking the way that it does when he chews. In our family, that's a silent dinner table.

When Mom gets up to clear the table, I leap up to help because I don't want anyone pointing out how much I hate all this house-work stuff as if it's because I don't wear dresses often enough. Besides, it helps change the tone of everything for dessert, and we have forgotten the whole conversation enough so that Dad pulls out the weekend football pool that he gets at work. It's the first round of the play-offs, and I'm still hopeful enough to believe that I can bet on the Patriots to make it to the Super Bowl. Dad says that his football sense overrules his loyalty to the home team, so he plays his card differently than I play mine. We argue a bit about whether or not the Patriots can get their ground game going, and then we turn our attention to the chocolate pudding Mom puts in front of us. The silence is broken, and when I go to bed I feel sure no one will notice what I wear to school in the morning.

"Do you have Phys Ed today?" Mom asks as I throw my backpack full of books on the kitchen floor by the backdoor.

"Umm, no. Why?" I pretend innocence and ignorance of Miss Monzelli's mandate.

"Well, because, we agreed that you'd save your jeans for gym days." Mom's trying to be as forgetful of the argument as I am.

"We agreed that I could wear whatever I wanted except for church and for Gram. We never agreed to anything about wearing dresses to school. Miss Von Smelly just poked her nose into some-thing that is not her business." Since this was not one of those times when giving in for the sake of keeping Mom happy was worth it, I made sure not to say *ain't*. I didn't want her to have any dirt on me in any way. Otherwise, I'd be stuck for good. I hoped she'd see this as one of those times when giving in for the sake of keeping ME happy would be worth HER while.

It wasn't.

"Angie, the school has its expectations and standards, and you have to . . ."

"Mom, it's not the school. It's Miss Monzelli! And she's an old witch anyway. Why listen to her?"

Dad walked in and silence returned.

I grew impatient and started pleading. "Mom, watch. No one will say anything's wrong if you just let me keep doing what I'm doing."

"Uh-oh, dresses again, huh? Tiger, why don't you just put on a dress, go to school, and do whatever it is you always do?" offered Dad, trying to be helpful and healing to the conversation.

"Daaadddd," I whined, hoping the tone said more than the word itself.

"Tiger, no one is asking you to change yourself. Nobody is going to stop you from being who you are. It's only your clothes we're asking you to change."

"Well, if it's only clothes, then why is everyone else making such a gigantic deal about what I wear?"

For a moment I grew hopeful when my dad had no answer for me, but then Mom filled the pause. "Because your teacher thinks you ought to dress up a bit more—like the other girls."

"Exactly," seconded Dad. "So why don't you run back into your room, slip those clothes into your backpack for after school, and put on a dress for classes?"

It was more of a commandment than a question, and I knew I wasn't going to get out of the house in my jeans. So I just glared at Dad a bit, then glared even harder at Mom, and stormed back to my room.

I had tried to be honest with my parents, but my honest opinions had gotten me nowhere. I didn't really want to cut school, although that option did come to mind. I figured I could change my clothes as soon as I got around the corner from the house. So, I put on the dress I hated most, the candy-wrapper one from Rico's wedding. It looked really stupid with my sneakers, and I felt like irking my folks because they were siding with Miss Von Smelly. I wore one tube sock with black and orange stripes and one with green and blue stripes, all of which completely clashed with the yellow and red of the dress.

I stomped my way back into the kitchen, no longer hungry for breakfast. I stood in the doorway as defiantly as possible with legs spread wide and arms folded across my chest. Mom and Dad looked at each other, unimpressed by me, and pleased as punch they'd won the argument. I stuffed my jeans and a T-shirt into my backpack as Dad had suggested, but I guess he must've been onto my plan to change before I reached the schoolyard because he offered to drive me to school.

Next thing I know, Dad's dropping me off in the school parking lot, and I'm facing a blacktop filled with my friends who have never even seen me in a dress, let alone in a flower girl gown, and I can't believe it. I'm angry as can be at Mom, Dad, Miss Monzelli, and any kid who dares to look at me. I turn to get back into the car, and when Dad innocently waves "So long, Tiger. See you tonight," I can't believe he's humiliating me this way. I see a few kids pointing toward me, laughing, and I want to punch them all. I don't know where to begin swinging, so I run inside to the girls' room, leap into the second stall, lock the door, and stand up on the seat so that no one can find me.

As I'm catching my breath, I discover that I left my backpack in the car.

Everybody has already seen me and I'm weighing my options while perched atop the toilet. Then I hear the bathroom door squeak open. By the clicking of tiny footsteps echoing across the tile, I know Miss Monzelli has stalked me down.

"Hello? Is anyone in here? Hello? Angela? Angela?"

I say nothing, but I think of how stupid I'll feel if she finds me hiding in the stall. I know she knows I'm in here. I quickly and quietly slide my feet down so that it looks like I'm sitting on the toilet, and I drop my underpants down around my ankles. "Yes, Miss Monzelli," in the sweetest voice I can put together. "I'm just, well, ya know, doing what I have to do."

"Oh, Angela, it's you," she says, as if she's surprised I'm here. "I saw someone sneak in, and you know you shouldn't leave the playground without permission. Unless of course it's an emergency. I suppose it's all right this one time if Nature caught you by surprise." She's trying to make me feel better, but it sure as cinnamon ain't working.

"By the way, I thought you looked very pretty when I saw your father drop you off."

That was the final straw. I wanted to scream, punch or puke at her. She sounded so smug in her triumph, like those TV preachers who have saved some stupid sinner from the clutches of the devil. But fighting Miss Von Smelly would be no solution. It would only help prove to her that I behaved unladylike. So I said nothing, and she filled the silence by explaining that she was going back out before the bell rang to line everyone up for homeroom. Again, the bathroom door squeaked and the echoing heel clicks out the door and down the hallway.

I hated the thought of being made a fool of by Miss Monzelli's dumb rules. I needed a way to make her own rules work for me rather than against me. So I sat for a bit, realizing I might as well pee while I was on the toilet. After finishing my piss, I stood and reached to pull my underwear back up. As I turned to flush, a comic vision flashed through my head. I quickly dropped my underwear back to my ankles and stepped out of one leg hole. With my other leg, I kicked it up into the air, then with one arm I reached out to first catch and then slam dunk my underwear into the toilet bowl. A quick kick to the metal bar flushed it all away. No more underwear!

Miss Monzelli could gloat all she wanted over her little victory because I knew I'd have the last laugh. I wasn't thrilled about the razzing I'd have to put up with in the meantime, but it would all be worthwhile.

I returned to the blacktop where everyone was lining up silent and military. Eyes flashed my way, and an occasional head turned, but always at the risk of Miss Monzelli taking away recess period for headturners to practice standing at attention. I always wondered what it was we were supposed to pay attention to.

I held my head high and looked at no one. I had a secret that would teach Miss Monzelli not to mess with my life or my wardrobe so I figured I didn't have to deal with any kid's questions or stares. I just strutted to my place in the back of the line, glad that my last name was Vickery so I was at the end of the alphabetical order that Miss Monzelli organizes her life by. I glared down at Eric Tydings who stood in front of me every time we lined up for anything. He turned with a giggle held under his breath, and I answered his jeering. "If you don't turn around and get rid of that jackass grin, I'm gonna make your teeth permanent fixtures in your stomach."

Eric quickly turned back to the front, and it was a good thing for him, because the line was filing into the school, and Miss Monzelli for sure would have slapped him with some detention time for not paying attention. And no way was she going to blame me for his mischief today. After all, I was wearing a dress, and in Miss Monzelli's book, girls in dresses act ladylike and stay out of trouble.

I spoke to no one all morning except to answer questions with "yes" or "no," because I had nothing much I wanted to say to anyone. We had lots of stuff to do, including a worksheet of word problems, some reading about astronauts, and a spelling test. I pretended not to notice all the attention I was getting—the muffled laughter, stolen glances and flat-out stares—but inside I wasn't missing a single sidelook or whisper. All the while I sat real careful not to let on that I wore nothing beneath my dress. I wanted to be sure that Miss Monzelli could not get word that I had no underwear on. I was determined that the whole school should see for themselves all at the same time, so I waited patiently for morning recess.

The recess bell finally rang at 10:30 just as I was completing an essay about my favorite animal. I had written all that I could think of writing about kangaroos about five minutes earlier, but I added one final sentence to my essay before putting up my pencil and folding my hands together on my desk top the way Miss Monzelli insists we all sit before she will consider allowing us to line up for recess. I wrote, "Kangaroos prove God has a sense of humor, because the only reason kangaroos exist is to jump around and have fun."

I signed my essay the way I always do at the end. Miss Monzelli hates it because she wants my name squished up at the top right corner of the page, neatly printed with her name and the date. She insists we use the "proper heading" on our work, so I do that, but I also let loose in big script letters at the end "by Angela Vickery" like a painter signing a masterpiece.

"All right, children. You may line up quietly in alphabetical order if you would like to go outside for recess." Of course everyone wanted to go out for recess, but Miss Monzelli always made it sound like an option and an invitation all at the same time that it was really, deep down, just another Von Smelly command.

We lined up, with me in the back again, and filed silently down the corridor to the double doors that lead to the playground. Once outside we were allowed to break file, and we scattered ourselves across the blacktop. Kevin Marino was close on my heels asking, "Hey, Angela. What's with the dress?" and I was answering only with an all-out sprint to the basketball court. Tyrone Freeman had the ball, and he was starting a game of 21 rather than choosing up sides for full court. Recess was too short for a game, and 21 gave everyone a chance to play because it's one big half-court game that leaves everyone against everyone scrapping to make a basket. You just have to keep track of your own score, and it's you against everyone any time you get the ball.

So I threw out my elbows the way I always did and made space for myself in the middle of the crowd huddled below the basket. The boys knew me well enough to tell from the scowl on my face that questions or jokes were completely out of order, so we all just settled in to play basketball. When Tyrone missed an outside shot, the rebound went off my fingers, and Stu Jackster came up with the ball. He cleared the ball out past the foul line, and I went out with him to play defense. He drove to my left, but his leg caught my knee, and we both went to the pavement. I landed sitting flat on my fanny with Stu sprawling across my legs. My dress was all in place, and Stu spit at the pavement beside me as he extended a hand to help me up. Meanwhile, the ball had gotten loose, and Greg Merrit had scored on a jump shot.

Greg got to take the ball up top because it's "make it—take it" where you get the ball back after you score a hoop. As Greg went to take a shot from the top of the key, I went back under to rebound. Sure enough, I came up with the ball, and put it straight up for a point of my own. It was my ball, at the top, and I took the ball left, spun around back to the right, and after two dribbles, I put the ball up and off the backboard for another basket.

My ball again. This time Tyrone decides to play me close, and as I move to spin past him, he gets help on the double team from Greg Merrit. BANG! Greg and I collide, and this time I'm on my back with my hightop sneakers looking down at me. Tyrone screams, "She's got no underwear on!" and they're all laughing hysterically. I clench my teeth almost as tightly as my fists and hiss out at them with squinted eyes "Miss Monzelli says I gotta wear a dress. Man, I'm wearing a dress, aren't I? You laugh at her, not at me, Tyrone Freeman. If any of you wanna laugh at me, you gonna have all your faces rearranged!"

Tyrone backed down on account we're friends, but Doug McDermott wasn't so smart. He starts chanting "I see London. I see France. Angela got no underpants." Once Doug gets going, everyone joins him, and I go right for his throat. He lands a half-punch the side of my head, and I throw one he ducks away from. Next thing I know, we're rolling around on the court, neither one of us landing any punches, but my dress is caught up high and my naked butt must be mooning the whole world just as Miss Monzelli arrives at the fight. Her voice is an extra two octaves higher than usual when I hear her scream "Angela Vickery, stop it! Stop this instant. Stop!"

Of course, I'm not stopping. I'm barely listening, but she tells one of the kids to run and get Mr. Stoller, the school principal.

Well, lots of fussing went on about this whole scene. The kids loved it. It was a scandal that had teachers and the principal unsure about what to do. After all, they had brought it on themselves. As Greg Merrit said, "You ask Angie to wear a dress and you gotta expect something crazy!"

Mr. Stoller lectured me a long while about fighting, but he never said anything directly about my lack of underwear. The school nurse gave me a whole lot of nurselike advice about being clean and wearing the proper undergarments. My Mom and Dad had a conference that afternoon with Miss Monzelli, but didn't say much to me about it.

The next day, when I arrived at breakfast in jeans and a Lakers sweatshirt, Mom asked if I wanted Wheaties or Grapenuts and that was that. Even after all the dust settled, Miss Monzelli never brought up the subject of dresses or underwear.

When the weekend arrived, Mom announced that Gram had invited us to the city for the day. I ran back upstairs to my room and happily put on my Magic Johnson dress. When I returned to the kitchen for breakfast, Mom and Dad looked at me, and then at each other, relieved.

I answered their unasked question by quickly turning, bending and lifting my skirt to show them my underwear.

"Looking good, Tiger!" cheered Dad as I turned around to face my smiling parents.

"What are you waiting for? Go on, get dressed. I want to sink my teeth into Gram's oatmeal cookies while they're still warm."

Part 2

EMPOWERMENT

SWEET PASS

Harriet L. Schwartz

Last basket!" an opponent yells. I head down court with my team-mates and we set up on offense. I cut through the middle, stop outside the key and receive a pass. One teammate sets a pick and another breaks free. I hit her with a bounce pass just beyond the reach of a defender and she turns, shoots and scores. Game over.

We exchange handshakes and high-fives, enjoying the adrenaline pump of a beautifully executed finish.

"Nice game," an opponent says, taking my hand as we walk off the basketball court.

"Thanks," I reply, confused by the visceral reaction that I am having, a reaction stirred by her strong grip as she looks into my eyes and continues to hold my hand. I hardly know this woman and besides, it's just a postgame handshake. What is stirring me up inside? Why am I so affected?

I sit down on the bench at the community center, tape my thumb and lace up my Nike high-tops. I stretch slowly, releasing the tension in my body. These pregame rituals help me to clear my head and focus on playing ball. It always feels good to be in the gym before we play, knowing that I'll see some friends and we'll get a good work-out. But there's more to it than that. To step onto the court is to step into a safe and constant haven. Ten years ago, I was a straight young woman about to begin college. Much has changed since then, but the game remains the same. The boundaries are clear and defined. The rules are understood. Playing time is finite. And I know instinctively how to play.

Single, isolated events that eventually made sense: the firm hand-shake after the game . . . the women who were able to touch some-thing deep within me by cracking the right joke or the right smile . . . the sadness I felt when I saw two women together at the amusement park, believed they had something special that I would never have. Finally, all the feelings and experiences came together one day, when I realized, maybe I am gay. In retrospect, the clues were there and so it seems like it should have been obvious before that moment, but it wasn't. So, at age twenty-six, there it was, a profound awakening. Initially this new understanding brought relief. Life finally made sense.

Then, some hard realities began to hit. Too unsure of myself to talk to anyone, I felt extremely isolated. The world looked different and I was full of questions. I realized that the frame of reference I had developed within my family, school and society gave me no sense of my history or culture as a lesbian. Eventually, I decided to go to a local bookstore that I knew had a gay/lesbian section. I searched the bookstore twice, making sure that I didn't see anyone I knew, and then I finally ventured over to THE section. I skimmed the titles quickly. I wasn't quite ready to buy a book that I feared would tell the world that I was gay (as if reaching for Rubyfruit Jungle *would trigger the store's lesbian alarm: "Attention all shoppers, we have a dyke in aisle three!") Ready for a fast exit, I found and quickly bought a book on counseling gay and lesbian clients.*

The first time I stepped onto the floor at the community center gym, one piece of this clearly defined and recognizable game was different: they were using a women's ball. Having played co-ed since high school, I had always used the bigger, heavier men's ball. So when I grabbed the first loose ball, and took a few shots, I was completely off—my shots were mostly long—missing the rim completely. Quickly I realized that the women's game would require a change in style, that this smaller, lighter ball, required a softer, more graceful touch. I would also eventually realize that while playing with this group of women, I would move from guard to forward or center and enjoy the thrill of developing a strong inside game. Aside from the different ball, though, it was the same game I had always played. Someone who knew the abilities of most of the players split us into teams. A teammate suggested that we match-up on defense so I found myself with someone who was about my size and appeared to have the same ability. We began to play. A teammate passed me the ball, and I knew what to do.

*   *   *

I walked into Zack's, one of two women's clubs in the city. Nervously, I sat down at the bar, ordered a drink and began to check out the scene. Look at all these women, *I thought. I was intrigued by this new world. Women holding each other . . . dancing . . . kissing. Unbelievable! Aware that I wanted to do more than sit at the bar and sip my drink, I began looking for someone to talk with and possibly ask to dance. As I looked around, it seemed to me that almost everyone knew each other and they all seemed quite comfortable and confident. I, on the other hand, felt lost. I couldn't tell who was with someone and who was alone. I felt like any opening line that I could muster would sound clichéd at best and stupid at worst. So, I just sat. Eventually, a woman sat down next to me and we started to talk. She asked me to dance, and we did.*

The game has begun and I am immersed. The flow of the game engages me and I forget that there is a world outside the gym. Adjusting my shot as the game progresses, I start to make cleaner passes and hit a few J's. I grab a defensive rebound and enter a zone of intense concentration. I take off down the court and realize that my teammates are behind and only three defenders stand between me and the hoop. I see the play unfold before it happens. Awareness of time and sound stops—only my vision of the drive to the hoop remains. I switch the dribble to my left hand, one defender disappears . . . ball back to the right hand . . . I stop, fake left, and a second defender drops off . . . I move forward to the center of the key and stop with my back to the defender and hoop . . . I pivot on my left and toss in a short hook over the hand of my opponent . . . time stops . . . nothing but net.

The moment transcends time. The movement transcends space. The integrity of the instant heals my spirit and brings peace to my soul.

A few months after coming out to myself, I am still not out to many people, so life feels fragmented. People at work ask how my weekend was and I say fine. I don't tell them about the emotional roller coaster of the last few months . . . the nervous thrill of my first date . . . the sharp pain I feel deep down inside as I deal with my hurt, confused, and angry parents who are struggling with the news I recently shared . . . the wonder I feel, now that I let myself engage with women on a level deeper than before . . . the isolation caused by most of the mainstream media—the television shows, newspapers, magazines and movies that show us virtually nothing but the straight life. Still not socially involved with the city's lesbian community, I live the gay life in the presence of a few special people: supportive gay and straight friends, my first lover and my therapist. But even with those folks and in the bars, I'm almost always aware that these moments will always seem like the exception to the rule, until my life is more integrated. I can enter the gay life evenings and weekends, in the company of some, but the world I spend most of my time in is still straight and the closet is closing in on me.

I turn and run back down court to set up on "D" after making the play. In the background, I hear a few teammates say, "nice play," "good moves." But mostly, I enjoy a private moment of satisfaction, knowing that without conscious effort, my body, mind, and spirit worked together for successful execution. I smile. A few minutes later, I am high-fiving a teammate who made a great pass, then I'm shouting "nice break" to the other team following a beautiful play. I miss a shot that I expect to make. "Damn," I mutter.

The physical release of playing sixty minutes is obvious. Play hard. Sweat a lot. Feel good. The emotional release is just as profound. The court is where I am most spontaneously emotional, rejoicing in the freedom of play and the company of friends. It's wonderful to see women play good ball and I delight in others' play—good shots, good passes, good rebounds, good "D," good hustle—whatever! I'm lovin' it and being a talker on the court, I let everyone know!

The emotional and experiential balance that I find in most of my life is here in the world of athletics. There are days when everything clicks and also days of discontent. The fast pace of the game that brings me joy can also bring frustration. Hoops should be fun and if I get this frustrated with myself and my play, I should quit playing altogether. Outside the gym, I am much more restrained, keeping my feelings in check. Moreover, I have enough anger and difficulty to deal with off the court, so why play the game if it leads to frustration? But I always decide to keep playing. This is one of the few places where I say what's really on my mind.

I call home and my parents ask how I'm doing. We aren't talking about much of anything these days, so I say, "Fine." I don't tell them how exhausting therapy has been, how scary the media coverage of the military ban debate has been, or about the wonderful evening I shared with my new girlfriend. A few days later, I talk with a close friend from grad school. I know that when I choose to come out to her, she'll be cool, but for now I just talk a lot about work. "How are your parents?" she asks. "Fine," I reply without a trace of the pain, anger and sadness that I know is somewhere inside me. The only thing that I feel is the tightness of my shoulders and the weight of the world.

Down by a couple hoops, one of my teammates calls time-out. We gather and talk strategy. We agree that our defense has been solid, but we need to score more. A few of us offer suggestions: "we need to set more picks" . . . "follow your shots—we need more offensive boards" . . . "keep cutting through the middle, keep them moving."

The dynamics of basketball underscore our need to play. On the macro level, there is a definite structure and within that structure the athlete must know the basics and understand strategy. However, on the most basic level, when it comes to playing the game, hoops is a game with a pace that demands spontaneity, and a freedom of choice that calls for creativity. The pace is quick, the action flowing, and even with a strategy in mind, the player must work on instinct, constantly acting and reacting with confidence and without time to deliberate. Basketball is a game that grants its participants endless room to play. In most situations there are many options, each with the potential to create the desired outcome. It is a game that accentuates each individual's style and personality. It is a game that teaches the athlete to play on instinct.

Just as in hoops, where we play within the rules, but operate on instinct, so it is with coming out. As I begin coming out to a family member or friend, I work within a structure. I examine the situation. Why do I want to come out to this person? Why now? How do I expect this person to react? What can I do to make it easier for both of us? What if it doesn't go well? The more confident and secure side of me wants to demand that people accept me for who I am. The more vulnerable side is still afraid of losing people who are important to me. Initially, my thoughts about coming out are logical and intentional. But when I get in the moment, and the opportunity to come out arrives, I toss most of that aside and trust

*my instinct, and if the moment doesn't feel right, I wait. Or, if I feel
confident and that there really is no other choice, I take the leap.*

*Time has passed and life has settled a bit. I have a much better
sense of who I am and what it means to me to be a lesbian. I am
more connected with the gay community here in the city and I am
out with most of my straight friends and many of my colleagues.
I may not feel the same urgent need for refuge in the gym, but
hoops remains, a significant and special part of my life.*

   *Those of us who gather for pickup games twice a week join in
celebration. We play ball together, admiring each other's strength,
skill, hustle, and desires to play hard and improve. It is not often
that our society values, appreciates, and encourages women in
these ways. And in much of our society, when a woman is an out
lesbian, that becomes her defining characteristic, overshadowing
her intellectual, spiritual, emotional, and physical strength and
character. But in the gym, we enjoy each other, the game, and the
freedom. Outside of the gym, we are all out in different ways and
to different degrees. But on the court, we can be openly physical
and playful. Through basketball, we meet and connect. It's an
alternative to the bars and it crosses racial, professional, religious,
and socioeconomic boundaries. We share a love for the game, respect for each other and a belief in the healing powers of play.*

   *Playing basketball with women reinforces my identity and rep-
resents the most profound realization that came along with coming
out. I enjoy a richer, more complete life, knowing and accepting
that I am a lesbian.*

The game is close and with only a few minutes remaining, everyone is playing hard. The opposition moves the ball quickly, trying
to beat our zone and find the open woman. With great anticipation
and quick hands, my girlfriend (who happens to be on my team
tonight) steals a pass. She drives down court, but with no clear
play, she pulls back and we set up. A few quick passes and we
have their defense moving. The ball goes back to my girlfriend. I
see her with the ball and work to get away from my defender. I
break free, move outside and yell that I'm open. She feeds me the
ball and I pull up and shoot, sinking the three-pointer.

   There's nothing like scoring on a sweet pass from your girlfriend.

ANOTHER LESBIAN JOCK

April Martin

I turn off my alarm at 4:15 A.M. every day and stumble to the bathroom planning the two-hour workout to come: I will fix that entrance edge on my camel spin, and correct that forward lean on my jump landings. At 5:20 I am on the ice, in a world that gives political correctness a slight shudder, but without which I would be bereft.

I did not grow up on the ice, devoting my childhood to early-morning practice with Olympic aspirations. I was never built like Kristy Yamaguchi and I will certainly never skate like her. I am a slightly chubby, forty-five-year-old psychologist and mother of two, with at best only a modest talent. I took my first skating lesson at the age of forty because I was looking for a little exercise, but it changed my life forever. Within a couple of weeks I was skating daily, and group lessons gave way to individual coaching. Every new step—the first back crossover, the first little waltz jump, was an occasion for such excitement that I didn't sleep for days. Public skating sessions were replaced by serious freestyle sessions. Music got chosen, programs choreographed, costumes designed, and competitions entered.

I am part of a group known in skating parlance as "adult skaters"—a term used somewhat derisively by many. It is less a reference to our current ages than to the fact that we began skating as adults. (Adults who skated as children are simply "skaters.") You can pick us out on the ice without too much trouble. We move more slowly, our jumps are lower, our limbs less stretched and extended, and the look on our faces may mix serious concentration with a bit of fear. It is unusual for an adult skater to ever achieve double-rotation jumps. Triples are unthinkable. When we compete, it is against other adult skaters. The United States Figure Skating Association has just begun to tolerate our presence in the skating world, but it can't be said to take us seriously. Still, we are athletes. We devote an astonishing amount of time, energy, commitment, and money to pursuing personal excellence, whatever that may look like to an observer.

It still sends a shiver through me to describe myself as an athlete. When I grew up, athletes were boys. I could never run fast and never learned how to throw a ball. All I knew about sports was that men watched other men play games on TV. Athletes had nothing to do with me.

That doesn't mean I didn't like to move. My most joyful childhood memories are all of movement. As a young child I was badly pigeon-toed, and would stumble over my feet. My parents took advantage of a ballet program in my preschool, hoping it would help me overcome my clumsiness. It did more than they expected—it sparked a passion. Whether ballet's appeal came from something in my genes—some tendency toward musicality and expressiveness, perhaps—or whether it was just the only avenue ever shown me for a girl to be physically active, I don't know. Biology, culture, or both, it became a part of me. Long after the ballet lessons had stopped, I was pirouetting around the living room, walking *en pointe* in my bare feet, and dreaming ballerina dreams. I begged for ballet lessons again in fifth grade and went to Miss Arlene's neighborhood dance school for a while, but by that time there was little family money for nonessential things and my interest was discouraged. By seventh grade my life contained no physical activity at all to speak of. The worst part was that I never even noticed what was missing.

I always had a very suggestible and malleable nature. Other girls might have reflected on the fact that we were robbed of the chance to strive for strength, skills, and physical goals, but I accepted it without question. The only goals I recognized for my adolescent female body were to look like a fashion model. It was a game with two measures of success: the mirror, and the boys who asked you out. My utter and complete failure in the mirror made for relentless anguish. I was short, chunky, had acne, and the vaguely ethnic features of my Italian and Jewish heritages. That Twiggy and I were of the same species was a taxonomic anomaly. And though boys were interested in me, the sexuality of it was confusing: the same attention that signaled my success could also get me branded as disreputable. Nevertheless, I relied on attracting male attention to get some affirmation of my worth. It never worked, and I remained convinced that the body I had just didn't measure up.

In the sixties we didn't even dance. My crowd looked down on dancing as a distraction from really grooving on the music. We were cerebral—political, literary, philosophical—and we were above petty vanities. The proof, of course, was that we didn't wear makeup or cut our hair.

This business of vanity is dicey. Figure skating is a celebration of beauty. It is also about exhibitionism, sequins and crystal, velvet and chiffon. It is about pointed toes and graceful arms. And about a feminine mandate: take fiercely honed skills, raw power, and courage, and mask them with an illusion of fragility and vulnerability. As I glide past the mirrored end of the ice rink in a spiral position I study the line my body creates, pleased to see a hint of elegance. I, who spent the seventies discovering the oppression of women, trying to recover from the notion that my worth rested in my physical appearance. I, who at twenty-nine fell in love with my life partner, a woman, and discovered a depth to passion and devotion that transcended the importance of social images. And who went on to become a committed lesbian feminist activist. Here I am, in a teensy skating dress, wishing someone would notice how terrific my spiral looks today.

I did try other sports. In my twenties a male friend took me jogging and helped me reclaim a body I'd abandoned. I still remember the thrill of wearing my first pair of sweat pants. It was like donning a sacred vestment forbidden to any but the inner sanctum. I am very bad at running, but I did it on and off for years because I loved to sweat. Though it gave me some lovely moments, something was missing.

For two years I played judo. My lover is nationally ranked in women's judo and I couldn't pass up the chance to learn from a champion who loved me. The skills of judo were wonderful, but I hated the aggression. It was fine when I was winning, but getting beaten up was awful. When I started trying to conceive our first child I gave it up.

Many of the people in my psychotherapy practice are living with HIV infection or AIDS. Most of my clients, as well as my friends and I, are living with the devastation of loss after loss in our lives. One woman spends her life in a wheelchair after a catastrophic illness. They are reminders of how quickly the joys of owning a body can be snatched from us. Other clients are recovering from childhood abuse, the ravages of racism, the sufferings inflicted by homophobia. All are seeing me because of pain in their lives. And though my work is deeply satisfying, it is intense. I am often immersed in heartbreak for many hours a day.

By contrast, what I do on the ice feels self-centered, superficial, and of little social relevance. I admit that I care desperately about landing a clean axel. I make guilty jokes about spending my children's college education money on it. The critical questions are whether my leg is sufficiently turned out, or if the new costume should be red. I have had to own up to a vanity and exhibitionism that would have shamed me at one time.

And yet within that showy, glitzy, extremely femme realm I have discovered something very close to love. It contains a celebration of joy, of movement, of music and the visual, of bodies and life. It has allowed me a new relationship with and respect for the body with which I spent so many years at war. It has helped me reclaim the ballerina of my childhood.

I stop briefly to reflect on the apparent contradictions: I have deepened and matured as a woman in a sport geared to little girls. And I am now nourished and replenished by a sport whose standards of femininity were once a form of bondage. Though I bring to the ice the painful bunions and chronically stiff muscles of middle age, I also bring one of its benefits: the increased capacity for living comfortably with contradictions.

My coach bellows across the ice, "You call that *speed?* My dead grandmother can move faster than that!" I bend deeper, push harder, feel the sweat start to run. There is deep pleasure in being pushed to my limits with the same gruff encouragement used for the serious competitors. I'm just another jock.

THE BELT

Alisa Solomon

Like a lot of scrawny schoolkids who got good marks, I took a lot of beatings during recess. Second grade—a particularly violent year—remains a repressed blur, save for three sharp memories: the assassination of JFK (as the only Jews in the class at Deerfield Illinois's Walden Elementary School, Jonny Gertler and I exchanged bewildered looks when Miss Wilke told us to "say a prayer to Jesus for the president's soul"); my first broken heart (when I learned I couldn't join the Cub Scouts because I was a girl); and an especially rough thrashing that left me picking gravel out of my elbows all through math class.

The bully, as always, was my big sister, a tough fifth-grader who was the best athlete in the neighborhood. She could hit a softball farther than any boy on the block, and trounce all takers at one-on-one under our driveway hoop. And, with less effort than she expended in chasing down and dismembering a firefly, she could pin my squirming 45 pounds of goody-goodiness to the ground and pummel me until I was gasping for air.

And so she did, repeatedly, in episodes surpassing plain old sibling rivalry, reaching into the realm of what might be classified as clinical abuse. I remember my teacher calling my mother to tell her, in hushed, judgmental tones, that my sister had been pounding me on the playground at lunchtime.

Strangely, I never seemed to hold much of a grudge against my sister. I idolized her, after all, and could see how unhappy she was. I knew she felt traumatized by my father's Dickensian demands. "Why don't you get good grades like Alisa," he'd say, and then lock my sister in her room to study for four hours at a time.

I can't remember how often she beat me. What I *can* remember is the unpredictability of her attacks, and the presentiment that I somehow deserved them existentially.

I never dreamed of doing the same to her. I gulped down my

rage without ever tasting it. As I grew older, I found I could stand up for myself intellectually, but in the face of real conflict felt utterly defenseless. Long after my sister stopped beating me, I was left with a far more formidable enemy: the sense of myself as a victim. It dogged me into adulthood, fed by the vulnerabilities I felt as a post-Holocaust Jew and, most of all, as a woman.

Practicing karate changed all that. One night in December, I had a dream: I was simultaneously myself at eight, and at my current age, thirty-three. My sister was chasing me around the house, gaining on me with every lap. Suddenly, I stopped, turned, and looked squarely into her eyes and said to myself—because I knew I didn't need to say it aloud—"You can't do this to me any more. I'm a black belt now."

During a karate class a few years ago, I caught myself by surprise one day in the mirrors that line one wall of the Seido Juku dojo, where I have been training since 1984. In the reflection of the forty sets of strikes being thrown by the men and women around me, I saw a knife-hand slice sharply through the air, and suddenly realized that it was mine. *What power,* I thought to myself, utterly astonished.

I'd always been an athlete—I played field hockey in college on a scholarship—so thinking of myself as physically capable was nothing new to me. But *feeling* powerful was something else. After class, I found myself crying in the locker room, as I began to understand how karate was unleashing something old and buried: my accumulated rage, grief, and fear.

That was not the last time I cried in the locker room, nor, I soon found out, was I alone. "The locker room is like a therapist's couch," says Sharon Shelton, an advanced brown belt at Seido, who has also shed her share of tears in that dank little room, where, day after day, the stories, the fears, the freak-outs get aired. And they have common themes.

Sharon was an abused child; one intermediate student is a survivor of incest; another was beaten so severely in her early years by her alcoholic parents that her motor skills were impaired. For these women, and countless others (one in three professional women in New York has been physically or sexually abused), karate helps to redress the damage.

Of course, you don't have to have been an abused child to feel threatened as a woman. Many of the 1500 women who are raped every day in America sign up for karate to address the trauma. Thousands of others who haven't been physically assaulted, however, join up to overcome the feeling of powerlessness engendered by being "hey-baby" -ed on every block. One senior student, who joined Seido because her life was being threatened by an unrequited admirer, explains, "I knew I wouldn't instantly be able to protect myself physically, but I had to have the sense that I was taking some action. The training was about mental strength." Though most women begin karate for self-defense, we soon learn that in the street, fighting back is not always the best response. It's the emotional workout, and love of the form, that keeps us coming back.

Karate is the only sport that guarantees you'll confront your demons. Sooner or later you'll have to put yourself in a position that feels victimizing: you'll have to put up your dukes and face some lithe but hulking man's hook kick heading for your face.

For most women, the idea of standing across from someone and attempting to hit him seems as foreign and awkward as trying to run for a bus on their hands. And for those who've survived assaults, sparring class is like returning to the scene of the crime. At Seido, the journey is mercifully gradual. We don't start fighting until green belt, which usually comes after at least eighteen months of training. I remember attaining that rank in late '85 with both trepidation and thrill.

At my first sparring—or *kumite*—class, a wiry black belt caught my gut with a sidekick, and I went down sucking wind. I bounced up (thinking of my favorite saying from our weekly Zen meditation classes—"Fall down seven times, get up eight times") and I charged him wildly. I didn't come close to landing a punch, but the point was I was fighting back. I'd never felt so exhilarated.

My teacher, Kaicho Tadashi Nakamura, calls karate moving Zen. His oft-repeated principle of *kumite* made immediate, visceral sense to me: It doesn't matter whom you're paired against, your opponent is always yourself.

After a few weeks of *kumite*, I started dreaming about my sister, whose bullying I hadn't thought about in decades. As I fought, the memories whipped at me like rapid-fire roundhouses. I found myself withdrawing into the familiar posture of the battered. I froze, making a fine flat-footed target. Suddenly, I was terrified of hitting back—God only knew what might come out if I opened the floodgates that had restrained my fury for so long.

What I really wanted to do was to stop the fight and announce to the world that my opponent was hurting me. It was the only protective action I knew. Picking up dodges and counterattacks wasn't enough to snap me out of that syndrome: to learn self-defense, you first must believe you have a self worth defending.

At Seido, that belief accrues over time. Unlike a lot of other dojos, which are typically run by marine-macho masters who punish students and create an atmosphere of terror, at Zen-based schools like Seido (which means "the way of truth, honesty, and sincerity") we're pushed, all right, but not to the point of injury—physical, mental, *or* spiritual. Just as students in their sixties aren't expected to be as pliant as the elastic-legged teenagers, no one is asked to overcome emotional limitations all at once. One woman who was a severely battered child says she hasn't been able to bring herself to buy the protective gear we use for sparring, much less exchange blows with a partner, even though she has been a green belt for two years. "I know sparring is there and I have to grow into it at my own pace," she says. "If anyone forced me into it, I'd have to drop karate altogether. I'm just not ready yet."

That our own pace is respected is itself a boost to self-esteem. As Sharon puts it, "Someone who has been abused is always trying to be good and please authority figures. In karate we have to become our own authorities."

And then, no small thing, there's the physical discipline. If the rest of the world bombards women with images of our weakness, at the dojo we're not only allowed to be strong, we're *expected* to be. We do push-ups on our knuckles, and stand in fierce regiments throwing a hundred punches. We haul off and slam the heavy bag—left jab, right punch, left spinkick, wham!—letting rip the all-important *kiai,* that gut-driven yell that sets the toes tingling, so releasing, so satisfying, so *subversive.*

Certainly kicking and hollering and acquiring biceps don't make us feel inviolable. But they do begin to make us feel like we have a *right* to be. It's empowering simply to assert that we deserve to be safe, and downright revolutionary to say that our safety doesn't depend on the protection of a man.

* * *

The promotion to black belt at Seido is a four-part trial. There is an evening of basic kicks, blocks, and strikes; another of *katas*, beautiful routines that make choreography of fighting; a third in which we have to answer questions about essays we've written that describe our philosophy of training. And then there is the coup de grace: the ordeal of fighting. One raw December morning, we arrived at the dojo at 6:30 to spar, in two-minute rounds, against every single senior black belt who showed up. There were forty-two of them.

The night before, I dutifully ate pasta, washed it down with Gatorade, climbed into bed at 9:30, and dozed right off. At 10:30, I was agitatedly awake, accosted by images of fists and feet flying at my head. Unable to dispel them, I got up and graded papers till 4. Two hours later, I was loping through the deserted streets to meet my fate.

With the ten men and three other women who made up my promotion group, I flung my feet onto railings to stretch my hams and threw flurries of punches at the mirrors, trying to bounce the nervousness out of my body. At 7:30 we lined up, each of us facing a group of three seniors. We'd fight them one at a time, then rotate to the next group.

My first dozen rounds, I managed to keep my cool. I blocked. I ducked. Often I took a blow. But I hung in there. "Hands up," I chanted to myself. "Throw combinations. Get in, and get out."

Then I rotated to the area where the most senior students lay in wait. After some thirty-five minutes of the most draining exercise I've ever known, I'd already lost control of my breathing, which is absolutely crucial, and was panting like a dry-mouthed dog. Kicks came at my head, punches at my body, sweeps at my ankles. Soon, my tears were commingled with torrents of sweat as one senior threw left jabs with such speed and ferocity that I couldn't block them, get under them, or find a way around them.

As we changed partners, my new opponent, who saw me weeping behind my fogged-up head-gear, touched the center of my belt and said, "Just breathe. In, out. You're here, now. You're nowhere else." I bowed gratefully, and when our fight began, planted a snapkick in her ribs.

More than an hour had passed. With every round, my legs

got heavier, my forearms more bruised and tender. I heaved on, carried by the *kiais* echoing around me. When I saw that I was three groups from the end of the line, I was astonished by a sudden surge of strength. There were only nine fights left; I went for it.

And then, somehow, ninety minutes in, it was over. It hardly mattered that if anyone had been scoring, I probably wouldn't have been given a single round. The important thing was, I hadn't said "no mas." I had *survived*.

One by one, the fourteen of us stood before Kaicho, and he tied the long, stiff cloth tightly around our waists. And then we went and bowed, one by one, to those forty-two senior black belts. They cheered; every one of us cried.

With my new rank of *shodan*, which means beginner, I discovered a new set of challenges, among them overcoming the old refusal to accept my own accomplishments. Nothing could have quite prepared me for the moment when I took my place in the front line, or for the way doe-eyed beginners looked at me in the locker room. Least of all could I have guessed that I'd feel—ambivalently—as though I'd been inducted into an elite order. The old, laughed-off rumor that Bruce Lee died because he revealed the secrets of his style to the West, suddenly made some sense to me. There's a palpable mystique about a black-belt class; everyone in it viscerally understands the sense of self-possession the belt conveys.

People who hear I've earned my black belt always want to know, "Have you ever used your karate?" So far, I've been lucky enough never to have been physically assaulted, so no, not in the sense they mean.

But we all use it, every single day. Sharon says it's because of karate training that she's gained the self-confidence to go back to school for her Ph.D. Nancy Lanoue, a third-degree black belt who has opened a Seido branch for women in Chicago, remembers getting up from her hospital bed after her mastectomy three years ago, and practicing a *kata* with her IV unit dragging along behind her. "I felt totally alienated from my body," she says, "and needed to know it would work again. It was deeply comforting to do that movement." And the woman too afraid to buy her *kumite* gear was shocked by her reflexive response to a man who accosted her in the street: "I dropped my bag, put my fists up and just stood there. He was so taken aback, he walked away."

Me? I'm surprising myself, too, with the inner strength I never knew I had: I'm sending this article to my sister.

OF HIGHTOPS AND HOME PLATES

Deborah Abbott

I am sitting by the river, by a wide lazy stretch of the American River. I feel lazy, too. A friend lies beside me on her belly, offering trail mix to some visiting ducks. Yesterday, our first on the water this season, was a long one. Up early, with just enough time to gulp coffee, we began hauling rafts to the eddy; pumping them up until they sounded as ripe as melons; rigging them with ice chests, medical supplies, emergency ropes, and bailing buckets.

We then greeted our passengers—a friendly group of men with AIDS—and assembled them in the boats. After final adjustments of the ten-foot ash oars, we were pushing off into the current. I gave a loud whoop of joy: back on the river again; the sun on my face; the muscles in my arms, my back and belly falling into that familiar rhythm. The water level was dropping, exposing more rocks than usual. So it was a "technical" day, requiring a sharp eye and more intricate rowing to avoid snagging obstacles. But all went well. The men got wet and silly, got tossed around the rafts through the rapids, with just enough mishaps to chalk it up to an adventure.

Today I'm feeling a little sore, somewhat weary and full of the contentment that rafting always brings. I cannot imagine my life without this distinct pleasure, without the challenges, that good fatigue. And yet, five years ago, I had never rafted, had never even sat beside a river for any time at all. Aside from an occasional swim, brief walks with friends, and some wild nights of lovemaking, the adventures I had had for much of my life had been in my imagination.

I was born with an insatiable curiosity, though, a lively spirit, and strong body. My mother didn't believe in children sitting in darkened rooms watching TV on sunny days and so fed me breakfast and shooed me outside. There was a pine woods close by and half a dozen girlfriends with whom to explore. We built forts to-

46

gether, climbed trees, dug holes, buried and unburied treasures, played ball, swiped food from our mothers' kitchens and generally ran amok. Nobody seemed to notice or care that I had one leg in a metal brace and wore only ugly brown hightop shoes. My friends walked a little slower for me, and Missy, who was the fastest sprinter and most ruthless slider, was my pinch runner. I felt good about my body. I had two sturdy arms, one extra-strong leg, and an endless supply of energy. Because I got included in everything, I barely noticed that I couldn't run bases, could only bicycle downhill.

In junior high, my adventures abruptly stopped. I spent most of seventh grade in an enormous cast in a narrow steel bed at Shriner's Hospital in San Francisco. Orthopedists took turns slicing me open, rearranging my bones, sewing me up, and promising me a brace-free future. I would walk "normally," they assured me, without a limp. My body, which had taken so much delight in climbing, skipping, and moving freely through the woods, now required a nurse to turn from back to belly. My leg, which had never suffered more than the usual bruises and scrapes, was now ribboned with incisions, penetrated by metal pins, and consumed with pain that even Demerol couldn't relieve.

I returned to school in eighth grade and got put into Adaptive PE. While my friends were across the field playing baseball, a game I loved, I spent week after week playing four-square with girls who had cerebral palsy and could not catch the ball. I was humiliated; they were humiliated. My well-coordinated, agile body was bored, unchallenged. I skipped class as often as I could, feigning cramps and headaches. I began to hate my "bad" leg.

I became an intellectual; I disdained "dumb" jocks. Being a clarinetist in the high school band, I had to go to football games. Between tunes I read Faulkner, Sartre, and O'Connor, rolling my eyes at the cheerleaders, the hulky players. I felt safer amongst the writers and artists. My leg was hidden beneath the cafe tables. I avoided beach parties, swim parties, and dances—any situation where my disability would be revealed. I had a witty mind, a quick tongue. I did a good job of distracting people from my difference. When friends walked ahead of me, I remained quiet, hoped they wouldn't notice, and concentrated on catching up.

* * *

I played this game, my only game, very well for twenty years. During this time I read many books, wrote a handful of stories, went to readings and concerts, and had countless animated conversations with friends. I kept busy with work, my education, and raising two sons.

Yet there was a growing restlessness in me. My lovers were mostly musicians who worked late into the night and slept until noon. I woke beside them as the sun rose, my insides screaming with impatience and the desire to move.

Somehow, despite my self-consciousness, I began to swim. I had learned to swim when I was two and recovering from polio. It was the only physical therapy I ever liked. I had fond memories of my big bear of a father carrying me on his back into the deep end of the pool, calling over his shoulder, "Kick, Debbie, kick!" It felt good, after all those years, to be back in the water. Once in the pool, my leg was mostly inconspicuous. I quickly developed speed and endurance and secretly challenged the swimmers in the lanes beside me. My friends began commenting on my broadening shoulders, my more confident stride.

One day, some time later, I was standing with a friend, admiring a tall, muscled woman pass by. I sighed and said aloud, "If it weren't for my leg, I'd surely be a jock." My friend looked at me, puzzled, and commented matter-of-factly, emphatically, "But Deb, you *are* a jock."

I was startled. I shook my head. There was no such thing, I knew, as a disabled jock. The terms were incompatible, as immiscible as water and oil. I had never seen a disabled athlete, though I had heard of one "courageous" man who had raced the Wharf to Wharf in a wheelchair.

Then I met a woman, an able-bodied woman, who was strikingly strong and physically capable. I was surprised to be approached by her, astonished to be seduced by her. Since childhood I had witnessed able-bodied people's discomfort with me, had grown accustomed to averted eyes and nervous smiles. I had experienced this avoidance particularly with athletic types. Disability is, after all, a jock's worst fear. Many jocks eventually become disabled from the accumulated stress of the game, retiring from their sport to become coaches, sports writers, and fans.

But this woman, who became my lover, seemed unphased by my leg. Her wounds were on the inside, she said simply, mine on the outside. She pulled my brace out from under the bed where I always hid it and appreciated it for the interesting and valuable device it is. She was tender with both of my legs, with all of my body, and I believe that she found it more attractive and loved it better than I did. She came to know it well and to understand its possibilities, its limitations.

One morning, very early, she brought me to Seabright Beach. I peeled off my clothes, pulled on my swim suit, took off my shoes and my brace. We walked arm-in-arm to the water, and for the first time in twenty-five years, I felt the surf swoosh over my bare feet. She held me as I walked into the waves, laughing and sobbing. The water was numbingly cold. I gasped as I plunged in and began to swim past the breakers. I was elated and terrified. I kept stroking. I looked back at the shore and said to myself, "There's no turning back now."

There has been no turning back. Over time, my lover taught me to row, to boogey-board. She literally dragged me up mountainsides, pushed me over boulders, carried me down river banks. Years later, I can say, with only slight hesitation, that I am a jock. I spend a good deal of time on my tandem, in the ocean, on the river, in the pool. I work springs and summers as a sea kayak and whitewater raft guide with a company that specializes in making trips accessible for people with special needs.

In all this time, I have met only one other disabled athlete, a woman in a chair who plays basketball. She invited me to watch a game, to join the team. I have not yet had the courage to go, or join. While I long to be part of a team, I am a klutz in wheelchairs, and honestly, I have a great fear of the things. One day I may need one, not just for playing in. My brace slows me down and constrains me in some ways, but I do not experience the profound barriers nor the stigma that wheelchair users do. Not yet. As I imagine myself watching a game from the sidelines, a huge grief wells up in me. Even watching my children play soccer, or my able-bodied friends play softball, can be hard. I get sad. I get mad. I feel excluded. I *am* excluded.

Being disabled and athletic isn't easy. I am constantly reminded of my limitations, confronted with my pain. Sometimes I want to go back to the world of concerts and poetry readings, to take refuge in that place.

But most often, I want to go back, way back. I want to be ten again, at bat, with Missy poised to charge to first base for me. I remember what a powerful hitter I was, how my friends had to scramble to the far reaches of the field for the ball. I want to be ten again, in my clunky little brace and my dusty old hightops, squinting at home plate from the pitcher's mound. I want to be regular, just one of the girls.

GAY GAMES III: REFLECTIONS OF
A CANCER SURVIVOR

Pat Griffin

When we arrived at the beach, the moon was still up, a huge orb hanging over the bay. The dawn sky was red and blue. The water was flat, a good sign. The air had enough of a bite for sweatshirts and pants to be comfortable. I walked my bike into the transition area, found my number on a rack and hooked my brake handles over the cross-bar. As I stretched out my shoulders, I surveyed the prerace preparations. Race officials moved about, cordoning off a lane from the water to the transition area. Others sat in a tent poring over computerized entry information. A couple of others sat on a log in the sand drinking coffee and talking in quiet voices.

The few other early arrivals for the triathlon were sorting out their gear, carefully laying out shoes, bike helmets, and other equipment needed for the bike and the run legs of the race. All of us were quiet, absorbed in our own thoughts. My stomach was fluttering and I hoped I would not have to shit again before or, worse, during the race.

My lover of eight years, Maryann, waved and smiled at me from outside the transition area. She balanced a camcorder on her shoulder ready to record the event for posterity. Her event, the marathon, was later in the week. Along with a small contingent of lesbian friends, we had been planning on this trip to Vancouver, B.C. to compete in Gay Games III for over a year.

The events of the year between my deciding to participate and standing here on the beach had taken me through places I had never expected to go. Six months ago I didn't know if I'd live to see the Gay Games, much less participate. I was operated on for ovarian cancer at the end of January.

"The lab reports are back, Pat." My surgeon stood beside my hospital bed with a clipboard propped against her stomach. "They found some cancer cells in the ovary." I felt like I was falling, spinning away from her. I was too stunned to cry or speak. All I could hear was the word "cancer" and all I could feel was the terror it raised in me. I felt dizzy and it seemed like something was sitting on my chest. I remember thinking that this couldn't possibly really be happening to me, not me. I am forty-four years old, strong, healthy, athletic, in good shape. Not me. I kept waiting for the punch line, but of course, she would never joke about this.

"The cancer seems to be contained in the left ovary, but I recommend that we do a complete hysterectomy just to be safe. And I'll need to check your entire abdominal cavity and lymph nodes, too, just to be sure. After the lab reports are back from that, we'll know about any follow-up treatment."

My mind was a few sentences behind her, as I tried to absorb what she was telling me. I have cancer. Or I had cancer and I might still have cancer. I felt dazed and alone. I wished Maryann was here. Cancer.

"Pat, you're going to do that triathlon this summer. I want you to focus on that. We're lucky. I really believe it was contained in the ovary we already took out."

My thoughts drifted back to my first appointment with Dr. Keene two weeks before, on my birthday. She was checking out the shadow an ultrasound exam had picked up on my ovary. Her daughter was a runner on the high school track team and we had talked a lot about sports while I lay on the examining table and she was busy between my legs, probing, feeling. I told her that I was planning to do a triathlon that summer. I was so scared about what she might tell me that talking about sports helped to calm me down.

She stood, pulled off the latex gloves, and stepped on the pedal of the waste can. The top lifted and she tossed the gloves in. I kept chattering away about triathlons as if I could keep her from telling me something I didn't want to hear if I just kept talking. Finally she spoke, "It is not a cyst. It is a mass. Probably it is nothing serious, but it could be ovarian cancer." This definitely was not what I wanted her to say.

"Pat, did you hear me? You are going to do that triathlon in Vancouver." I tried to pull myself back to the hospital room. I wanted to be somewhere else. I wanted to be someone else.

My second surgery went well. The cancer was contained in the ovary and I did not need any follow-up treatment. My training began in the hospital shuffling up and down the hall as many times a day as I could, holding a pillow over my stitched, stapled, and very sore abdomen. Over the next few months I moved from walking to jogging, added biking and swimming, and focused myself on recovery from surgery and preparation for Vancouver.

Over the next few months I took a crash course in menopause. I learned to cope with hot flashes. I also discovered how useless most books about menopause and hysterectomies are. So many left me with the sense that my life was going to be filled with emotional and physical trauma and dysfunction. Most of what I read I found to be total bullshit. Some books assured me that I was still a woman, a concern that had not even entered my mind. Others cautioned about changes in sexual response and the ability to have orgasms. I got angry about the heterosexism in all of the books. Only one book said anything about lesbians and hysterectomies or menopause (one paragraph of speculation because, of course, no one had studied the experiences of lesbians). I learned to manage the terror that my three-month check-ups with Dr. Keene caused. Did they really get it all? And I absorbed new identities: postmenopausal woman and cancer survivor. Through it all I ran and biked and swam.

Training gave me focus and direction. It got me outside and gave me time alone to be thankful for my health and the love of my partner and my family and friends. As summer came, I realized that I would just barely be ready to complete the mile swim, twenty-mile bike, and seven-mile run in Vancouver. My goals became participation and enjoyment. I wanted to finish the triathlon and have a great time doing it.

As I sat on the beach in the Vancouver dawn, I smiled to myself. Yes, Dr. Keene, I am going to do this triathlon. It may not be the fastest time ever, but I am going to finish it and I am going to savor every moment of it.

By the time the starting gun went off and we ran into the cold water of English Bay, the sun was up and shining brightly. After the initial chaos of so many bodies bumping and splashing, I found open water and smoothed out. The swim is my best leg and I loved the feel of the water against my skin as I settled into a rhythm. Here I am, I thought to myself, doing the triathlon in the Gay Games. Just like you told me I would, Dr. Keene. I'm alive and well and doing this thing with all of these lesbian and gay sisters and brothers from all over the world swimming around me.

People cheered for all of the swimmers as we emerged a little disoriented from the sea. I stood up and wobbled out of the water in the glare of the morning sun. I ran up the beach to the transition area to find my bike. I felt full of joy for the beautiful day, and thankful for all of the people shouting encouragement. The bike leg took us around Stanley Park three times, up a grueling hill each time. I rode with this silly grin on my face. Even sucking air up the hills, I felt grateful for the burn in my chest and legs. What miracle or accident of fate had given me the chance to do this, I wondered. And how could I keep from taking life and health and joy for granted ever again.

Coming into the transition area to prepare for the run, my legs felt wobbly. I was hot and sweaty. And I was having a great time! The run took us around Stanley Park, much of it on the sea wall. Fresh sea breezes kept me going as my energy began to ebb. Rounding the last turn I saw the finish line a half a mile away. I could see the crowds of people waiting there, some of them my friends, and my partner looking for me among the runners.

All of a sudden I felt a catch in my chest and tears filled my eyes. I felt so alive and so proud to be who I am. At the same time I laughed at myself for being so sappy and so emotional about this race. But then, why not?

How many women did not survive cancer this year to realize a dream? How many lesbians were too filled with fear or self-hatred to come to the Gay Games and feel this incredible surge of pride and spirit? I thought about Meg Christian singing "The Ones Who Aren't Here" at Carnegie Hall. I felt the presence of lesbians and gay men who, because of fear or illness, weren't able to be there running with me. And for a moment they were with me. I carried their spirits and their spirits carried me, on toward the finish line, laughing and crying with joy and a profound sense of humility.

Part 3

POLITICS

LESBIAN ATHLETES

Betty Hicks

The rewards of her athletic triumphs of forty years ago provided the backdrop for our interview—her silver trophies etched with tenderly polished patina, the meaningful medals speaking of her international achievements in her chosen sport. The walls of her upper-middle-class condominium in a sunny upper-middle-class community are crowded with autographed pictures of her famed contemporaries.

Except for some matronly plumpishness replacing what once were the beautifully toned muscles of the top woman athlete in the nation, she and the sun, the wind and the years, have been kind to one another. She emphatically refutes the myth that the women athletes who were in the vanguard of professional sports for women were leather-skinned, tough-talking, testosterone-laced diesel dykes. She is gentle, warm, attractively feminine—and a lesbian.

She enthusiastically agreed to my interview request, provided she and her sport would remain anonymous in the article. Her chosen pseudonym will be Carol, avoiding any name that would duplicate those of the women champions of her era.

"Why write about women athletes?" a college physical education teacher asked me angrily when I told her I had proposed to write this article. "Why not write about lesbian actresses, or doctors, teachers, lawyers, journalists, or closeted housewives?"

"Write it!" was the consensus of women from several relevant professions, "because lesbian athletes are not understood." Carol agreed. "Unlike actresses, doctors, teachers, lawyers, and journalists they are carte blanche stamped with the lesbian label. They are subjected to slanderous inquisitions and harassment about their sexuality, usually by straight males milling around the periphery of their arenas. They are frequently slighted or insulted by

Editor's Note: This piece was originally published in 1979.

the media, and queried in print about why there are so many les-
bians among them. Thus, most lesbian athletes cringe in their clos-
ets, frightened for their livelihoods, the future of their sports, the
welfare of their sister athletes.
"Do you believe there are compelling reasons to write about
lesbians in sports?" I asked Carol.
"Even if there should be no other, there is a very legitimate
quantitative reason," she smiled. "There are so many of us."

In 1975 reporter Lynn Rosellini wrote a series of articles for the
Washington Star on homosexual athletes. In the second article,
"The Lesbian Label Haunts Women Athletes," she claimed that
gay women athletes number well above the 5 percent national
average of homosexual women.

"Rosellini was 55 percent off in my sport," says Carol. "I don't
know how she conducted her poll, but it wasn't the way a group
of us did recently, by counting the ones we know are gay."

"It's easier to count now than when Carol was a star," observed
a lesbian who stars in a professional team sport, whose census
among her compatriots revealed 80 percent gays. "The athletes
feel freer among themselves, even though they are—like myself—
just as closeted publicly as they ever were."

"The issue reaches beyond mere numbers," continued Carol,
who is 5'3" tall and fine-featured, hardly the amazon of homophobic myth. "There are innumerable questions about lesbian athletes that have never been asked. I am not at all sure society wants
to know the answers. Except perhaps in heavily academic texts,
discussions of our most important problems have been avoided."

She enumerated the questions she believed to be significant:
What is the psychosociological basis for the preponderance of lesbians in sports? What are the stereotypes and myths about women
athletes? How can we destroy these legends? Do sports create lesbians, or do lesbians simply do better in sports because they are
independent, psychologically strong, and self-sufficient?

"And what is the *real* cause of all the harassment we get?" she
added. "Why are straight males so pantingly curious about what
we do in bed? What rewards does society offer to lesbian athletes
who create the best cover-ups? And what have been our experiences with the media?"

Lynn Rosellini did not ask any but the most superficial questions; other writers have only minimally touched on the sociolog-

ical ramifications of being a woman athlete in a culture that imposes artificial sex roles upon both sexes. But all of the reporters who have done feature-length stories on women athletes in the past several years have emphasized the lesbian connection, that women athletes are automatically stamped gay unless they are married or beauty queens. Then they cluck their literary tongues and say, "My, my! It's too bad, because they're not all lesbians."

In a superb article on women golf pros in a 1971 issue of *Look*, Vivian Gornick admitted that "Everyone to whom I mentioned my assignment said bluntly: 'Find out if they're dykes.' "

"The questions persist," reported *Newsweek* in a women-in-sports cover story in 1974. "Who are these women who compete and live together on closely knit tours? . . . Are they lesbians who hate men or rejected heterosexuals who want to get back at men? . . . Do they sneer at sexiness, glamour, and marriage—or do they secretly covet a 'normal' life?"

"Almost every female sports star in U.S. history," wrote Rosellini, "with the exception of an occasional outstanding beauty, has been reported to be homosexual at some time in her career."

Women athletes are perpetual targets of homophobic attack, most of it from straight males. Carol recalls that there wasn't a week of competition in which she did not have the question tossed at her in some form as to the nature of her sexual activity. One young woman golf pro recalls, "When the *Star* articles were published, my boss got a gleam in his eye and asked me, 'Do you know any of those gay women golfers?' His dream was to watch two lesbians making love."

A personable straight male, a high executive who endorses the all-they-need-is-a-good-lay (by a *man*) method of therapy for lesbians, constantly interrogates his assistant about the women under contract to his company.

"His guesses about who is straight and who isn't are *so* bad," she laughed. "He's just gaga over this one international beauty who is a confirmed lesbian. Yet he is suspicious of another athlete—a big woman, a bit masculine, stronger than most of the gays—who is so active with men she scarcely has time or inclination to train for competition."

Carol was once invited to a preexhibition dinner with an older male coach in her sport. "Tell me," he began, cocking his eyebrows suggestively, "you're healthy young women. What do you do for sex out there?"

"Well," she said solemnly, "we masturbate a lot."

Vivian Gornick wrote in *Look* that "It is the dearest wish of the golfers' collective heart to put this matter straight" (note the pun)—that is, to blame their image on a knot of alleged butches who inaugurated the women's professional golf tour and who, the story persists, are to blame for the durable rumor that LPGA really stands for Lesbian Professional Golf Association. (Ironically, the strong, intelligent, attractive golfers for whom Gornick expressed the most admiration are gay.)

According to Lynn Rosellini, "The LPGA can trace its image difficulties back to 1950, when it was founded by a group of rangy, muscular women. Then, as now, society tended to link athletic women with lesbianism." Pro golfer Jan Ferraris added, "That's why we never got much money. Who wanted to come out and see women who look like men?" (Ferraris was two years old when the LPGA was incorporated.)

In fact, of the so-called truck drivers who started the LPGA, four were petite and "feminine"; three of these were straight. The founders ranged in size from 5'2" to 5'7½" and from 102 to 143 pounds. Three of them were married; one of *them* was a lesbian. The percentage of lesbians among the total original group? Exactly what it is estimated to be today: 60 percent. But Rosellini made no effort to examine the etiology of the diesel-dyke myth. Perhaps it was too "plausible" to invite skepticism.

However, Radicalesbians, a NOW splinter group, has successfully analyzed the cause of the legend's existence in a magnificent position paper written in 1970, entitled "The Woman-Identified Woman." "Lesbianism," they explain, ". . . like male homosexuality, is a category of behavior possible only in a sexist society characterized by rigid sex roles and dominated by male supremacy. . . . The investment in keeping women in that contemptuous role is very great. Lesbian is the word, the label, the condition that holds women in line . . . a label invented by a man to throw at any woman who dares to be his equal, who dares to challenge his prerogatives . . . who dares to assert the primacy of her own needs. . . . A lesbian is not considered a 'real woman.' And yet, in popular thinking, there is really only one essential difference between a lesbian and other women—the essence of being a 'woman' is to get fucked by men. . . . Are we going to continue the male classification system of defining all females in sexual relations to some other category of people? . . . As the source of self-hate and the lack of real self are rooted in our male-given identity, we must create a new sense of self . . . not in relation to men. For this we must be available and supportive to one another. . . . Our energies must flow toward our sisters, not backward toward our oppressors."

If the woman is an athlete we are assured the "male classification system" will be imposed. Tragically, many female athletes also have deplorably low consciousness levels. In their embarrassed haste to proclaim "*We're* straight," they panic and start pointing fingers.

One straight golf pro offered to give a reporter for a national muckraking magazine a list of gay women in golf. The writer was talked out of publishing it by a straight woman journalist who was sympathetic to the gay golfers' plight. Another unidentified golf pro told Rosellini bitterly, "The gay ones never hear about the problems it entails or the disgust it creates with sponsors or the galleries."

As Rosellini pointed out, "It was particularly galling to some golf veterans several years ago when the fledgling, yet 'feminine' U.S. women's tennis tour surpassed the golfers in total prize money. It is not surprising, then, that golfers are more sensitive about lesbianism than tennis players."

Rosellini's observation that the lace on their panties instantly brings more bucks to tennis players is a visceral-level judgment. Several factors produce more revenue for tennis players, the primary one being that tennis enjoys more TV exposure because it is far cheaper to televise a tennis tournament than a golf tournament.

As if heterosexual golfers sniping at their sister players weren't enough, some straight tennis players have joined these adversaries. "For a long time," tennis pro Julie Heldman told Rosellini, "the image of golf was one of homosexuality. What was the image of tennis? Gussie Moran. So they associated tennis with wiggling your tail. There's been only one Laura Baugh, but there's been a stream of masculine-looking golfers."

On the contrary, there has been a stream of Laura Baughs in golf: the Bauer sisters, Betty Mims Danoff, Diane Garrett, Betty MacKinnon, Nancy Lopez, Susan O'Connor, Marlene Floyd, Mary Cushing, Jan Stephenson, and more. They far outnumber the classic dykes, of which, admittedly, there have been a few.

Why has this reality been ignored by the lesbian baiters? Although golfers were her favorite targets, Rosellini quoted women athletes from a gamut of sports concerning the problems encountered by gay women athletes. Some were evasively, nebulously defensive; others merely added to the torrent of energy's backward flow.

"Reporters don't ask Arthur Ashe who the gay men on the circuit are," said tennis pro Julie Anthony resentfully. "But they ask the women players which women players are gay." Marathon runner Kathy Switzer said, "For years women athletes have been suffering from prejudices because people assume they're gay. I can never understand why society throws roadblocks in the path of people who want to live their own lives."

"But society does throw roadblocks," countered Rosellini. "In a culture in which plain features, a muscular build, and a competitive instinct are often equated with lesbianism, female athletes become 'dykes.' And lesbians in sport have yet another reason to stay in the closet."

Julie Heldman's mother, Gladys, the publisher of *World Tennis* magazine and one of the founders of the women's pro tennis tour, fired an hysterically homophobic shot: "I don't want to buy a racket if a homosexual plays with it. I can't conceive of the average mother wanting to send her son or daughter to a camp run by a homosexual."

"There *have* been best-selling rackets endorsed by homosexuals," challenged a lesbian tennis player, then laughed. "Doesn't Gladys Heldman know the manufacturers sterilize those grips? And Dr. Spock would assure mothers that before they ship their children off to tennis camps run by homosexuals that the kids' sexuality has already been cast in concrete. Heldman evidently forgot: One of the most revered tennis coaches of all time was a lesbian who managed nonetheless to produce some very fine straight champions."

"There is only one situation that continues to anger me," states Carol, and that is men who, between sips of Scotch and soda, seductively try to draw her into their confidence with the same question she used to hear every week. "Mister," she now answers, "if you need to call us lesbians, you are the one with the problem."

"I do not get angry at most of the camp followers who pursue us," says Carol.

"Camp followers" are upper-middle and upper-class women,

usually married to prominent businessmen or professionals. Children? Of course. Junior leaguers? Naturally. PTA? An obligation. Hospital volunteers? A must. Superstraight, right-wing club members, their eyes must be shielded from the sight of lesbian athletes. A number of these camp followers have had significant admiration for Carol.

"One night we had dinner at her home," recalled Carol about one such woman. "Husband out of town. Kids in bed. She was only a tiny bit drunk. 'It's wrong! It's immoral!' she protested, simultaneously telling me how much she cared for me. At that same instant she embraced me and traced her tongue around mine."

It is only when the camp follower decides to reject her heroine—out of disinterest or guilt—and runs to the sanctuary of home and husband screaming "That lesbian attacked me!" that Carol becomes angry. "I am intolerant of hypocrisy," she declares, eyes snapping, "particularly when a lesbian athlete is professionally damaged because of it."

"Star women athletes become 'extensions' of their married women admirers," notes Barbara Fellman, a California gay therapist. "It is entirely possible that some of the rumors about lesbian athletes chasing women club members around locker rooms result from fantasies. These women would like to be chased but are not. So they fantasize that they are."

Myths beget myths. One solemnly perpetuated rumor warns young athletes that if they enter high-level competition they will magically turn into lesbians. I once overheard two top collegiate women golfers, seated on a teeing-ground bench, chatting about the LPGA tour.

"Boy," said one, "I don't want to turn pro and go on that tour. I don't want to be a lesbian."

"Me neither," echoed her companion, a tone of fear and repugnance in her voice.

Another amateur woman golfer recently asked me, "Is it true, like my club pro says, that the tour will turn you into a lesbian? My father is worried." My response was that the tour cannot "turn" a person into anything she was not already before she went on it, which appeared to frighten her.

Why is it that when a young woman moves energetically, vigorously, even violently in dance, swimming, gymnastics, or tennis she is considered graceful and feminine? A female in a designer dress can swing a tennis racket in the center court at Wimbledon before the Queen of England and count her income in hundreds of thousands of dollars. But if she competes with equal skill and grace in the "masculine" uniform of a professional softball player, she works for slave wages, often in grungy ballparks where the outfielders can smell the portable toilets when the wind is wrong.

"The phenomenon of packaging and labels involves 'sex-role identity,' " explains Barbara Fellman, "those traits and behaviors most people believe characterize males and females."

Janice Kaplan, writing in the *New York Times,* observed, "We like our female athletes in huggable packages. When they're cute, they're not threatening. But when victory constantly goes to the very young, it's a sign that something is wrong.

"The reason for cherishing the more vulnerable and childlike of female athletes has less to do with sports than with psychology. A female athlete who has not been allowed to grow up is a delightful toy. She is not a challenge and she is not a threat. Men can recognize that she has talent without admitting that she is a real athlete. She receives pat-on-the-head praise. Apparently, we still find it easier to infantilize women than to accept them."

Beyond the fundamental branding imposed by our culture, women athletes must also buck what Dr. Roberta Bennett describes as "society's exploitation of sports as a 'social-control mechanism.' " A professor of physical education and women's studies at San Francisco State University, Dr. Bennett claims that "Sports are used to sort males into their roles."

Before a child can be sorted, it must be labeled. The efficacy of the fool-'em-with-packaging was emphasized by a psychological study in which young parents were asked to describe fully clothed anonymous babies. Those babies that were dressed in blue were perceived as "strong" and "alert" while the babies swaddled in pink were "soft" and "little"—regardless of the actual sex of the child.

"Society functions on packaging," said Fellman, a marketing fundamental long exploited by women's tennis. She summarized some of the studies of children during their developmental years, from which have emerged children's concepts and views of their own sexuality. This research affirms that sexual orientation is determined in the preschool years.

"As early as the first year," continued Fellman, "boys are re-inforced for exploration and for gross motor activities, while girls get approval for staying close to mother and for fine motor activities. Even three-year-olds become aware that society supports behavioral differences based upon gender. From nursery school on, children are encouraged in same-sex-typed behavior. By the sixth grade sanctions against opposite-sex-role behavior are internalized. Children do better in tasks believed appropriate to their sex. They also do significantly worse on tasks labeled appropriate for the opposite sex.

"By puberty both sexes have been conditioned to believe that masculine attributes are more socially desirable. Girls are praised for same-sex-typed behavior. Only occasionally are they praised for opposite-sex-typed behavior."

The media routinely delivers this message. In one episode of "The Waltons," Mother Walton solemnly warned young Elizabeth, "There comes a time when a boy would rather see a girl in a fancy dress than with a catcher's mitt." For the girl who won't slip into the fancy dress, the social penalties are enormous.

Basketball star Carol Blazejowski, interviewed on TV during the 1978 Women's Superstars Competition, recalled growing up as an athlete: "As a child, playing with the boys, I really suffered from the verbal abuse." Earlier, she had told *womenSports* magazine about the taunts from the boys: " 'You're nothing but a tomboy! Why don't you go home and make babies?' I'd go home crying because of what people said. But I kept my goals in mind; I persisted."

By the time children reach adulthood, the messages are militantly translated. Researchers have shown that adult males are far more likely to equate opposite-sex-typed behavior with homosexuality. It is significant that both men and women perceived a demonstration of the same assertive behavior by either sex as more aggressive when it is exhibited by a woman than by a man.

No recent in-depth study of women in sports has examined the cultural values that question the right of women to participate in athletics. In *The American Woman in Sports,* authors Ellen W. Gerber, Jan Felshin, Pearl Berlin, and Waneen Myrick observe, "Sex-role steretopes don't have to relate to reality, as long as woman's role is idealized within the home. . . . In sexist social view, the very participation of women tends to downgrade an activity, and sport is much too important and stands for far too many valuable social norms for that to be permitted. . . . Most pernicious of all, women in sport are so adversely affected that they are no longer considered real women."

Sport is reserved for men, and the women who seek to enter the arena court the lesbian label. Dr. Alan Bell of the Kinsey Institute benevolently explained away the bull-dyke image for Rosellini: "The preponderance of homosexual females . . . are passive and traditional females." Then he added, "Sports has always been a haven for lesbians."

Dr. Harry Edwards, a sport sociologist at the University of California at Berkeley, states that women athletes "are forced by cultural definitions to choose between being an athlete (thereby facing barely hidden suspicions as to the degree of their heterosexuality) and their womanhood."

Straight golf pro Carol Mann told Lynn Rosellini, "Women attracted to athletics in my generation were usually not very attractive. They had deep insecurities about their physical image and were attracted to something where they could get some acceptance. I was tall, very ugly, super ugly, with no identifiable figure. I enjoyed boys, but they wouldn't ask me out. I had trouble with my sexual self-image for a long time. So I buried myself in golf. That happened to so many players on our tour."

Many of the women athletes I interviewed said in chorus, "I was an athlete before I knew I was a lesbian." They considered themselves no more, no less attractive than their peers. More often than being rejected by boys, they had themselves rejected the boys in favor of concentration on sports. Society, of course, considers this unlikely.

In 1973 Nancy Williamson and Bil Gilbert published a largely excellent three-part series on women athletes in *Sports Illustrated,* notorious for its shunning of sportswomen. "Behind the myth that participation in sports will masculinize a woman's appearance," they wrote for their predominantly male readership, "there is the even darker insinuation that athletics will masculinize a woman's sexual behavior." The authors then made a crippled effort to refute this myth, citing a study by Dr. Christine Packard, a London consultant on sexual dysfunction, that suggests sports create the opposite effect. Dr. Packard found that "*girl* [my emphasis] athletes tend to make better lovers and are much sexier than less active females." This fortuitous finding, deduced Williamson and Gilbert, indicated superior *heterosexual* behavior, clearly the opposite of "masculinized" sexual behavior. It obviously did not occur to either author that lesbian lovemaking, rather than being "masculinized," is *emasculated;* a majority of "girl" athletes who are sexier as a result of sports direct their superior desire and lovemaking talent toward other women.

In 1973 *Ms.* magazine published two articles on women in sport. In "Giving Women a Sporting Chance," Brenda Feigin Fasteau wrote: "One of the potent means of discouraging women from participating in sport, was the unenlightened suspicion that a woman's interest in athletics violates the docile female stereotype and indicates lesbianism (remember the rumors about gym teachers?)." In "On the Playing Fields of History," Marjorie Loggia wrote: "The historical choice has been simple: woman or athlete? To choose the latter meant risking censure—the pejorative 'tomboy' for the child, 'dyke' for the woman—plus suffering the paradox that the better a woman became, the worse became her self-doubt."

The automatic gay label affixed to women athletes is intricately entangled in the sociology of sports for males. The question of why the sexuality of women athletes is suspect is not a simple one to address, yet it has gone unanswered because its simplicity has been assumed.

"Sports serve a function in our country which is parallel to initiation rites," explained Dr. Roberta Bennett in a paper presented for the Western Psychological Society. "Protection of sport from the intrusion of women is as critical to the power structure as is the protection of the church from heretics. In order for society to maintain its structure, the young must be made to fit.

"Games become an expressive model for testing parental and societal messages about a child's 'proper' role. The game form itself becomes a learning situation in which the child is educated on the values and competencies required of her/him by the culture. Through game forms, each child receives society's messages."

In Dr. Bennett's view, the exclusion of females from sports is systematic and pervasive.

"For centuries, certain myths about how girls should play and about women in sport have served to keep women out. . . . We have been told that women must be kept out of sport and games of physical skills for our own well-being. I propose to you that this is the greatest myth of all . . . that women have been kept out of games of physical skill only to preserve these games as an exclusively male domain.

"What good is a male rite of passage if females are participating in it? What good is it to train the male to succeed in today's power structure, to develop group solidarity, if females are to become a part of that structure? The war against women in sport is one of the most vicious of the misogynistic battles being fought today."

"Physical skills are imperative in the development of a positive self-image," says Barbara Fellman. (Research has shown that women athletes develop more desirable self-images than do non-participants.) "But little girls are told: 'Be careful, don't get dirty, don't get hurt.' Thus, valuable behaviors for developing self-esteem are negated. The factors necessary to development of self-esteem are considered 'masculine' in our culture."

"The battle will remain vicious," predicts Dr. Bennett, "because the legal and power plays are not working well."

The weapons are myth, slander, and the creation of guilt. Some women athletes are still snapping at the bait of distortions of physiological truths, widely used as an effective barrier to keep women out of sports. Pro golfer Jane Blalock, in her autobiography *The Guts to Win,* whispers confidentially that when women golf pros shoot a bad round it's probably because it's "that time of the month." (Blalock confessed that she tries to plan her own tournament schedule around her menstrual periods.)

"For a man," comments Dr. Bennett, "it's called 'having an off day.' It's one of the established myths that cyclic changes and menstruation prevent women from performing all-out." Although research has emphatically disproved this, Bennett notes that "Unfortunately, myth has a far more pervasive influence on popular belief than does science. It serves excellently as a tool of social control."

If the promulgation of physical untruths fails to deter girls who enjoy sports, what other methods can the straight-male establishment use to keep them out of sports? The guardians of male-only sports now turn to "scientific psychological research" to show that sportswomen have more "masculine traits" than their nonathletic sisters.

"What is this all about?" wonders Dr. Bennett. "Sport inculcates characteristics considered requisite for success by males in our society, so why should we expect female athletes to have personality profiles resembling nonparticipating women? And why are these 'masculine' traits desirable in a man but not in a woman? These personality tests have shown that the characteristics, attitudes, and preferences that society values in a woman become locker-room jokes if found in a man.

"In our culture there is perhaps no more slanderous remark than that which questions one's sexuality. Dance is a woman's thing; thus, a male who is a dancer must not be a male. Sport is a man's thing; thus, a woman who is an athlete must not be a woman; therefore she must be a lesbian. This line of reasoning has been, perhaps, more effective than any in keeping women out of sport. For many lesbians who are still closeted, it means removing one's self from any activity that may threaten one's cover. For straight women, it has been translated from 'sportswomen are lesbians' to 'women's sports are *for* lesbians.'

"But why do you resent the lesbian label," protest the homophobes, "when you admit there are in fact a preponderance of lesbians in sports? Doesn't an athlete almost *have* to be a lesbian to succeed? Don't sports turn women into lesbians? Why otherwise are there so many there?"

During a recent major women's sports competition, eight women athletes representing several sports grouped informally at the luxurious home of two of them, sipping beer, rapping about being gay. "Let's see if there are similarities in us," suggested one star, "if there *is* a pattern." They explored parental relationships, examined their childhoods, talked of their first awareness of being attracted to women. They spoke of the heavy social pressures to be straight or to pretend to be straight. Their exploration revealed no pattern they could identify. "I think it's just the way you are," said a clipped Australian accent. The conversation drifted into typical tour small talk about who was not doing the laundry properly and who would go to the grocery store.

In "The Woman-Identified Woman," Radicalesbians answered best the question of why there are so many lesbians in sports:

"What is a lesbian? A lesbian is the rage of all women condensed to the point of explosion. She is the woman who, often beginning at an extremely early age, acts in accordance with her inner compulsion to be a more complete and freer human being than her society . . . cares to allow her. . . . At some level she has not been able to accept the limitations and oppression laid on her by the most basic role of her society—the female role."

The lesbian athlete is fighting an all-out war against the restrictions of sex roles.

"When I was eleven," recalls a lovely, soft-spoken softball player, "I played baseball with the kids until Mom would yell at me to come eat. And I used to kick their butts, man! They couldn't hit a fly I couldn't catch; I could hit flies they couldn't catch. Then, when it came time for Little League, who was in the stands watching those little turkeys? And it pisses me off now that it didn't piss me off then. But I had no reason to be pissed off, because I did not know I was being cheated, that something was wrong. I always wanted to be a boy because I couldn't do those neat things boys could. Now I'm glad I'm not a boy, because only girls can be lesbians. Maybe if we didn't have to plow through so much crap to become athletes in the first place, more of us would be straight."

I sought out Pat Elliott and Carol Berendsen, two of four co-authors of the pioneering sex manual Loving Women, for more insight on the lesbian athlete. Both are former physical educators and experienced observers of the arena in which female athletes perform.

"Women athletes will rarely achieve an egalitarian relationship with a heterosexual male," observed Berendsen, "because once the average straight male has perceived that a woman doesn't need stud service, it's scary for him."

"The woman athlete's personality is a type the male can't deal with," interjected Elliott. "Marriage as a lifestyle is not suitable for most women who have achieved in sports. Isn't it ironic that traditionally stated objectives of athletics are to make a person self-sufficient and strong, that the Great American Dream tells the athlete to hope, strive, plan, sacrifice, work, achieve? When the woman athlete does this society sticks a purple star on her forehead."

Where can the strong, coordinated, "aggressive" woman turn for social approval? "So-called masculine traits often associated with lesbianism—independence, aggressiveness, and competitiveness—are welcome in sports," wrote Lynn Rosellini in the Washington Star.

* * *

Recently I watched a group of young athletes perform a dance choreographed by Abner Doubleday. I admire the courageous grace of women softball players. If they wore leotards instead of sliding pads and sanitary hose society would reward them with bouquets instead of brickbats. If they had turned their skills towards the "feminine" sports many of them would now be wealthy women. Why are there so many lesbians on that field? I asked myself. Why did they become left fielders or pitchers while the "straight" country-club woman who actually prefers other women became a wife and mother? Possibly all of these women are close to one another on the continuum of sexuality.

A young woman with gay tendencies who likes sports but is short of top-level talent, lacks the motivation to acquire championship skills, or is deficient in the kind of independence and fortitude required to resist social pressures to cram her into a stereotypical mold, will probably complete her cultural assignments to be a wife and mother. She will not become a lesbian athlete. The woman athlete's lesbianism has comparatively little to do with her enjoyment of the juxtaposition of clitoris with clitoris. It has a great deal to do with talent and courage, with seeking the companionship of others with like capabilities and motivations. The same inner strengths that make her a champion have fueled her resolve to express her sexuality as she feels it. The lesbian athlete may be the ultimate articulation of women's liberation.

In her novel *Flying,* Kate Millett wrote, "If women are vulnerable to the dyke baiting we are vulnerable to everything, a paper movement [the women's movement], helpless even before words. . . . The media is delighted to exploit one's sexuality. . . . We will never be free unless we relinquish the comfort of our disguises."

I do not know a lesbian athlete who would debate that statement. Nevertheless, a major portion of lesbian athletes' fortitude and energies must be directed toward maintaining straight facades. Millet also wrote, "The movement cannot be queer, dykes the papers call us. No, straight we rush to assure them, showing wedding rings and children, pushing the prettiest ones forward to go on television." Lesbian athletes perform the same protective ritual. For those women who choose to compete, regardless of society's exhortations not to, the penalty is severe; their paychecks reflect a direct correlation to the "femininity" they project.

"To most lesbian athletes," wrote Lynn Rosellini, "coming out is not yet worth it"—although she indicated that in recent years gay women in sports have become increasingly overt about their sexual preferences. One gay woman tennis player told Rosellini that she's sure the straight women on the tour knew she was gay; they just didn't discuss it. "The public, however," said Rosellini, "is not likely to be as tolerant as the women in tennis. So, like other gay women she practices small deceptions."

"Coming out is a continuous process," observes Barbara Fellman. "If you are gay you are faced with an ongoing decision as to coming out. It's never completed, unless you wear a purple star on your forehead."

"We never discussed *it* thirty or forty years ago," Carol told me, "except very privately, between couples." She spoke matter-of-factly about the burdensome facades she and her sister competitors were forced to project. World War II created a convenient camouflage for many of them. A woman's "fiancé" could be overseas—the irreplaceable male lover shot down in flames over Tokyo. "I even wore an engagement ring one year," remembered Carol. "But I'm a bad actress; I could not read my lines with convincing sincerity. So I 'broke the engagement.' " (Although women athletes will lie to hide their homosexuality, few actually resort to marriage.)

Barbara Fellman regrets the psychological price of the facade: "It can interfere with an athlete's developing her full potential. They are hiding from one another, hiding from the public. The energy spent playing those games could go better into something else. The traveling and competitive lifestyle are stressful enough, without the additional weight of the facade."

Dr. Roberta Bennett is fatalistic: "It's a no-win situation for the woman athlete. You have a whole additional trip laid on you. Because of the sheer ugliness of the rumors and myths, women in sports have to fight on a far different level for their right to participate."

Several women athletes admitted to me that they have gone to bed with male groupies. Often the men stated crassly that they were curious to learn if the alleged lesbian could be lured into the sack, if it was true about those dyke athletes. "I was sure that was the way to convince this guy that we were not lesbians who hated men," one woman athlete recalled with distaste. "His departing statement was, 'I still think it's true what they say about you.' "

Carol now realizes that when she was at her peak she felt enormous pressure to perform well, to achieve, to gain respectability, "combined with the weight of that damned facade. I know now that trying to create the veneer of straight-hood and femininity—I detest that word for its superficiality—availed nothing. We were guilty without trial, no matter how many men we bedded down with, no matter what efforts we made to flirt with and date and pretend and kiss the tittering straight males who handed us the trophies at the final presentations. It was the epitome of exercises in futility."

Carol believes that what helped her to survive and to continue functioning was that her success in sports gave her an arsenal of good feelings about herself: "How strong those feelings must have been to give me the guts not to crumble under the taunts and threats of those KKK-type homophobes."

Ever since the Greek Olympiads, when women apprehended in the vicinity of the stadium were condemned to death and hurled off a cliff, the words "women" and "sport" have been accepted as being diametrically opposed. "The woman-in-sport concept is a social peculiarity," explains Roberta Bennett. "Women in sport have had few choices, none of them appealing, if we wanted to participate. We could participate in those movement forms which are acceptable because they are considered feminine or we could participate according to our own desires and then develop the elaborate apologetic to affirm our feminity. Or we could simply *not* participate. We had to assure society that women in sport are, thank God, 'just like everybody else in bed at night' (a comment attributed to runner Chi Cheng)."

Bennett is vigorously critical of the "defensive posture of women in sports." The myth purveyors say women in sports are masculine, muscular, aggressive, dominant, lesbian, success-oriented. "What if they are?" retorts Bennett. "Why should so many pages be devoted to defending, excusing, begging, or apologizing for the desire of girls and women to pursue all forms of movement activity?" In no other male domain women have tried to enter has "the resistance been so vocal and so violent"; in no other domain have well-intentioned women and men been so uniformly defensive. According to Bennett, "We are still trying to reassure society that it is OK for women to play, gain skill, excel in all the uses of our selves—united body, spirit, intellect, emotion."

I asked Carol if the scene were any brighter for the lesbian athlete now than it was forty years ago. She shook her head.

"It is no different today," she answered, "though many women
athletes have deluded themselves into thinking it is. Young athletes
have such a zilch sense of history. The exception is that today they
are paid a great deal more for carrying their heavy facades around.
Numerically there are more lesbians now, because there are more
participants. Perhaps their production of cover-ups is more prolific
and more imaginative than ours was. Their exposure to the media
is greater; the accessibility to more fans has increased. But the
myths are not dead. The legends persist.

"No," she concluded sadly, "the picture for the lesbian athlete
has not changed."

Carol smiled. "It is quite a relief," she said, "to reach an age
when people no longer maliciously speculate about your sex life.

"Of course, because according to one more of society's myths,
you no longer *have* any sex life!"

THE COMPETITIVE CLOSET

Victoria A. Brownworth

With a dramatic rise in salaries, scholarships, and prize money in women's sports, a new, dangerous "game" is taking hold: dyke bashing. Victims range from established stars to aspiring college recruits and in the end include everyone involved in women's sports.

The impact of antilesbian discrimination in women's sports is far-reaching. Women in college sports can—and do—lose scholarships because of their sexual orientation. Others who are training in college for the Olympics or other international sports competition are deliberately passed over for inclusion on teams, making the move to professional sports almost impossible.

Professional sports are no easier for the lesbian athlete. In professional sports, where tournament purses can reach into the millions, loss of revenue is a very serious fear of any athlete considering coming out as a lesbian. Product endorsements, prize money, and positions as coaches, trainers, or sportscasters after retirement are all threatened.

"There's just so much homophobia out there," says a national sportswriter who asked not to be named.

One professional woman golfer, who requests anonymity, says, "I thought this was a safe haven, a lesbian sport. There is no question that this is the gayest of sports—come to a women's golf tournament, and all you see are gay women everywhere. Yet there is this idea that nobody knows, nobody *should* know, and if anybody finds out, somehow the whole sport will just disintegrate."

"Homophobia is everywhere, but it's sometimes very subtle," says Jane LaForce, an openly lesbian sports trainer in Los Angeles.

But some in women's sports contend that discrimination against lesbians is necessary. "As unfortunate as it is that this sort of harassment goes on," says a coach at a Midwestern college, "these girls really bring it on themselves. It just isn't important to be openly lesbian in college and tell everybody that you like other girls and so forth. I don't think it's discrimination if these coaches keep these players off their teams. It's for the good of the team. And frankly, in the long run, it can only benefit women's sports."

THE PRICE OF GOING PRO

Martina Navratilova and Billie Jean King are reputedly the only publicly known lesbians in women's professional sports. And though there are many lesbians in the sports world—insiders even call the Ladies Professional Golf Association (LPGA) the Lesbian Professional Golf Association—few are out of the closet. The LPGA was founded in 1950 by Babe Didrikson, who, during her athletic career in track and field and in golf, earned several Olympic gold medals, broke world records, and received the Associated Press world athletic award seven times. Didrikson's affairs with other women on the LPGA circuit were fairly well-known, and she had a long-term relationship with another woman founder of the organization.

Navratilova came out in 1983, only after hitting the pinnacle of her game as the top-seeded women's tennis player in the world—twelve years after defecting to the United States from Czechoslovakia. King was outed in a palimony suit brought by a former lesbian lover. At the time, she denied being a lesbian.

The financial rewards of professional women's sports have risen astronomically over the years. In 1980 the total purse for the LPGA circuit was $5 million. In 1993 the purse was an impressive $20.1 million. The U.S. Open tennis tournament also boasts a significant increase in winnings for women. Awards, which amounted to $16,000 in 1974, reached $402,150 in 1993.

With tournament purses increasing in size, lesbian athletes have high stakes in keeping their private lives in the closet. Says the national sportswriter: "After covering women's golf for the past ten years, I can tell you what the *L* stands for in LPGA. The tournaments are very big with the gay crowd. But get one of these gals to stand up and say she's a lesbian publicly, and she's out of the game. Martina and Billie Jean—they're exceptions. It's more likely you get the Maggie Courts claiming that dykes are killing women's sports. And it only takes one statement like hers to get everybody scurrying back into the closet."

During the height of the 1990 professional tennis season, former tennis great Margaret Court, now a born-again Christian, announced to the news media that women's professional tennis was rife with older lesbian players such as Navratilova who "preyed" on younger players. Court, winner of twenty-five Grand Slam tournaments, was quoted in a variety of national newspapers and tabloids as saying that lesbianism was so rampant in women's tennis that parents were refusing to allow their young daughters to go on tour.

Lesbianism, said Court, was killing tennis. "Because of the lesbian influence, there are now some players who don't even go to the tournament changing rooms," she asserted. "There's a group of lesbian-bisexual players on the circuit, and they're the ones who get at the youngsters with their example." Court said that Navratilova, who was photographed jumping over the stands to kiss her lesbian lover after winning the women's singles at Wimbledon in 1990, "hasn't been a good example" for young players.

Weeks after Court's accusation, other players were quoted in the London tabloid the *Sun,* among them Gabriela Sabatini, who said, "I don't even like to take my clothes off in the dressing room. I feel safe only when my parents are around, because I'm very young and some people may take advantage. You never know in this sport." Other complainants included Steffi Graf, Jennifer Capriati, and Monica Seles.

Jack Hutslar, director of the North American Youth Sport Institute, added to the furor by claiming that in professional women's tennis, "there are considerable lures and temptations put out by lesbian players that can entrap these young, impressionable girls."

Others find the statements by Court, Sabatini, and Hutslar way off base. Women's Tennis Association (WTA) publications director Doug Clery was the first to react to Court's accusations—a full year after she made them. Clery called the retired tennis star's statements "an example of personal bigotry. There are many players of different sexual orientations and preferences [in the WTA]. The WTA did not respond to Court and saw no reason to respond because these were the statements of a bigoted person who has nothing to do with the WTA."

"I don't know what possessed Court to make those accusations," Clery continues. "She's someone who's never been active in the WTA. She wouldn't even know about these things. It seemed to be a case of someone past her prime wanting to get her name in the papers. The fact is, at a tournament a lot of the players are already dressed [for the game]; they arrive dressed from their hotel rooms."

Clery says that although the WTA has no official antidiscrimination policy based on sexual orientation, "there have been no official complaints to us. We also haven't had any complaints of the sort Court claims there are."

The LPGA echoes Clery's comments on Court. Public relations administrator Beth McCombs says, "How did she know? How would she know about these other players seducing younger women, and how would she know these younger players are being kept off the circuit? Anyone who knows anything about sports would wonder about her accusations."

McCombs angrily denies there is any discrimination on the ladies pro golf circuit. "I don't think there are any lesbians on the golf circuit. We don't have an [antidiscrimination] policy because we've never had the problem. Fortunately, it hasn't become an issue because it just hasn't happened." Any complaints that might arise in the future would be handled by LPGA president Judy Dickenson, according to McCombs.

Some lesbian players, however, claim homophobia is rampant on the LPGA circuit.

"I'd like to be able to come out, and I know a couple of other women would," says the professional woman golfer. "But to do it takes a kind of maverick quality that I just don't have. I'm afraid—I'll admit it. I'm afraid to even be talking to you. What if you decide to print my name? Or what if someone figures out who I am? This is my job, this is who I am, this is where I want to be, where I've worked all my life to be. I'm just not willing to be a martyr and give it all up. It's painful, it makes me unhappy, but it's the way things are. Period."

ENFORCING THE COLLEGE CLOSET

The issue of homophobia in college sports was raised publicly in March 1991 by Rene Portland, who was then coach of the top-ranked women's college basketball team in the country, who said lesbians had no place on her team at Pennsylvania State University. According to former players and Betty Jaynes, the executive director of the Women's Basketball Coaches Association (WBCA), if Portland uncovered a player's lesbianism, the player was benched and dismissed from the team and would lose any scholarships.

Portland's antilesbian bias even translated into fear for straight players. "Rene told us when we came on the team that she didn't go for the lesbian life-style, that she didn't want it on her team—wouldn't tolerate it," says a former Penn State player, who asked not to be named. "I'm not a lesbian, but when I played for her, I was afraid she might think I was and take away my scholarship. I started changing the way I dressed, started going out with a guy I didn't like—just to stay on the team. It meant my academic career, that scholarship."

When the Portland story made news across the country during the National Collegiate Athletic Association finals in April, Portland stopped answering her calls, and Penn State did a quick shuffle on its antidiscrimination policies. But although the story was picked up by much of the mainstream and gay and lesbian media, none of the reports went beyond Penn State to the broader issue of homophobia in women's sports.

Following the Portland controversy student demonstrations resulted in Penn State officials considering—and eventually voting down—the addition of a sexual orientation clause to the school's antidiscrimination clause. The majority of colleges and universities have no such protections, and there are no state or federal laws to protect intercollegiate players from discrimination based on sexual orientation.

Federal Title IX laws were instigated in 1977 to protect against discrimination on the basis of gender in intercollegiate sports, but most legal experts in the area of antigay and antilesbian discrimination agree that they cannot be extended to include sexual orientation. And even when colleges have antidiscrimination clauses in their charters, few students file complaints. Only two have filed against Portland, yet several former players contend that there have been at least that many lesbians dismissed every season that Portland has coached the team.

The WBCA also has no antidiscrimination policy, but Jaynes says the organization has held seminars on homophobia. As for Portland, Jaynes comments, "Her stance is well-known. Some coaches would agree with it, some would disagree."

In fact, Portland's attitude toward lesbians is so well-known that some players take her stance into consideration when applying to colleges. Meggan Yedsena, who was named the most valuable college basketball player of the season in Pennsylvania in 1991, says that she had considered Penn State because of Portland's stand on lesbians. Yedsena, who now plays for Arkansas State University, says, "I like that she took that stance. It's pretty much a big issue. [Portland] is trying to create an image for women's basketball. They are trying to get the stereotypes erased."

Mary Ann McChesney, a spokeswoman for the Women's Sports Foundation in New York, a national information resource center and archive, says the foundation is opposed to antilesbian discrimination because "we are against discrimination in any form." She also notes that the foundation has a file on coach Portland "and would be happy to receive other information on lesbians in women's sports or discriminatory policies or acts against them."

A THREAT TO FEMININITY

There are some who believe that at the core of homophobia in women's sports is the issue of femininity.

The equation has always been simplistic: sports are masculine; therefore, women in sports are masculine; therefore, women in sports are lesbians.

"Some women's sports have always had the stigma of lesbianism," asserts an athletic director at an Eastern college, who asked not to be named. "Basketball and softball, particularly. Golf—look at Babe Didrikson, the Olympic athlete and founder of the LPGA. She was a notorious lesbian. Any sport that requires real physical power, not just prowess, will have that stigma. In the traditionally 'feminine' sports like ice skating, field hockey, archery, or even gymnastics, there just isn't the same aggression needed to perform."

The most "masculine" American sports—baseball and football—are off-limits to women both in college and on a professional level. And although women's college basketball is increasingly popular, there is no professional women's basketball league.

Since the winter games of 1968, the Olympics have required all women athletes from any nation competing in any sport to take the so-called sex test—chromosomal testing that determines the sex of a competitor. Male athletes are not tested. A U.S. Olympic

Committee (USOC) spokesperson, who refused to be identified, says the test is "to get rid of speculation."

"There was one recorded case of a 1932 participant, Stella Walsh, who was shot in 1980 and found to be a man," says the spokesperson. "There are oddities of nature—some people are born both sexes. No one has failed at the Olympic Games since we began testing. But we test for drug use; why shouldn't we test for sex?"

One Olympic trainer, who requests anonymity, says, "Most [women] who have trained for their whole lives in a sport have defeminized somewhat. Hard training stops menstruation. It builds up your pecs and flattens your breasts. It gives you intense muscles in your arms and thighs. Yes, some of the women look more like men with their bodies all built up. But that doesn't make them men, and it also doesn't make them lesbians."

BODYBUILDING SCANDAL

The link between homophobia and defeminization was made apparent in a sports scandal that erupted in 1984 at the Caesar's World Cup, the largest female bodybuilding competition with the largest purse for any such competition—for women or men—in the world.

An Australian competitor, Bev Francis, who had been expected to win, placed eighth after the judges decided that her body bulk was unfeminine. A documentary, *Pumping Iron II: The Women,* illumines the fear the judges had of Francis, who is heterosexual, because she had built up her body to the level of a male bodybuilder. The International Female Body Building officials had even instructed the judges prior to the competition that Francis was too muscular. As a consequence, two judges gave her a single point out of a possible 30 for her performance. Said presiding official Oscar State in his instructions to the judges: "We have to define femininity. [The winner] should be a woman who still has a feminine aesthetic but who has the muscle tone to show she's an athlete."

"It would be a total disaster if Bev Francis won. She doesn't look like a woman; she does not represent what women want to look like," judge Anita Columbo said before the competition.

The difference between first and eighth places in the competition was $24,600. Francis received $400; the winner, Carla Dunlap, received $25,000, a title, and a series of endorsements. Dunlap, who was a strong supporter of Francis, says, "Who's to say what the definition of *feminine* is as it applies to our sport. The crowd loved her. They thought she was terrific. It was the judges who were afraid of her."

Another member of the competition, who asked not to be named, says, "From the day we hit Las Vegas, everybody knew the judges were afraid of lesbianism. Bev isn't a lesbian. I am. But because I have a more traditional feminine look, no one questions me. But the judges are afraid of what people will say about the sport. Bev should have won. She didn't because everybody was afraid the public would think we were a bunch of bull dykes." Francis has since stayed away from the competition, as have other "masculine" women.

Los Angeles sports trainer LaForce contends that homophobia in women's sports is inextricably linked to notions of femininity. "There is social pressure from everywhere for women to be more feminine," she says. "In sports, women have to exhibit more masculine qualities, like power and aggression. This causes a stir. People associate sports with men, not women. Parents want their girls to be feminine. They see women's sports as full of stereotypical lesbians—women who are too masculine. So they get afraid."

TROUBLE IN SCHOOL

The fear is rampant in women's college sports, according to both athletes and coaches. On campus there is a belief that lesbians have an advantage over straight women; since lesbians are presumed to be more masculine, they are thought to be stronger.

Some coaches believe lesbian participation distorts the nature of women's sports. "I try to discourage lesbians from my teams," admits one women's coach at a Southern university well-known for its competitive teams. "It isn't that I'm necessarily against lesbians. I'm a lesbian myself. But I think there's a stigma attached to the game itself when there are too many lesbians involved. People feel they have an unfair advantage in terms of their physical abilities, and they think they intimidate the other players.

"And I don't like it when lesbian players attempt to come out to me," she continues. "I just don't want that. My private life is very separate from my professional life. I don't want to lose my job for being a lesbian or for being a bad coach. And in my experience, too many lesbians in women's sports make for a lot of problems that create bad teams and bad team playing and have an overall detrimental effect on the sports themselves."

Others believe homophobia has had a chilling effect on women's sports. Clare Lamont played intercollegiate sports at Ithaca College from 1980 to 1984 and was an athletic trainer there and at Cornell University, both in Ithaca, N.Y. "At Ithaca [College] I was out, but nobody ever really talked about it," says Lamont, an all-American field hockey player.

Lamont remembers one frightening incident. "It was a [basketball] game between Cornell and Dartmouth, and there was one woman taking a foul shot, so it was very quiet in the place," she recounts. "I remember someone yelling out 'You dyke' or 'You butch.' And I remember seeing every woman on the team shudder. I shuddered too. It was just so exposed. You know, you're taking a shot, and you can't hide your strong arms. But the thing was, there weren't any lesbians on the basketball team that I knew of. It was just the kind of thing that people said about women players. And I think that's part of why there's so much fear of it. The straight players don't want people thinking they're gay."

Carrie Jacobson, a star soccer and field hockey player at Adelphi University in Garden City, N.Y., and the University of Maryland (UM) in College Park and Baltimore between 1983 and 1987, says there were "lots of incidents of name-calling at both schools.

"*Dyke* was used as an insult on and off the field. There was certainly a [negative] attitude toward lesbians. You joined a team, and you made friends, and everybody assumed you were straight. But if they found out you were a lesbian, then they were very distant to you. One girl outed me the last semester I was [at UM], and all the people on the team stopped talking to me."

Jacobson now plays rugby semiprofessionally. It is a wholly different experience, she says. "It's the most open sport for lesbians. Even the straight women are supportive. And it's a big sport—rugby clubs are all across the country, and we play in other countries as far away as New Zealand. It's great because it's one sport where no one can say you can't play because you're gay," she says.

When Daphne Miles transferred to George Mason University in

Fairfax, Virginia, in her sophomore year in 1985, it was to play basketball. She was recruited to the team as a starting player—a star with a full athletic scholarship—by coach Jim Lewis. But within a semester she was being benched for all but two minutes of every game.

"I went from being one of [Lewis's] pets to sitting out game after game," she recalls. The change occurred when Miles moved into the apartment of another team member, a known lesbian. "Jackie was actually just my roommate, but everyone assumed because she was gay that we were lovers."

That assumption nearly jettisoned Miles from the team and brought the wrath of the coach down on her for the duration of the following semester. "If you were a lesbian, you just didn't play," she says. "He had me in his office almost every day . . . and had freshman students on the team spying on us."

Lewis, says Miles, went so far as to call her mother during the semester break. "I never knew exactly what was in that conversation—I wasn't ready to come out to my mother at that time— but she said to me that she thought I was being influenced by the wrong sort of people at the school. He was always trying to talk me out of being a lesbian. He just didn't understand it." Miles finally left the college because of the harassment.

Coach Lewis and George Mason University athletic department officials refused comment.

Another lesbian athlete, who requests that her name not be used, faces similar harassment. "I've been on a women's basketball team for three years. I transferred here because I was recruited to play and they gave me a tuition scholarship," says the player, who is currently at a Southern university known for its competitive teams. "The second semester I was on the team, other players told my coach I was gay. I think they told him because I was new, I was a really good player, and I'm black. There are only three girls on the team who are black. There's a lot of tension at this school about black athletes, and there's even more about gays. So he benched me for every little thing after that. If my socks weren't white enough, I'd get pulled from the game. The other players, including the other black girls, haven't talked to me in three seasons. It makes it really hard to play a game. But I can't leave because I'll lose my scholarship. I can't wait to graduate and get out of here."

ISOLATION IN THE OLYMPICS

Cindy Olavarri was terrified of coming out in college when she was on the crew and track teams at the University of California, Berkeley, and the fear didn't stop when she entered professional sports. Olavarri, an Olympic qualifier for cycling who has participated in almost every major cycling competition in the world, says homophobia and women's sports go hand in hand. "When I was competing as a cyclist, I was really afraid to tell anyone that I was a lesbian [and afraid] that it would mean I wouldn't be picked for an Olympic team," she says. "Everyone on my team was straight. I was on a U.S. national cycling team for four years. It's very political. If you have any sort of strikes against you, you don't make the team.

"When you're cycling, you want to go on the big tours, you want to go to Europe," Olavarri continues. "We room together, ten women to a room. It's not a problem for me, but it might be for other women. There were a couple of women who were out who were on the circuit in the U.S., and other riders would make comments. It was clear that unless they were winning everything, they wouldn't be picked for a team."

Olavarri had none of these problems when she participated in several sports in two rounds of the Gay Games, an experience she found very different from the homophobia of other competitions. "It's not as competitive, obviously, as qualifying for the international Olympics, but it felt very good to be competing with other lesbians, to have none of the pressures of pretending to be straight in addition to the pressures of competing," she noted. "We all were very connected to each other—as you're supposed to be in sports. There was none of the artificial distance created by homophobia."

Currently, Olavarri is a fitness director at a health club in San Francisco. She points out the difference between her experience at the Gay Games and in competitive sports. The major difference is the isolation of the lesbian athlete. "You spend four months with these women. I couldn't tell the truth about who I was, who I was calling or talking to," she explains, adding, "your other teammates don't want to know you're a lesbian. And the sponsors don't want to know either."

Says another coach, who has trained several Olympic athletes and asks to remain anonymous: "I would love to be able to come out and have every lesbian in sports come out. I think if that happened, there would be a lot less of this kind of underhanded and subtle discrimination. But stereotypes are hard to break down. I wouldn't know how you'd even begin to go about it.

"A lot of my athletes have come from all-woman colleges," the coach continues. "There used to be a stigma attached to that. These changes take time. Unfortunately, there's only a certain number of years when you are strong and healthy enough to play well. We have to view sexual orientation the way we viewed color differences, because we are losing a lot of great athletes to prejudice and bigotry. If the United States is going to be an international force in the sports world, then we are going to have to find ways to make those changes happen sooner."

PAID TO PLAY A GAME

Mariah Burton Nelson

The story of how I got fired from the Women's Pro Basketball League for being a lesbian—which is akin to being fired from the National Basketball League for being black—is the most lucrative and least known story of my athletic career. Lucrative because an earlier version of it was purchased twice: first by what was then called *Women's Sports* magazine, then by *Ms.* magazine. Least known because both magazines "killed" it, citing fears that advertisers would jump ship if the magazines deigned to mention lesbians.

I'll begin the story at the end, or near the end, of my brief stint as a pro basketball player. At San Francisco's Civic Center Plaza, in the summer of 1979, I felt the binocular burn of two eyes staring at me and turned to see who it might be.

There were a lot of possibilities. I was standing among 200,000 other people. The Gay Pride Parade had just marched peacefully through San Francisco, and now we were gathered at Civic Center Plaza to listen to music, hear speeches, and express sorrow and outrage at the recent murder of supervisor Harvey Milk. I was standing to the left of the stage, swaying happily to the music of Linda Tillery. Turning, I scanned the crowd for familiar faces. Finally, I saw on a raised media platform, a television reporter who knew me, and waved weakly. My career as a professional athlete flashed before my eyes.

Just a week or two before, the reporter had interviewed me for a television spot about professional women. In 1979, even female lawyers and bankers were newsworthy, but as a female pro basketball player I was a particular anomaly. During the interview, the reporter posed some antagonistic questions typical of that era (and, unfortunately, still typical of this era): Does playing basketball threaten your femininity? Do you have a boyfriend? Do the men in your life approve of your playing basketball?

"No, basketball doesn't threaten my femininity," I told him, adding pointedly, "but it does seem to threaten some men." I was young (twenty-three), angry, and emboldened by the lesbian and feminist environment in which I had come of age. To the question about male approval I said curtly, "All of my friends approve of my playing basketball or they wouldn't be my friends."

I didn't come out to him because I hadn't come out to my coach on the San Francisco Pioneers, and didn't intend to. The coach had clued me in by telling me our uniforms were made by "a bunch of faggots." He also insisted on calling us girls, though we asked to be called women. "This is a business, not a women's lib thing," he said bluntly. Later in the season, at a home game, a group from Berkeley unfurled a large banner reading "Lesbians Against Police Violence"; the security guards made them take it down. All of the owners and coaches in the Women's Pro Basketball League were men. Evidently it was *not* a women's lib thing.

But Gay Day had become a four-year tradition I was not willing to forego. When, at nineteen, I came out of the closet, I came roaring out, waving banners and carrying torches and making a spectacle of myself. Within months of beginning a relationship with Stephanie, a basketball teammate, I was speaking to high school classes about the joys of being a lesbian. Stephanie founded a Gay Counseling Center on campus. None of this seemed to bother our Stanford coaches, who let us room together on road trips, or our teammates, many of whom, one-by-one and two-by-two, came out themselves.

The gay liberation movement was in its pre-AIDS, giddy, innocent infancy. Anita Bryant had lambasted homosexuals but we lambasted back until the orange juice company dropped her as a spokesperson and she retracted her homophobic comments. The Briggs Initiative proposed firing all of California's gay teachers as well as straight teachers who publicly supported gay colleagues; voters defeated the bill.

I devoured books: *Rubyfruit Jungle, Sappho Was a Right-On Woman.* I discovered, preserved on microfilm at the Stanford library, issues of *The Ladder,* the lesbian newspaper from the fifties, and made it the subject of a paper for a women's history class.

Feminism, even more than the gay movement, validated my life-long observations and my rage. With great glee I read books by Robin Morgan, Toni Morrison, Marge Piercy, and Susan Brown-miller. I joined a consciousness-raising group. I helped organize a women's film festival and taught a course called Women and Body Image.

On my embroidered jeans jacket one button proclaimed, "A Woman Without a Man Is Like a Fish Without a Bicycle," another said, "Teenage Lesbian," and a third, a small red one, announced: "I'm menstruating."

In these heady days it seemed natural to me that sports teams— groups of strong women who enjoy their own bodies and each other's—would provide an outlet for my feelings of empowerment and love for women. In high school, I had played on a predominantly lesbian basketball team that traveled throughout the southwest. During one car caravan from Phoenix to Gallup, New Mexico, the VW bug I was riding in repeatedly played just one cassette tape: Helen Reddy's "I Am Woman."

For three years at Stanford I was the team captain, and its leading scorer and rebounder. I felt loved and respected, almost revered. In my bedroom I hung a poster that showed women swimming, running, and cycling. "Women in Sports," it said: "We Can."

Yet even before that fateful Gay Pride Day, I had been rudely awakened to the fact that women's sports were not always the lesbian/feminist mecca I wanted them to be. At a summer basketball camp during college I had been the victim of a witch hunt. A group of fourteen-year-old campers accused dozens of counselors of lesbian atrocities, primarily public kissing and fondling. My alleged crime was showering with another counselor. There were details: I had supposedly spread soap suds all over her body. It sounded like fun, but inappropriate, and I didn't do it. I was horrified at having to explain to the camp directors that, though I was gay, I had not committed the crime. To their credit, the directors— themselves closeted lesbians—ultimately gathered all the campers and counselors and lectured them sternly: "If you're going to be in sports, you're going to have to learn to get along with lesbians."

After Stanford I was drafted by the New Jersey Gems of the fledgling (and short-lived) Women's Pro Basketball League, and also by le C.U.C. (pronounced "Le Kook"), a French pro team that traveled throughout Europe. Let's see: France or New Jersey? The decision was not difficult.

But in France I discovered, much to my horror, that I was not the best basketball player in the world. The fall from Stanford star

to foreign sub was a steep, miserable descent. Because of a quirk
in the French rules, once I was designated backup center I was not
even allowed to dress for about half of the games. I'd watch glumly
from the bleachers, adding a sad, self-pitying voice to the singsong
cheers: "*Allez, les filles.*" (Go, girls.) My teammates began to resent my relatively high paycheck, and told me so. I further of-
fended them by not shaving my legs, not eating meat, and not
drinking wine. To make matters worse, the woman I fell in love
with—the starting center—informed me that she was in love with
me too, but Jesus would not approve. She then refused to speak
to me.

Eight months later, when I arrived back in the States, the New
Jersey Gems still "owned the rights" to me—meaning I could not
play for any other pro team until they sold those rights. I agreed
to play the last third of the season with them on the condition
that I be traded to San Francisco the following year.

In New Jersey I began to recover my athletic self-esteem. Yet
my last paycheck—for $1000—bounced. And the gay players
would not talk openly. When I asked, two specifically denied their
relationship, making me feel slightly crazy as well as angry and
isolated.

So it had dawned on me that the "real world" was not going
to embrace me as lovingly as idyllic Stanford had. When I saw the
television reporter, and saw that he'd seen me, it occurred to me
to call him up and ask him not to tell my coach that I'd been at
Gay Pride Day. But the contradiction of showing up at Gay Pride
Day, then diving into the closet was too great, so I didn't call.

Three weeks into the regular season, I was fired. (They call it
being put on waivers, which means that another team is free to
buy your contract, but basically you're out of a job.)

"Why?" I asked the coach. I was shocked. I had been playing
with confidence, and had expected to start at center.

He looked surprised. "You're not tall enough," he said after a
moment's thought.

I stared at him incredulously. "I'm the tallest person on the
team!" I protested. Two teammates were exactly my height; no
one on the team was taller.

"Oh. Then you're not quick enough," he said lamely.

I learned from a teammate who was close to the coach that the
reporter had indeed told the owner of the Pioneers (I never quite

got used to calling him "my owner") about my appearance at Gay Pride Day. I had not mentioned the incident to the player, and she had no other way of knowing about it. She responded to me sympathetically but made a mad dash for the closet herself, immediately introducing a "fiancé" to the team.

About half of my teammates, I estimate, (including the two tall ones), and at least half of the players in the league were gay. But no others were politically active.

One gay friend was fired along with me; I think they thought we were lovers. When the two of us walked out of the gym that day, into the unusually bright San Francisco sunshine, I was in a stupor. My friend led me to a cafe, where she alternately told chatty, cheerful stories and ranted against the stupidity of our coach. She was already in graduate school, and was to some extent relieved at the prospect of not spending so much time in gyms. She hadn't been enjoying the serious, stifling atmosphere of the professional sports scene. She didn't particularly mind an early departure.

I was devastated. I had thought I'd play in the U.S. pros for at least a year or two, and had given up a shot at the Olympic team with that in mind. I clung to the same dream that led so many naive young women to postpone other careers and to accept bad coaching and bounced checks during that three-year life of the WBL: continuing to play the game we so loved. France had been a disappointment, New Jersey a brief redemption. I wanted more. A Stanford graduate with a psychology degree, I nevertheless had no other career plans.

For three days, I lay in my bed in shock. I was unable to move, unable to feel. I didn't cry. I just lay there. Teammates kindly came by to visit, and for them I lugubriously hauled myself out of bed and into the living room, where I thudded into a beanbag chair. They treated me as if somebody had died.

Two local feminist newspapers learned of the firing but I refused to talk to them, fearing further repercussions. Though I hated the idea of being closeted, my passion for basketball temporarily won out.

Finally my agent called: the California Dreams, of Los Angeles, had invited me to try out. I didn't feel particularly excited. Still depressed, I did not want to move to smoggy L.A. After almost a year in France and New Jersey, I wanted to be home, and because of Stanford, home had become the San Francisco Bay Area. Nevertheless, this opportunity was knocking, and no one else was at the door.

Relinquishing a then-precious symbol of feminism, I bought a razor and shaved my legs. This token attempt at conformity failed when, at the first day of practice with the Dreams, an old friend called across the gym: "I can't believe you shaved your legs!"

Almost immediately, the Dreams sent us to John Robert Powers Charm School. Their intention, of course, was to teach us to portray a feminine (that is, heterosexual) image. Leg-shaving I could do; charm school I could not, so I quietly boycotted, but my teammates reported that they learned such useful skills as how to walk upstairs sideways.

Then, just when I was getting used to the idea of living in L.A., the coach arrived at my door and asked to speak to me alone. I was sharing the apartment with other players, so I invited him into my bedroom. There we sat stiffly on the twin beds, facing each other. "I'm sorry to tell you this," he said kindly, "but we've traded you to the Dallas Diamonds."

"Why?" I asked.

He explained that they needed to let go of one center, and the others had no-cut, no-trade contracts. "I'm sorry," he said again.

I stared at him dumbly. I did not want to go to Dallas. With no warning, all the tears I'd held back in France, and New Jersey, and San Francisco, came pouring out. Great, heaving sobs shook my body, and when I tried to speak, the words were muffled through uncontrollable gasps. Uncomfortable, naturally, the coach stayed with me, not touching me or trying to comfort me, which would have only heightened my embarrassment, but simply sitting on the opposite bed, listening. Thankful for his kindness, I tried to explain that my tears weren't really about these particular California Dreams—they were about a larger dream, and larger losses, and a simple desire to be home. I wanted to tell him more—about the woman I'd loved in France, the Gay Pride Day, the "faggot" remark. This desire to talk to someone—even a man I'd only known for a few weeks—made me realize that I was terribly lonely.

But once I regained my composure, I agreed to go to Dallas. Homesickness and loneliness aside, I still had that dream. "What the heck," I told the coach, drying my face and beginning to laugh at my outburst, "It'll be an adventure."

In Dallas I shared a two-bedroom apartment with Michelle and Valerie, who knitted, watched a lot of television, ate Spaghetti-O's, and carried Bibles in their gym bags. One of them generously offered me what had been her bedroom. "Valerie and I will sleep together until you find your own place," she told me.

I believed that ruse until I woke up in the middle of the first night freezing. It was November in Dallas—cold—and the bed was made with just one thin blanket. Clearly no one had slept in it for months.

The Diamonds wanted me to stay but didn't want to pay my moving expenses. Instead of sending me to San Francisco to get my things, they wanted me to wait until we flew there for a game two months hence. I was still living out of the gym bag I'd brought to Los Angeles nearly a month before. Rather than turn the matter over to my agent, I pointed out to the owner that under the terms of the contract, the Diamonds were obligated to pay the expenses. He then put me on waivers, explaining that I was "too aggressive off the court."

And so it was that my life as a professional athlete ignominiously came to an end. This time there were no tears. I felt as if I had been released from bondage. My agent soon informed me that the New Orleans team was interested, but I told her that I wasn't. I had run out of tolerance for men who called us girls, for ignorant reporters, for gay teammates who hid behind Bibles, for coaches and owners who seemed threatened by outspoken women. Also, after years of jumping, running, and pivoting, my knees were very sore and, as it turns out, permanently damaged. On the flight home to San Francisco from Dallas, I promised my knees I would quit. Then, as I began to imagine life beyond basketball, my spirits began to lift.

For one season I coached the junior varsity at a local high school, a job I enjoyed tremendously, but the varsity coach, herself a lesbian, made it a condition of employment that I not come out to the girls. A college coach—yet another closeted lesbian—invited me to interview with her after that, but I declined.

I turned instead to writing—a lifelong dream predating basketball—where, as in the case of the two "killed" versions of this story, I still sometimes feel stifled by homophobes. But publishers are increasingly making way for the voices of openly lesbian authors, and in my books I've been able to integrate my passions for women's sports, for women's rights, and for women. I was also recently hired to coach high school girls basketball, which makes me one of the first openly lesbian coaches in the country. I hope to write a book about that too. It's become clear to me that sport, with its physical empowerment and lesbian potential, is an inherently feminist act. Another feminist act is telling the truth. I'm doing my best to combine the two.

TAKING UP SPACE

Louise Sloan

I first heard Martina Navratilova described, years ago, as a woman who was beating all the other female tennis players because she had developed "unnatural," "masculine" strength through weight training. Now, years later, weight training has become more acceptable for women, and Navratilova has turned out to be one of the world's greatest athletes. But the idea that she is somehow "unnatural" persists, partly due to her open homosexuality: despite her stunning ability, she is considered by some to be an embarrassment to women's tennis. So much of an embarrassment, in fact, that after Navratilova's record ninth Wimbledon victory, former tennis champion Margaret Court felt it necessary to call a press conference denouncing Navratilova as an unfit role model for younger players, due to her "admitted" lesbianism.

Not all strong, "masculine" lesbians are jocks, and not all strong, aggressive women are lesbians, but women's sports seem as good a place as any on which to focus a discussion of lesbianism and women's sex roles.

For Mara, a "butch," out-of-the-closet lesbian friend of mine, involvement in sports, particularly contact sports, is an essential part of feeling alive—alive in a way that has traditionally been reserved for men. To her, being a "butch" jock isn't about being hostile to men. It's about being human, feeling her body is absolutely her own, and taking up a big enough space for it to fully develop in.

She explained that sports teach you "what impact your body has in the world"—"that you are actually inhabiting [your body], rather than being one removed from it, worrying about being looked at."

Contact sports also teach you something about self-defense, Mara said, "what it feels like to hit someone and knock them to the ground." This is a feeling most men and boys know, to some extent. To be a trained athlete is "to be able to carry your body

95

as a weapon, which is not something that can be taken away from you or used against you."

At a university women's speakout against sexual violence a few years ago, Mara urged the crowd of young women—many of whom had recounted brutal experiences of incest and rape—to reclaim their independence, their sense of self and their bodies by making themselves physically strong and by feeling free to take up as much space as they wanted.

Yet Mara knows from experience that there are serious consequences to taking up space in this world, if you're a woman—even more if you're gay. Women's sports are plagued by rumors of lesbianism, and another athlete friend of mine says she has heard through the sports grapevine that one of the reasons women's sports are so underfunded is that possible sponsors believe no one wants to watch a bunch of unnatural, "mannish" women running around.

"Since women's sports is an adjunct to men's sports, the ['mannish'] definition is always already there," Mara said. Men's performance is the standard of excellence, she explained. Women's sports is a classic double-bind: you become involved in sports as part of a drive to excel, but as a woman in sports, the better you get, the farther away you get from what are considered excellent qualities in a female.

This can be a big problem for many women athletes, socially. "Looking at a woman who is as competent as they are, I don't know if it makes men feel gay, or what," Mara said, but negative social attitudes toward physically strong, aggressive women "puts heterosexual women athletes in a bind." These women need to cultivate strength and aggression in order to succeed as athletes, but as heterosexuals, they want and need men in their lives. The result of this dilemma? "You have these women trying to over-compensate for their 'unfeminine' athletic abilities by becoming ultra-feminine in every other respect," said Mara, "so they don't get cheated out of the sexual part of their lives." Often, too, they subtly pressure their peers to "be as straight as possible," to avoid the possibility of "masculinity by association."

Yet in Mara's experience on college sports teams, about 20 percent of the women were lesbians. Among team captains, it was more like 80 percent. Why so many lesbians? I asked. Mara theorizes that it has partly to do with being able to focus one's energy on achieving excellence in the sport, without having to worry about the negative impact it might have on your love life. Not having to divide your attention between physical excellence and femininity "really frees you up to follow sports," Mara said. "Naturally, these women are going to punch through to the top." But when these winning women are particularly "mannish," or if they're open lesbians, like Navratilova, straight athletes get angry: "They're doing what they're supposed to [being feminine], and you [the dyke] are winning," said Mara.

These dynamics, as well as the constant presence of homophobia, mean that staying in the closet, at least within the team, is the norm for lesbian athletes. For the many lesbians that become team captains, Mara said, being closeted is the way they achieved leadership status. But that puts them in a "killer bind": either feeling like a constant liar or coming out and "risking everything that you're building your life around."

So what was it like for Mara to be out, on a team? First off, she said, "I don't think of myself as 'out,' as contrasted to something else—I think of myself as just being me. But I fit so well with the cultural stereotype of the 'dyke,' that 'being me' *is* being out." So, she said, when she has been the target of homophobic abuse, "it's not as if I think, 'I could have done things a different way.'" For Mara, whatever it is that makes her "dykely" is inseparable from what makes her herself.

Having grown up in liberal Seattle and having come out in Santa Cruz, Mara is not apologetic about her sexual orientation because it doesn't occur to her to be. And that—"the idea that being gay can be as organic and normal to someone as being straight"—is "profoundly unsettling" to many people, Mara said.

There were consequences, for Mara, to being an unsettling presence on the team. After she came out, her crew team—especially the women who were closeted lesbians—kept a safe distance from her. "It's really painful," she said, "when, day after day, you sit down to stretch out on the mat, and no one sits near you." Would-be liberal teammates gave themselves all sorts of excuses ("It's not because she's gay, she's just not my type"), but it all boiled down to the same thing: homophobia. "Being frozen out really wrecked me as an athlete," Mara said. She remained on the team for a while, but, as a team, "you have to be together or you just don't win." And as a team player, Mara said, "I'm very dependent on the emotional support of my teammates." When that support is not forthcoming, she said, "you have twice the work."

Mara ended up a scapegoat for her team's collective homophobia and sexism, and perhaps, too, for the whole team's discomfort at being females involved in a "masculine" pursuit of physical excellence. She also "took the fall" for the numerous lesbian team members who were in the closet.

Yet as Mara made it clear, all women athletes, not only lesbians, suffer from the sexist attitude that physical strength and aggressiveness—and excellence—are "masculine" characteristics. And although other athletes may not share Mara's experiences and opinions, I have seen, firsthand, the damage done by the kind of attitudes she describes.

I have a teenage friend who was always a tomboy. She loved sports and excelled at them, and by junior high was running track with the high school boys. There was talk of track scholarships. There was talk of the Olympics. But there's a limit to how much physical prowess is acceptable in a female. When she wanted to work with weights to increase her strength, her otherwise-supportive mother asked, "But how are you going to look in an evening dress?"

Eventually absorbing the message from her peers and family, and sick of being mistaken for a boy and not getting dates, she started curling her hair, wearing makeup, acting less aggressive, dieting—and slacking off in sports. Soon she was so underweight she got sick and had to quit track.

Now, a couple of years after high school, this young woman is very feminine, and has happily landed herself a boyfriend. She's still struggling with anorexia, but she's getting better. Of course, there's no track. There will be no Olympics. But she'll never again be mistaken for a male. Physically and psychologically, she no longer takes up "too much space."

CHANGE-UPS

Maria Noell Goldberg

I was one of those girls who gave girls a bad name. My throwing arm traced its trajectory along a course best suited, not to propelling baseballs, but to swatting flies. Balls sailing toward me were treated with the same caution any sensible person uses when an object careens through space in her direction. I ducked. Or stepped sideways, glancing casually into the sky as if a particularly interesting species of bird had just flown overhead on its way to a more hospitable neighborhood.

Perhaps because I grew up on a small island surrounded by water, and trees you couldn't see over the tops of, perhaps because it was the fifties and sixties, sports and love were both ideas whose definitions were so limited they left much of my own experience outside the scope of recognition and naming. Sports meant balls and teams to me; love meant boys and men. My friends and I recognized no other kind of sport, no other kind of love. Given the narrowness of these definitions, no matter how feverishly we played, our activities were never sport; no matter how much yearning we directed toward each other, our longing was never love.

While my brothers faced each other across the lawn and sent balls sizzling through the air at each other, my best friend Cathy and I stood on the end of the dock trying to master our hula hoops. Once spinning, it took the subtlest hip thrust to keep the hoop moving, circling our waists, orbiting around the planets of our bodies. My brothers and most of the other boys we knew were hopeless when it came to the hula hoop. They'd step into the circle of bright plastic, raise it to their waists and give it a spin, but synchronizing that spin with the movement of their own bodies seemed to require a patience and a particular kind of focus they were unable or unwilling to muster. After a couple of awkward gyrations, they'd drop the hoop and go back to more manly pursuits.

Although a few boys mastered the hula hoop well enough to

turn it into an endurance test, or to fantasize about setting a new
world's record, boys had no use for them. Their rejection made it
largely a "girl's game." Like my brothers, they preferred practicing
the small skills that would eventually lead them to baseball and
basketball teams. They faced off as combatants armed with mitts
and balls aimed at testing each other while Cathy and I, like many
other girls, practiced skills that would lead nowhere as we perfected variations in hula hoop speed, rhythm, and orbit. We faced
each other, not as combatants, but as mirrors in whose surfaces
we saw shining back at us the easy pleasure we took in one another's company. In our variety, we also saw the possibilities of
what a girl might be.

Cathy was my best friend through grade school, high school,
and the first years of college. Her legs were solid and strong, her
thighs as big around as her waist. From the hips down, she was
as muscular as her older brother. Proud of his strength, he used
his burly thighs to steal bases and charge across basketball courts
to shoot lay-up after lay-up. Cathy used hers to ride her bike to
my house around curving roads that skirted deep wooded ravines,
calling me before she jumped on her Schwinn so I could clock her
and chart the seconds she shaved off her arrival time. She did
cannonballs off the end of the dock, climbed trees, raced the neighborhood dogs. She used those sturdy legs to ski on snow and water, jumping above earth and wave and seeming, for all her muscle
and the pull of gravity, to fly.

I ran. Small and light, I imagined myself a girl from a Haida or
Kwakiutl tribe as I cut a fast, silent path over the crumbling layers
of the forest floor. I could swim across the lake and back, hold
my breath under water longer than any of my brothers, carry the
rocks we used for the foundation of the forts and dams we built,
and shoot holes into the center of every Spaghetti-O that dotted
the cans we shot off stumps in the woods with B-B guns. I nourished these skills out of a fantasy of survivalism, the conviction
that I did not want to depend on anyone to keep me whole and
that even in the 1950s, the world did not seem such a safe place
for girls. I ran to escape boys chasing me to pull up my dress
during recess, perfected my marksmanship and tracking ability
should I ever decide to live alone in the woods, and practiced
holding my breath and stilling my body out of a sense that a cloak
of invisibility might be a more useful garment than a party dress.

Whatever images of femaleness Cathy and I tried on, it never occurred to us to envision ourselves as athletes. The potential for athleticism may have been there, but the models necessary for shaping and directing whatever skill, speed, focus, and endurance we possessed were not. The pictures presented to us about what it meant to be female (read feminine) did not include images of women in sports. To my knowledge, Donna Reed never chucked the family dinner in favor of a few games of tennis. Emily Post and Betty Crocker dotted our childhood and adolescence with advice on cooking and courtesy, but had nothing to say about running full out to a finish line. And while Ike spent a lot of time on the golf course, Mamie Eisenhower always looked dressed for a tea party in heels, white gloves, and hats the size of salad bowls.

The notion of women in sports was an oxymoron since sport and the determination, competitiveness, and sense of agency that sport entails were not included in the territory of womanhood. More specifically than just balls and teams, sports meant males. As a child, even one with brothers, I paid little attention to what the boys were doing, preferring the gestures and sounds of other girls, but I did recognize that most of what the boys played were called "sports"; most of what the girls played were called "games."

Dimly, I was aware of a handful of women who were doing more than playing "games"—Maureen Connolly, in spite of the diminuitive "Little Mo," did win a grand slam in 1953, and Tenley Albright became world figure skating champ in the same year. I knew about Florence Chadwick even though in many ways her accomplishment seemed as distant and unrelated to me as the English Channel she swam across. Yet because of a snippet in one of the rare newspapers I glanced at in 1951, and a few fifteen-second announcements on the radio, her swims across the Channel in '51, '53, and '55 entered my consciousness. She swam. I swam. So I remembered.

But even swimming was never framed for me as a sport, a pleasurable challenge in which I could test the measure of myself or participate in the making of myself. Swimming, too, was about survival. I complained just once as my mother dropped my brothers and me off at the beach club for our lesson in the rain. "We'll get sick," I said as I climbed out of the car into the chill drizzle. "We'll get terrible colds." I gave a few preliminary sniffs as if already in the grip of an incipient virus. "A cold is better than a drowning," my mother answered, rolling up the window against the damp gray day. "I don't want to look outside some afternoon and see one of you bloated and floating on top of the lake."

The fact that the beach club had a swim team and that I could have been on it was blotted out by the shadow of drowning that now entered my mind each time I entered the water. Cathy was on the swim team until the boys began snickering and teasing her about the size of her legs. "Here come the tree trunks," they'd shout, making chain-saw noises, cutting her down to size. From that summer on, Cathy, instead of using those glorious strong legs to propel her through the water she loved, tried to diet them out of existence.

I, too, had loved the water up until the moment of my mother's comment. I was infinitely strong, cutting the water with my diving body, infinitely alive with the silky feel of water grazing my skin. I paddled and splashed and played as if the possibility of danger had never entered my mind. Swimming had been about play. Now it was about survival.

In the conversion of play to sport, the stakes get higher. In the conversion of child to girl, the stakes are higher still. Cathy learned it first but I soon caught on that just as one has to learn the rules and talents that make one a winner in a particular sport, we had to learn to be girls. From television, from the comics and romance novels we hungrily devoured, and the plaintive songs of heartbreak we listened to on the Top 40, we breathed in the directives and expectations about what was required of girls, the rigid codes of appearance and behavior we could not afford to ignore. If you failed at a sport you were a loser on a particular playing field, but if you failed at being a girl you were—in all quarters—an outcast.

Cheryl appeared in our school in the tenth grade, her hair slicked back into a DA that resembled Elvis's. She wore a pleated gray shirt every day and the same white short-sleeved shirts the boys wore, the sleeves rolled up to expose the lean, wiry muscles of her arms. She wore undershirts instead of bras, and we knew from watching her change into her graying gym shorts at two o'clock every day that she never wore a girdle—that important symbol of maturing womanhood—like we all did.

No one ever spoke to her, even in gym class where our natural tendency to huddle, to touch and lean into one another broke down some of the barriers of cliquish hierarchy that existed in the halls. We whispered about her, though, stunned and outraged by her difference, her refusal to comport herself in the "appropriate" fashion of the day.

Gym class in high school was the location of the greatest tension between what young women were physically capable of and the exhortations of teachers, parents, and every other social arbiter of the day. Cheryl's presence among us seemed, in the brief year she attended our school, to heighten that tension. The lanky Miss Stokes may have gotten a few of us to move our feet and run, take aim at a basket and shoot, but most of us were expert at feigning the vapors and waiting for the bell to ring. Even those who played hard enough during gym to actually need a shower at the end, never played baseball or soccer after class was over. Physically, we may have tested and stretched our limits when we were younger, but now the fever to give our all to something had been deflected into the full-time job of dressing and acting the part of a girl.

Cheryl alone was determined to use that hour for all it was worth. She stole basketballs from our unresisting hands and did push-ups long after the rest of us had given up, refusing to stop until Miss Stokes tenderly leaned over her and lifted her up. She hit home runs and ran the bases twice, never looking at any of us, making us feel that for all our obvious talk about her she didn't know we existed. While I know now our condemnation must have pained her, she seemed to have carved out a unique self that no amount of our hissing could shake.

We understood, even if Cheryl seemed not to, that in order to succeed as girls much of what we had been and done as children could not follow us into lives bound by the necessity to be feminine. Even my mother, a tough, funny, and troubled resister of her own diminished life, taught me that a woman's strength must not be displayed in public. She loved gardening and thought nothing of digging up and moving young trees from one corner of the yard to another. She learned carpentry and added rooms to our house. She dug a ditch the length of a football field from the hilltop behind our house to the lake below, filled it with gravel and lined it with French drains to divert the rainwater that regularly flooded our basement bedrooms. But these were private acts, part of the secret life of our family that arose out of necessity because my father was not "handy around the house." When she went out to the grocery store or church, my mother's cracked gardening hands were neatly covered in white gloves, her slim muscular arms hidden inside pearl-buttoned cardigans. When asked to help carry a box, boat, or lumber for a neighbor in need—acts of which she was supremely capable—she anxiously scanned the horizon for a man.

I had my own secrets, facts of my existence that, having no name, were hidden even from myself. I was blind to my own desire, blind to the lesbian selves Cheryl and the lonely, dignified Miss Stokes most likely were. My careful study of them, of Cathy and all the girls and women on whom I had crushes was belied by the amount of time I spent courting the favor of males. I preened for them, dated them, and because I am a slow learner even married a couple, all the while failing to notice that it was women to whom my attention was drawn, women who inspired and consoled me, women who helped me shape and know my Self.

By the time my brothers and I were young adults, they were still practicing change-ups, signaling one kind of pitch, then executing another as they tried to fake each other out. I was engaged in another, deeper form of deception, one from which I awakened slowly and late.

Like my mother and Cathy, I had developed skills and strengths that could have been used in the service of sport but were so charged with the possibilities of life and death I kept them hidden like a small arsenal of secret weapons. While sport demands a public display of skill, I nourished my endurance, speed, and strength in secret so that I might pass as an acceptable young woman.

Yet these qualities—strength, physical and mental determination, the hard-won comfort that has come with living and loving fully from the heart of my body, the willingness to dig deep into my body's power in moments of love, work, life—have survived their time in the closet. In the absence of a particular sport to call my own, I live out my athleticism just as I live out my love of women, that disowned longing which was fed, not consciously but mercifully, by springs deep within me that slowly, patiently, and finally worked their way to the surface.

Part 4

OUR HEROINES, OR, MARTINA

I SAY 'ANCHORS', NOT 'ANNOUNCERS', CAUSE THE **ANNOUNCERS** WERE GREAT... TWO EX-OLYMPIANS WHO LOOKED LIKE BLOWDRIED GEEKS BUT TURNED OUT WONDERFUL. LOOKS AREN'T EVERYTHING.

THEY SAY BATTLE DOESN'T HIT WELL ENOUGH BUT SHE HOLDS TH' NCAA ALL-TIME RECORD FOR KILLS-THAT'S OK IN MY BOOK!

WEISHOFF TO SERVE! WHAT A TEAM THAT WAS IN '84—SILVER MEDAL—WEISHOFF, RITA CROCKETT, ROSE MAJORS, SUE WOODRUFF...

REELING OFF FROM MEMORY

WHAM!

SEE YA! BEST RALLY OF THE OLYMPICS AND TEEE SANDERS NOT EVEN **BREATHING HARD!!**

THEY KNEW WOMEN'S VOLLEYBALL FORWARDS AND BACKWARDS. THEY WERE FAST, RAPTUROUS, NOT A HINT OF SEXISM, CONDESCENSION, JINGOISM. THEY JUST LOVED THE GAME.

AND THEN, OF COURSE, THERE WAS THE TEAM.

THEY HAD SPEED, POWER, LIGHTNING REFLEXES, COMIC-BOOK VERTICAL LEAPS, SPIKES THAT BOOMED THROUGHOUT THE PALAU ST. JORDI AS THEY HAMMERED THEM DOWN.

LORI ENDICOTT. CAREN KEMNER, THE WORLD'S TOP PLAYER. THE UNSTOPPABLE ODEN SISTERS. LIANE SATO. RUTH LAWANSON, THE HEPTATHLETE. PAULA WEISHOFF, 1984 MEDALIST.

KEMNER 7

I FELL IN LOVE WITH ALL OF THEM.

CONFESSIONS OF A CONFIRMED COUCH POTATO, *or,* THE LAMENTATIONS OF A LATENT SPORTS DYKE

Jaye Zimet

I have always considered channel-surfing to be a sport. Well, not exactly a sport, but definitely an art. Sitting, or more correctly, lounging on my favorite piece of furniture; being one with the smooth, black Italian leather; melding into the small mound of throw pillows; the hard plastic remote resting lightly in my hand, ready instantly for the next command, the next whim of its master.

CH. 7

Golf. The question in my mind is—Is golf an actual sport? Sure, one probably walks several miles around the links during the course of the game. It takes skill and strategy and exact calculations; but I think of it more like a game, a game like chess, bridge, or billiards, requiring intense concentration and precise movements. My definition of a sport is a game where you sweat, and occasionally bleed. Football, baseball, basketball, hockey, tennis, boxing, sex.

Of course, when I happen to land on golf—always by accident, I might add—I find myself watching for a while, transfixed by the tranquil surroundings. A wave of calm washes over my prone self, and my thumb slides away from the channel button. I am standing, surrounded by lush greenery, on a meticulously manicured lawn, putter in hand, legs gently relaxed, feet hips-width apart, elbows slightly bent, head down, a bead of sweat rolling down my neck. The crowd is hushed for this last putt, the putt for the title, the putt for the money. A few practice swings. No, I'm too tense. I back away from the ball, roll my head slowly, then readdress the ball. The crowd quiets down again. I inhale deeply and exhale

111

slowly as I release my stroke—Damn, too hard, I think, as I watch, helplessly—the ball rolling too high. I can't watch—my eyes lose focus—*choked.* Tears start to form out of frustration and humiliation. I blew it. But the crowd roars suddenly, and people rush to me, screaming—it dropped!

Much pandemonium ensues; the result of an unknown, unranked woman wearing black bike shorts, with hairy legs and a crew cut winning this *men's* event. Fuck the inequality of this separatist sport, "*Veni, vedi, vici!,*" I yell at the reporters over the din. But more exciting than the startling upset, the money, the adulation, is the fact that every young dyke in America is having a wet dream over me. Likewise.

CH. 31

Show jumping. I like the fairness of this sport. Both men and women competing equally in the same events, for the same money. Even the horses are deemed equal as far as gender goes, and are separated by experience only. I can watch show jumping without the feminist guilt that arises when I watch almost all other sports—although classist guilt does come up. But I'm Jewish, so I have to have some guilt associated with everything I do.

I used to love to ride. The beauty and grace and power. And control. The perfect sport for a control queen, such as myself. What is it about girls and horses? Something Freudian, no doubt. I can't wait to hear my therapist's response to that question. Actually, I know what her response would be. "How would *you* answer that question?"

CH. 24

Hockey. The Islanders. Growing up in Great Neck, JAP-ville, U.S.A., was a horrifying experience for a teenager who wore no makeup, had short hair—not the buzz cut of my later years, but hey, it was the seventies—didn't shave the parts that were usually shaved, wore jeans, T-shirts, and work boots as a rule, and whose idols were not Cheryl Tiegs, Farrah Fawcett, and Cher, but Kristie (Buddy) McNichol, Chris Evert-Lloyd, and Billie Jean King. And Billy Smith, the Islander goalie. I didn't have a crush on him, but I think I wanted to be him. Well, not be him exactly, but be like him, be the Islander goalie. The last line of defense, the puck stops here.

Goalie is the perfect position for a woman to break into the majors. One needs to be a good skater, have excellent balance, and have good hand-eye coordination, all of which I had before the effects of being a couch potato set in. While one needs to be fairly strong, goalies generally are not involved in checking or fights, with the exception of B.S.—stray too close to his crease and have your knees swatted at by a heavy goal stick. My hero! A female goalie did almost break into the majors this year, and I say *almost* with a sense of inevitable dread, knowing full well the chances of upsetting any patriarchal monolith. She, of course, was used briefly, as a media draw, and then sent down to the minors when the season started. Another woman being exploited for profit, *quelle surprise!*

But my fantasy started in 1972, with the birth of the Islanders, and thus preceded all this. I would be so athletic, graceful, quick, intuitive, etc., that they would have to hire me, and therefore I would be the first woman in the NHL, like a white, Jewish, female Jackie Robinson. And somewhere on Long Island, an insecure teenager with a buzz cut would have posters on her wall of k.d., Martina, and me.

CH. 2

Tennis. Martina. I love Martina. I love the fact that she walks out on court in shorts, as if in silent protest to the conventions of gender. I love her for being out. I love her persona, her stamina, her strength. I see her before me, nude. Lying there, wanting me. My hands run down her tanned, taut skin, outlining each individual muscle. She is like no other woman I have been with. She is so much stronger, yet I am on top of her, with her wrists in my tight grip. I feel her power beneath me, between my legs, knowing that she is *allowing* me control. Legs intertwined, hips grinding, bodies straining, sweat mingling with sex; now this is sport!

Do you douche?
Damn.

CH. 4

Basketball. Any thought of basketball, even the NBA, makes me think of Nancy Liebermann. Also a hero of mine. Well, I guess

any female sports figure who commanded national press was a hero
to me since there were so few. Basketball should be the one sport
that would *not* induce fantasies from me, being on the short and,
shall we say, plump side. *Au contraire,* I see myself as a power forward, elbowing my way past towering guards, knocking them on
their collective butts. Maybe not blocking shots, but stealing balls
with my quickness and agility. But back to Nancy. I can't say I've
followed her career or even know where she is now, but I seem to
remember her being a commentator for the Olympics, women's
basketball, of course, and her being referred to as Nancy Lieber-
mann-Klein. What the hell is that? She got married? What happened to the rumors about her and Martina sharing a house in
California? "Roommates," as they referred to them at the time.
Don't tell me she went the way of Billie Jean King, who declared her
affair with a woman "a mistake." Probably Nancy didn't refer to it
at all. Didn't acknowledge it publicly. Just another invisible lesbian.
The object of jokes and rumor and innuendo in the girl's locker
room of Great Neck North Junior High. Along with Billie Jean, and
all of our P.E. coaches. I wonder if there were rumors about me.

Looking back on those junior high days, I find my fascination
with the girls' coaches amusing and obvious, especially since I'm
such a loud militant dyke now, or so I've been called. That I could
be so unaware of who I was and could misinterpret my feelings
toward women seems pathetic. But one of the difficulties about
coming out or even acknowledging to myself that I could be *that
way,* was that there were no role models. I knew of not one acknowledged lesbian. All I had was the locker room talk. *Did you
hear about what happened to Billie Jean King at the Dutch Open?
She was caught with her finger in a dyke.*

I was never one of those girls who stared at the others getting
undressed, I was far too shy. I admired the girls who were athletic,
since I wasn't, but didn't have crushes on them. I longed to be like
them: fast, strong, comfortable in their bodies. When I had a crush,
or some more ethereal, undefined longing for someone, it was always someone there had been *that* rumor about. Miss Pamillo. I
often wondered about the story of her living with another woman.
Another P.E. teacher, I imagined. I thought about what it would
be like to live with another woman; the loving looks across the
table, the casual way they would have with each other, the oneness
of the relationship.

My other fascination was with a girl named Sharona. She was

the biggest jock in the school, boys included. (This was Great Neck, after all.) Now *she* was actually rumored to have slept with another girl at sleep-away camp. I was in total awe. I would find myself seeking her out, just to talk or hang out. How I wanted to ask her. Ask her what it was like. What did you do. How did it feel. I was not ready to use the information even if I had it, my sexual identity being totally unformed, but I still wanted it. I wondered so long and hard about Miss Pamillo and her "friend," about Sharona, and Nancy and Martina. Why did it take me another eight years to put this information together and realize I was a lesbian?

CH. 11

Why Ask Why?
Unlike this commercial, I have to ask why. I don't want to mindlessly accept the way I grew up. Would it have been easier for me to come out if Billy Jean had said that she was a dyke, and proud of it? Or if Martina had come out when I was in high school? If *Desert Hearts* were released in 1975 instead of 1985, would I have had the nerve to date women in junior high, or high school? Probably not, judging by the overriding social unacceptability of homosexuality. But I needed someone to identify with, someone to help me put a name on what I was feeling. It would have been nice to have been less confused, not mistaking friendship for love, or love for lust. And maybe if I had things figured out, I would have gone out with Sharona. When I think about her now, I can't help but imagine that she turned out to be a big ol' dyke. I can see her now—short, solid, strong, living on the fringe of Park Slope. Maybe into s/m. Wearing a leather biker cap . . . *Oops, that's my ex, Susan.*

CH. 14

Swimming. Oh, those big, butch, small-breasted, broad-shouldered, testosterone-laden Eastern European women with short blond hair!

CH. 10

Women's Volleyball. U.S.A. vs. Japan.
I miss Cheryl—what *is* her last name? You know the one. The

one who died during a match in Japan from some mysterious blood ailment. Wait, wasn't it rumored that she and Nancy and Martina . . .

CH. 47

Football. Why is it that the entire world population refers to soccer as football, footbol, fútbol, or some such name? I'm sure this has a lot to do with the current state of soccer in the U.S. We are probably the only industrialized country in the world that does not have a professional football league, I mean soccer league. It's a good thing that we're hosting the World Cup in 1994, or else we would never play.

Soccer also strikes me as a sport where women should compete with men. Stamina and finesse. Of course, I'd have to be the goalie. Hmm, this seems to be a recurring fantasy. Something about preventing men from scoring . . .

This is the one sport that I played well in junior high. Comparatively well, that is, I being the only person in junior high who knew the rules—a slight advantage. In fact, I knew the game better than Miss Goess, the P.E. teacher who oversaw the soccer games, whose sexuality I didn't even *want* to know about. Once, when we were playing an intramural game (now there's a word you never hear after you've left school), and the ball was out of bounds, she actually told the girl to put the ball down and *kick* it in bounds. It took me ten minutes to convince her that the ball should be thrown in, and even then, I think she gave in rather than prolong the argument.

I always played on the same side as Sharona. She was defense and I was, of course, in goal. It was a great vantage point. From there I could just stand around and watch her, how she moved other girls out of her way, how she loped down the field. When I thought about her at night, I would always picture both of us on the soccer field, drenched in sweat, like some advertisement for an American girl version of *Another Country.* This was one of the rare opportunities I had to share the field with Sharona. Most of the time she played on varsity teams, and I refused to try even for J.V., hoping to avoid total humiliation. I suffered enough in gym class, running the third or fourth slowest 50 meters. I should be thankful that I wasn't *the* slowest. But on that field, together, she made me feel like we were playing varsity together. I'll always love her for that.

I wonder if those rumors about her were true.

Click

LOSING WIMBLEDON

Laurie Ellen Liss

Where were you the day Billie Jean King pronounced her "affair" with Marilyn Barnett "a mistake" on national television? The expectation that you might remember is a far-reaching one, though it's not exactly like the day Kennedy was shot (that's the day I was born, what's your excuse?). My high school yearbook was distributed to all us seniors on that June day in 1981. Underneath my 1" × 1" photo, team and organizational affiliations, was a quote:

> Never confuse motion with action.
> —Billie Jean King

A five-word formula for success, and how I saw myself in the world. It resonated throughout every tennis match, every debate, mock court, chem lab experiment. To put it into being meant that I had found the "Big M," for "momentum," that unexplained place where one is at a personal best and seemingly undefeatable. "The Big M." An idea I first heard uttered by Billie Jean King.

The day Billie Jean King went on national television and declared her affair a mistake was the day we all knew the rumors were true. Where were you? I was on Harris Field tossing a frisbee, looking over my shoulder at the softball diamond, running the bases one final time. I was the picture my classmates turned to and made cracks about, not the photo, but the quote. I was, effectively, "outed" (my long-haired boyfriend notwithstanding) by association. Tennis. Softball. Confirmed on television, local and national. My classmates declared their gossip about me fact—like Billie Jean King, I must be a lesbian too. A funny fact to have eluded me.

College. More tennis. More softball. A pickup game of basketball. Or football. The arm never betrayed me. I left the photos of Billie Jean King on my wall at my parents' house, mostly because

I didn't have that dream anymore. The one where I made it to the final at Wimbledon and happily lost to Billie Jean King. Happily because she deserved to win. Athletic prowess aside, she had pointed the right fingers and yelled above the noise. In my dream she was playing her last Wimbledon, and I was going to ensure her finale came with the fanfare of championship.

As it happened, that time in-between high school and college I fell in love with a woman. I had the dream only once that summer. I won.

MARTINA AND ME: A TRILOGY

Rachel Lurie

Part I

SEPTEMBER 24, 1989

GAME, SET, MATCH . . . AND STILL LOVE, OR,

WHY MARTINA'S LOSS MAKES ME SAD

I have a hard time talking about sad events in my life. It was at least a week before I spoke to anyone about the loss I felt when Lucille Ball died. So it's important to sit down now and reflect on what a bummer it was to see Martina Navratilova have to slam down her racket in disgust after she gave away the final in the U.S. Open to that twerp Steffi Graf.

See, Martina isn't just the greatest woman tennis player ever, she's a symbol for dykes everywhere. A muscular, athletic woman who admits to loving other women. Quite a rare commodity in the realm of famous and watched people. And a true inspiration for every dyke who's ever hit a slow-pitched softball and dreamed of greater things.

But of course no one really talks about it much. We don't see the camera focus in on Martina's significant other during the big matches. And when the camera showed Billie Jean King, now coaching Martina, chewing on her nice short nails during the tension-filled match, of course no one alluded to *her* lurid past or the possibility that maybe something was going on between the two tennis idols (I don't think there is anything going on between them, but certainly Mary Carillo, CBS's very dykey commentator, could have raised some questions and eyebrows about something other than how much Ivan Lendl spent on his house in Greenwich, all as a gift for his fiancée).

"Women's tennis" got bonus TV time this year with the golden tribute to Chris Evert who was throwing in the towel after twenty

120

years of making aces. The best thing about the tribute was that they stopped using her husband's last name as a tag-on to her long-revered tennis handle. But we sure got the picture of her illustrious career, both on and off the court, complete with her thwarted engagement to Jimmy Connors and later a real marriage to that Lloyd guy. Yeah, Chrissie was good, and her name was easier to pronounce for North Americans who rooted for the home team in her outings against Martina. But the anticipation of a "Dyke vs. Het Showdown" never made it into the blathering discourse of the commentators or sportswriters. And some people never even made the distinction. Once when I was playing basketball with the brothers on the West 4th Street court, my teammates, always preferring nicknames to real ones, dubbed me "Chris Evert," which goes to show, really, just how much our culture is at a loss when it comes to big-name women athletes. Only women tennis players (and track stars around Olympics time) make it into the sports pages or bar screens, and even that only once or twice a year.

What will happen when Martina heads off into that retirement sunset? Will we see footage of her and Rita Mae Brown, complete with an analysis of the nasty trashing Brown gave both Martina and the women's tennis circuit in her novel *Sudden Death*? Will we hear how Nancy Lieberman coached, trained me and loved Martina back into a competitor, at the expense, some say, of her own basketball career? Will we hear that Lieberman couldn't really *have* a fucking career in women's sports because no one in this country will pay to watch women play graceful, fast and aggressive b-ball because they can't slam dunk?

Like everyone else watching that championship match last Saturday, I was convinced Martina had it all wrapped up. She was playing flawless, at-the-net tennis, making mincemeat out of that blond bomb-out (who bad-mouths Martina's "lifestyle" but has as a doubles partner Martina's *real* successor on the court, already dyke-watched Gabriela Sabatini). Martina was pumped up and so was I, calling my friends to tell them to turn on the TV, Martina was five minutes away from *creaming* Steffi.

But then Martina's game started to soften: Steffi broke her serve and started to come back. Perhaps most symbolically, Steffi changed from her sweat-soaked *lavender* skirt into tennis whites between games, all fresh in anticipation of a third set. Every unforced error had Martina scowling, cursing, pounding her racket in anguish. And I shared each emotional grimace because, god-dammit, Martina *is* the better tennis player, not to mention the better woman, and she was sinking fast.

If Martina won, she was winning for all of us, every dyke (and even more so for those of us who wear glasses) who wants to say, "Look, we're here and we're winners, even champions. We live in your straight world but play by our own rules and we can still come out on top." And even in a world where we sometimes have to grope for heros, Martina is a valid, three-dimensional one. When Pam Shriver asked her to play in an athlete's benefit for George Bush, she readily refused saying "I've been a lot of things, but I could never be a Republican."

But Martina did lose the heartbreaker last week and stupid Steffi got to run off the court for the trademark victory kiss with her overbearing father. And I sunk in my couch, grumbling, saddened, snapping off the TV. But it won't slow my admiration for Martina: out, emotional, gracious in defeat and a thrill to watch. Yeah, you've been a lot of things Martina, but you could never be a loser. And don't worry honey, we're behind, or should I say, beneath, you all the way.

Part II
DECEMBER 3, 1989
SELLING OUT AT THE VIRGINIA SLIMS CHAMPIONSHIP

Martina Navratilova choked again in the final of a major tour-nament, losing last Sunday to her nemesis Steffi Graf in the Vir-ginia Slims Championship. But this time I'm not so quick to feel sad or disappointed about the lesbian idol's missed opportunity. Thanks to an *OutWeek* press pass I got real close to the women's tennis scene for the duration of the tournament last week, sitting courtside for the matches, drinking coffee with the cynical press pack and asking questions up close and personal at a pretourna-ment press conference. The sadness I feel after all this is not about Martina's waning days of glory, but about lesbian invisibility in what should be our turf—women's sports—and the open antag-onism and homophobia perpetuated by one of the few pieces of mainstream culture we belong to.

Of course there was plenty of excitement to be had all week

long at Madison Square Garden as the "richest" and biggest women's-only sporting event in the world unfolded. For the first time ever, scalper's tickets were in demand for the sold-out semifinals on Saturday (where Martina made short order of the hot Spanish upstart, seventeen-year-old Arantxa Sanchez and Graf struggled against Gabriela Sabatini and a hostile crowd rooting for Sabatini, last year's winner). The lines to the women's rooms (it seems like there are twice as many men's rooms than women's at the Garden) were fifteen minutes long, allowing many an old college teammate to run into another. I ran into a friend who noted: "This is a weird crowd: you've got the tennis nerds and the dykes." Quite a few of those dykes skipped the lines altogether and headed into the men's rooms unnoticed.

And these dykes, not surprisingly, added our own dimension to the event. Between matches on Saturday, outgoing Women's International Tennis Association President Merritt Steierheim received a recognition award as the woman presenting it to him first described how utterly unqualified for the job Steierheim was when he took it on four years ago. "But he took control of the WITA the way a patriarch takes control of his family," she groped, completely oblivious to how offensive this remark was and equally naive as to why the crowd of 18,000 greeted her words with a spirited round of hisses and shouts of "Patriarchy Sucks."

What planet do the people running these events live on? It is a fight for women to get any respect in the testosterone arena of sports, and as long as men and ass-kissing women are running the show, we aren't going to get anywhere. Athlete/advocate Billie Jean King, who in her entire career won as much money as Steffi Graf made in the last two years, saw this fight for what it was and took it on. And it got her ostracized among the same people who stand at center court and give awards out to the "great white fathers" for their "advancement" of women's sports. But it also worked, because now Graf, who seems to have no sense of the history of the game she keeps winning in, rakes in nearly $2 million a year.

It's the sponsors of the sport which determine the size of the take, but they also control the image, which is, after all, what affects those of us who work real jobs. Back in 1981, Avon stopped its sponsorship of women's tennis in the wake of the lesbian "scandals" of Billie Jean King's "palimony" suit (Marilyn

Barnett wanted a pay-off for a relationship that lasted seven years)
and Martina's very public relationship with Rita Mae Brown. A
friend of mine joked that what's more likely is that Avon backed
out when they realized none of the dykes were using their prod-
ucts, but nevertheless, a clear signal went out to the only profitable
segment of women's sports that any acknowledgment of lesbians
in their midst was bad for business.

No matter that we're the ones who buy the tickets. Virginia
Slims is owned by Philip Morris Companies, number ten on the
Fortune 500 list with annual revenues rivaling the Pentagon
budget, so the net from the tournament's 94,000 ticket sales probably doesn't even cover their corporate lunches for the year.

Bill Goldstein, the tournament administrator and VP for Sports
Etc., the promotion company for the tournament, balked at the
idea of hitting the lesbian market directly by advertising in the gay
press because "it's too sensitive."

"Obviously there are some women who are lesbians and some
who are not," he pointed out to me. "Making the connection [be-
tween lesbians and women's tennis] offends the athletes and it
reinforces their concerns to affirmatively advertise in a lesbian
publication."

Apparently, at last year's tournament, "people took notice" of
a group of lesbians who bought a block of choice seats and, gasp,
were given the usual privileges which come with such a purchase.
So Bill Goldstein, who was thanked profusely by everyone at the
tournament who ever got in front of a microphone, thinks denial
and invisibility is the best way to handle this "sensitive" issue.

I decided to go straight to the players themselves with the ques-
tion: "Does lesbian interest in women's tennis offend you?" And
I had my chance at the pretournament press conference held in an
Upper West Side sports bar on November 13.

After fielding the very tennis-focused questions from reporters
about the demise of the Berlin Wall and the reunification of Germany, Steffi mumbled "Oh, don't get me into this," after I had to
repeat my question. "People should stand up for what they want,"
she managed to articulate, "but I like boys very much." Well, we
all know Steffi's depth does not extend beyond the backcourt, so
I can't say I was too surprised.

Then it was Martina's turn, but the staffperson standing guard
was ready for me this time and shouted out "time's up" as soon

as I asked my question. "I'm so glad I don't have to answer that," Martina sighed out loud to herself. "It's not about *you*, it's about the sport," I said in my defense. "It's not about the *sport*," she spat back.

Now, I know about Martina's struggles with being out all these years as a celebrity, and how she feared being publicly identified as a lesbian would threaten her right to citizenship in the U.S. And it's exactly her willingness to stand up to all that which has made her a lesbian hero. So why should she stop now? When I cornered her to apologize for seemingly putting her on the spot, she peered down at me and chastised, "Your question was out of line."

But what's out of line is the denial of the lesbian force in women's sports, among both athletes and fans. No, we haven't come a long way baby, because every time we agree that our lesbian identity is something to keep hidden or avoid talking about, we are chipping away at our own survival, allowing our oppressors to keep us locked in a closet of shame. And Martina Navratilova did thank her lover Judy Nelson in her postmatch speech (calling her "my friend"). This struggle is not about any one athlete taking a stand, although every act to do so should be applauded as the courageous move it is. The place we need to be is where this information can't be used against us, where it isn't unusual or courageous to talk about it, but perfectly normal.

Part III
SUMMER, 1993
MARTINA: A DISTINCTLY LESBIAN CHAMPION

It's a long time since my strained and awkward encounter with Martina at that press conference in 1989 and part of me can't help but wonder if maybe that meeting played a small part in her political evolution. Swatting away us critics of the closet like so many tennis balls, she's proved to be the perfect role model of the politicized lesbian celeb, reaching out as a kind of queer ambassador to the straight world. All the while, she's maintained a great deal of power over the agenda, realizing, I guess, that she simply had nothing more to lose by any further revelations of who she is or what she believed. My admiration is deep. Regardless of all my righteous tones, what would I do in her position? Would *I* have jumped into the stands at Wimbledon to hold my lover at the proudest moment of my career? Or would I have only thrown her a knowing glance, tears of joy streaming down, but staying put on Centre Court, silenced by the overbearing presence of royalty and TV cameras? I'll never know. But Martina Navratilova did leap into the stands to embrace her partner after her ninth Wimbledon victory, and in that moment of pure emotion reshaped the framework of every little girl's sports success fantasy and every dyke's visibility goals.

What were the things that brought Martina to this public place? Her lesbian identity has haunted her during her twenty years on the tennis circuit; tabloids have hounded her and her "gal pals"; parents of players have humiliated her, and commentators don't know quite what to make of her rippling muscles or her Team Navratilova entourage of coaches and friends. And in this era of excessive sports marketing, she brandishes no significant endorsements. Gatorade's not going to have flashy commercials telling kids to BE LIKE MARTINA because her very name *means* queer. But finally, she's settled in proudly behind the banner and there seems to be no turning back.

She's in a unique position to force the mainstream world to take a look at things as she sees them. This past July, when she lost in the semifinals at Wimbledon, thus keeping her from the anticipated finals showdown with Steffi Graf and a run at her unprecedented tenth win, Martina appeared at the postmatch press conference wearing a T-shirt with a pink triangle. *New York Times* sports columnist George Vecsey wrote about it: "Navratilova has worn her heart on her sleeve for a long time. Yesterday her heart was on her T-shirt." He quoted her explaining the shirt's meaning: " 'This, the pink triangle? It's a symbol of the gay movement, the upside-down pink triangle. Since Hitler marked gays in the concentration camps with a pink triangle, now it's the inverted pink triangle.' . . . She was proud of the pink triangle, proud of herself. She was glad to be alive. And she wasn't giving up."

Her choice of wearing the pink triangle at a moment of intense personal loss is profound. Wearing it shows where she's getting her strength and solace from—from the community that's there when others leave us; those who we ultimately come home to when we need comfort or we're out of the spotlight. But it also shows how intensely solid she is about her own identity. No longer does she have to struggle for some tenuous respectability by hiding who she is. She can proudly cross the boundaries between her tennis life and her lesbian identity, knowing, and making it known, that the two could not and would not be separated.

No one, no matter how homophobic, could deny her her place as athletic legend. In twenty years, she's played, and won, more singles matches than any other tennis player, male or female. During the 1980s, she finished number one in the world for six consecutive years, and has never fallen below number five. She basically couldn't lose in 1983 and '84, winning 55 matches, losing 1, and then taking the next 74 for an all-time record. *Time* magazine summed it up well: "Her standing as the all-time greatest in her sport seems beyond challenge." Remarkably, she's still playing, and the July 1993 semifinals loss to a player twelve years her junior is hardly something to be ashamed of. The level of greatness, the drive, ambition, discipline and intensity, has to adorn other aspects of her life. She herself has drawn metaphors between her game and her life, saying she's a "risk taker who sets herself up to be vulnerable" both on and off the court.

She certainly has known the betrayal of other lesbians. When jilted Judy Nelson, her lover of nine years, sued her for half her net worth, Martina was once again dragged across headlines as a lesbian monster, a homewrecker who seduced this one-time Texas beauty queen into throwing away her husband and kids for a life on tour with a lezzie tennis star. From what I understand from the reviews, Nelson can't even come to her own defense in her book *Love Match,* written for that expressed purpose. Martina, for her part, went on camera with Barbara Walters, and—in one of the most watched television programs of the year—offered a rather revealing picture of her relationship, complete with a heart-warming, if anguished, sense of loss. There are rumors now that Nelson and Martina's more famous ex, Rita Mae Brown, are shacking up on some grand farm somewhere. I read about it in *Lesbian Connection,* but that small mag cited "The Larry King Show" as the source for this dish. Not only is this information a replay of that odd blend of lesbian incestuousness and double-crossing, but this particular juxtaposition of media outlets also shows how Martina iconography (and gossip) swerves back and forth across the lesbian fringe and mainstream boundaries.

Since the Judy Nelson debacle, and undisclosed settlement that

sent her on her way, Martina has really come on strong in her
political persona. When Magic Johnson revealed his HIV status,
she was vocal and righteous about the double standard for women.
She noted the political and social price any woman sports figure
would pay if she confessed to having hundreds of sex partners in
any given year, as Magic had. "She certainly wouldn't be honored
with an appointment to a presidential AIDS Commission," Martina told Phil Donahue, offering a perspective no one in the sporting world had dared. They were all too busy thinking themselves
amazingly liberal for even continuing to mention Magic's name,
not because of his (heterosexual) sexual exploits, but because of
the A word.

More recently Martina has risen to the queer call by actively
working to overturn her home state of Colorado's antigay Amendment 2. She also gave her name to a National Gay and Lesbian
Task Force fundraising letter focusing on lifting the ban on gays
in the military—a letter which also brought together a larger picture on the current gay rights movement and its fight-the-Right
mandate. Even if the letter was ghost-written, I trust she agrees
with the sentiment: "When the history of this time is written, I
hope you and I will be able to look back and say, yes, we were
there. We were at the side of those whom we love when they
needed us most." She spoke at this year's March on Washington,
wearing freedom rings and a black T-shirt with the sleeves rolled
up, and she appeared in a tux jacket for the Gay Games tribute
in her honor. She's always sure to use "we" when talking about
gay people, in everything from *Ladies Home Journal* to TV talk
shows.

These are the signs of a dyke very much at home with herself.
And very much fed up with the closet. It seems like for all eternity,
we watch for signs from queers in public places. We wait for a
wink when watching the Academy Awards. We have always stood
ready to decipher the codes we use to identify ourselves to each
other, particularly when coming from famous quarters. But the
strength of the gay rights movement now is in our visibility. Our
triumphs no longer have to be passed on through some coy ritual—in fact, they can't be. When we see a big, strong woman,
who is out and famous and surviving, it lets me know the most
important thing: that I'm okay too. And that being different
doesn't have to keep me from being great.

The questions about Martina's playing days are: when will she quit, and to whom will she pass the torch? The teenage locker room atmosphere—with the odd mix of fame, fortune, pressure and puberty—must be one volatile place. Plus it's tough enough being a girl jock, because you're immediately suspect for being some kind of outcast from your gender. And the boyish, butch girls—like I was—have it tougher still because we know we'll never fully outgrow the taunts and failed expectations. But someday the lesbians on the sports circuit won't have to hide or feel ashamed of their sexual desire for other women. And they'll have Martina to thank, the woman who already has allowed girls to dream of having muscles, of winning a championship and jumping into the stands to kiss their dream girlfriend.

And off the court, she is showing us that though we might make some bad choices—have loser girlfriends and questionable haircuts—who we are is always something to come home to. In that interview with Barbara Walters, Martina said she'd like to have kids, "to pass on these genes." But her message and legacy is the most maternal of all: who we are is a wonderful, special thing. We don't need to be ashamed or afraid of our difference or our gifts. Our surviving, our persistence, our drive, makes us great. It is a champion bloodline she is passing on, and it runs through *my* veins too.

HOW I (ALMOST) MET MARTINA NAVRATILOVA

Bonnie Morris

In December of 1985, I received a wonderful present from my friend Camille: tickets to see Martina Navratilova play in the Virginia Slims Tournament! It was held in Washington, D.C., where I lived, and I walked about gleefully with the precious ticket snug against my hand.

On the afternoon of the tournament, I had an idea. Why not send flowers to Martina as a gesture of good will and Amazon pride? I dashed to the nearest florist and paid a ridiculous sum for a bouquet of the largest lavender blooms available. I could deliver these flowers to backstage officials when I arrived at the tournament, and Martina would know that the women of Washington were behind her all the way. But how would she know, really . . . unless a note accompanied the flowers? Very well, I'd write a note wishing her the best.

But what could I say that other fans had not yet said?

With the flowers glowing in the back seat of my parents' Toyota, I roared out of the florist's driveway and headed for the library at American University. I'd come up with a brilliant scheme: I would write Martina a good-luck note *in Czech!* Surely this would distinguish me from her other fans. Beaming with self-importance, I strode into the foreign languages department of Bender Library and reached for the English-Czech dictionary.

Within minutes I realized that I was a starstruck peabrain. Lacking the remotest knowledge of Czech grammar and conjugation, I could use no verbs in my note. I frantically lumped nouns and forms of greeting together in a truly insipid pattern. For hours, I strained and sweated over the dictionary. Finally I had crafted a short note (in lavender ink of course!) that said, in formal Czech, something like "GREETINGS EXCELLENT TENNIS BALL. AMAZON WOMEN HELLO FROM WASHINGTON CITY.

BEST GAME TONIGHT PLEASE YES. SPORTS OF WOMEN TRIUMPH. FRIEND PEACE FORTUNE, BONNIE."

I tied the card to the flowers and returned home to eat a tasty meal with my jocular parents.

The tournament was held at George Washington University, where I had attended my first lesbian dance at age nineteen. I entered the sports arena with complete confidence. After all, had I not sent flowers to Judy Collins on two occasions and thus succeeded in meeting her? Perhaps I'd have the pleasure of meeting Martina too, if only I behaved calmly.

I looked around for a security guard. Unfortunately, it wasn't that easy. This was not just *any* tennis match; this was the Virginia Slims tour—and the streets outside the arena were jammed with protesters who objected to the tobacco industry's sponsorship of women's sports. I paused to chat with an attractive demonstrator, who urged me to burn my ticket and join her in the struggle.

Due to the confusion, noise, and tension of the anti-cigarette demonstration, dozens of security guards paced through the arena. How would I find the one who could lead me to Martina's dressing room? I had to appear nonthreatening, placid—or better yet, official as hell. I had to shift into actress gear.

Of course! Pasting a yuppie smirk on my face, I approached the nearest guard and announced that I was a courier from the Potomac Tennis Club and where should I deliver Ms. Navratilova's bouquet? The security guard waved me downstairs to the "backstage" area—and suddenly I was outside of the players' dressing rooms.

At this point I had no plan, but before I could scheme anew I was confronted by an enormous man wearing a gun and several badges. He wished to know my business. I opened my mouth and tried to speak. Suddenly I heard myself sneer in a phony Czech accent, "Hallo. I am from Czech Embassy. We have forgiven Martina for defecting. Our women's sports bureau wishes Martina to have these flowers. You will please deliver."

The word "embassy" has great power in Washington, D.C. Moreover, I was conveniently dressed in a folksy outfit that might pass off as Czech if one was unfamiliar with East European fashion. And, to clinch my act, I had a note written in authentic Czech! Ungrammatical, yes! Incomprehensible, yes! But could the cop prove that? I stood in a posture of crisp dignity, flaring my nostrils and intoning like a mantra "Embassy . . . embassy."

Within seconds, another security guard appeared and gave me an awed smile. He took the flowers and the card from me and said, "I'll see that she gets these, ma'am. We appreciate your stopping by."

"Hnn, ya," I nodded gravely, my left eye straining to see over his head and into the dressing room. I saw: towels. But no other flowers. Only I had thought to send flowers. And I knew mine would be the only fan letter in awkward, earnest, Lesbian-American-Czech.

I turned around, took the stairs three at a time to my seat in the arena. And watched Martina win.

INTERVIEW: MARTINA NAVRATILOVA

Michele Kort

RuPaul, in red, white, and blue-spangled supermodel drag, is a hard act to follow. Maybe that's one of the reasons tennis super*star* Martina Navratilova, in forearm-revealing T-shirt chic, took such a deep gulp of air before striding to the podium and addressing the marching minions in Washington, spring 1993.

"I am not going to cry, don't even try . . ." she warned, like a schoolmarm, as the throng gave her a swelling ovation. Maybe she was referring to her emotional courtside past, like the time she boo-hoo'd at the U.S. Open in 1981 after losing a hard-fought match to Tracy Austin—but winning the formerly hard hearts of the New York crowd.

This crowd had loved Navratilova, who turned thirty-seven in October, for years, swooning over her butch athleticism and femme vulnerability and her ever-more-open sexual preference. They'd stuck with her through the "bisexual" years, through the recent bitter galimony lawsuit filed by her ex-lover, and now this appearance was a reward of sorts: no longer just a famous "known" lesbian, Martina Navratilova was finally a member of the *community*.

"What our movement for equality needs most," she began, numbering herself with the Washington million, "is to come out of the closet. . . . Let's come out and let all the people—read heterosexual—see what for the most part straight and square and boring lives we lead. . . .

"My sexuality is a very important part of my life," she continued, ". . . but still is a very small part of my makeup. In any case, being a lesbian is not an accomplishment, it is not something I had to study for, or learn, or graduate in. It is what I am, nothing more, nothing less."

The applause for that line was probably heard at the White House, if not all the way back in the former Czechoslovakia, from whence Navratilova defected in 1975 at the tender age of eighteen.

She left to compete at the highest levels of tennis without government control, but now she tells us there may have been other reasons as well (read on).

At first she was pudgy, inconsistent, and temperamental, but eventually she molded herself into a cool, sleek hitting machine, overpowering opponents with her mighty serve, deadly net game, and slithery backhand slices. Archrival Chris Evert had to start lifting unladylike weights to keep up with her. Indeed, every woman tennis player post-Navratilova realized that the little skirts they wore belied the sweaty work they'd have to do to compete in the game the expatriate had restyled in her own image.

Besides her legendary on-court exploits (165 career singles and 162 doubles victories; 9 Wimbledon singles titles and 4 U.S. Opens; 74 straight match wins in one stretch; seven years ranked #1), Navratilova drew attention for her love life and mouthiness as well. The revelation of her affair with novelist Rita Mae Brown nearly threatened her quest for U.S. citizenship, and she seemed to backpeddle in describing her next "friendship" with basketball star Nancy Liebermann, who became her trainer as well as (it's no longer an open secret) lover. Then came the seven seemingly blissful years ensconced in Dallas and Aspen with former Maid of Cotton/mother-of-two Judy Nelson, who upon their Martina-initiated breakup sued Navratilova for half her earnings (and revealed a videotaped agreement backing up the claim).

Meanwhile, Navratilova became a gadfly of sorts, speaking out about everything from recycling to AIDS. When Magic Johnson announced his heterosexual exploits along with his HIV status, Navratilova decried the double standard that allows male athletes to sleep around with impunity while females would be tarred as sluts. She also didn't want anyone to forget that if Johnson had been gay, the public would have been far less forgiving.

"I've been doing benefits for AIDS since before it was politically correct," she says on a sunny August afternoon in Manhattan Beach, squeezing out her words between healthy bites of fruit, pasta, and green salad in the players' lunch tent. She's just come from a practice session for the annual Virginia Slims tournament, which is the hard-court version of the Dinah Shore golf tournament in terms of lesbian attendance.

By week's end, Navratilova will have beaten Arantxa Sanchez Vicario in a come-from-behind match to take her eighth title in

Manhattan Beach, surpassed $600,000 in winnings for 1993 and $19 million lifetime, and cast doubt on the computer that ranks her only fourth in the world (behind Steffi Graf, Monica Seles, and Sanchez Vicario). Fifteen years her junior, Sanchez Vicario will have lauded Navratilova in her Spanish-is-my-native-tongue syntax: "She is the best volley in all history. You are the one who has to make all the run and the passing shots." And everyone will be wondering if this woman will *ever* have to retire from tennis (though she won't promise more than another year on the tour).

But right now, Navratilova, her neck weighted down with crystals and a chain full of pride rings, relaxes into a conversation that's mostly about life away from tennis. This interviewer had spoken with her at length twice before and found her cool and guarded; this time, she was warm, charming, and remarkably open. As she said herself at the March, "By coming out . . . we make ourselves personal, touchable, real. We become human beings. . . ."

I heard you had a great time at the March on Washington.

It was unbelievable. I would have paid to have been there. I was a wreck doing the speech, but I wanted to be a part of it.

You were nervous?

Wouldn't you be, talking to a million people? And I was reading something I wrote myself—the ego it took to think they would want to listen to what I had to say. But I figured if they booed me in the middle of the speech I'd say, "Hey, don't blame me, I'm just a tennis player!" Apparently they did listen, because people told me they came out because of the speech. That whole weekend would make you want to come out, because you felt part of a bigger group. You didn't feel so alone.

Did the March feel like a sort of debutante ball for you, being so publicly out?

Almost, I guess. It was nice to be able to be public and not feel like an outcast, an outsider, embarrassed about who you are. Which I've felt—not in the sense that I'm ashamed of being gay, but I've gotten the feeling in public that people are staring at me and my date, or whoever I'm with, thinking—"Oh, that's Martina's latest." I may not even be with that person, but people assume we're together if it's a woman. There's a sexual undercurrent, or undertone, of judgment. And it was just so nonjudgmental to be a part of that weekend in Washington. There we were, and we had something in common, but we're beyond the sexuality. It's the straights who really concentrate on the sex part, and gays don't pay attention to it. It's not the most important thing in our lives.

How did you feel being the brunt of Liz Smith's rumor about you and k.d. lang?

Oh it was ridiculous. If it had just ended . . . but then they pick it up in Europe, they pick it up in magazines, and because she wrote it it's *fact* now. Paparazzi took pictures of me and my sister in Rome, and wrote that it was me and k.d. lang. And then two weeks later they said it was me and Cindy Nelson—and it was still my sister. It snowballs and you can't get rid of it. Then Liz Smith writes a retraction, but by then the magazines have picked it up, and they don't print a retraction. It's just annoying. I think it was Lea Delaria who made a joke that people were happy these two lesbian women found each other—as if there are only two in the whole country. You have to laugh at it—we were the only gay people in that place, therefore we must be together. And I wasn't even with k.d., either going or leaving. Liz Smith had all the facts wrong. k.d. was with her mother. I did see her at a postbash party.

But you are *friends with her.*

Absolutely. I adore her, I love her. I want to be a groupie and see her perform. I want to be a groupie for Melissa [Ethridge] and the Indigo Girls as well. I'm a good groupie, period.

Athletes always want to be rock stars.

And vice versa, rock stars want to be athletes. I want to learn to play an instrument. But not to be in a band—just to play.

By the way, do you know Liz Smith?

I think I met her a long time ago, with Rita Mae. And *she's* gay.

You also recently appeared at a Gay Games fundraiser in New York where they raffled one of your rackets for $18,000, and then you offered a tennis lesson that went for $30,000—how was that experience?

Unbelievable. A woman at the same table with me bought the lesson. She's from Atlanta, and that's where I've been for a month, playing Team Tennis. But I said she had to come to Aspen for the lesson. I said I'd throw in a dinner. I didn't know who was going to win it, but I figured I'd have fun.

And Billie Jean King was at the Gay Games fundraiser and spoke. Is she inching further out?

She's inching out. I think she doesn't care. I don't know.

Could you have appeared so publicly at gay events a year ago?

I've been out, but I haven't sort of been waving the flag. I was always told to lay low so I wouldn't throw off potential sponsors. Not pretend to be someone else, but just keep quiet. I finally realized I wasn't getting any deals anyway, and I was tired of laying low. I speak out on all the other issues, and this one is as important as any of them to me.

I sort of got thrown into the spotlight as well with Amendment 2 happening in Colorado, because I live there. All of a sudden everyone wanted to talk to me; all of a sudden I'm this expert on gay rights.

You don't support the Colorado boycott, though—why?

Because it's like throwing the baby out with the bathwater. Two wrongs don't make a right. All those cliches work, because you're only initially hurting the people who are *for* gay rights. The people that are against them are the last ones who will get hurt economically. If all the people who believe in gay rights say, "We're not going to go there," and gays move out of the state, then these other people achieve what they wanted—which is not to have to deal with gay rights. And if they [achieve] it, what prevents other states from doing the same? Pretty soon, are we just going to be [limited to] one state?

You say you aren't going to worry about speaking out in terms of sponsors, but have you continued to pursue sponsorships without success?

I just don't get any answers. Things are always happening, but when push comes to shove they go sign Chris [Evert] or Jennifer [Capriati] or somebody noncontroversial. I think it's even beyond the gay issue—it's just that I'm controversial. Have you ever heard Michael Jordan speak an opinion on anything he feels strongly about?

But do you think the climate will change for gays in sports? Will someone coming out after you have an easier time getting endorsements?

At a lot of companies it would be a nonissue now. Look at Banana Republic, or The Gap. They don't give a shit. It would depend on the company, really. People just don't want the stigma attached to them, and it may not have anything to do with endorsements. Someone may not be endorsable anyway, they may not have that big of a name.

You said before in The Advocate *that there were maybe five lesbian players among the top three hundred on the tour.*

In the top one hundred. Probably it's a little higher. It's not that sports makes you gay, but you're more exposed to those feelings because you're around women more. You have a choice. So maybe the percentage is a little higher, but I could go over the top one hundred and one year there may be five lesbians, one year there may be ten.

But no one's coming out.

No. And there are some gay men tennis players, but no one's come out. It will be interesting to see when another athlete comes out, because I'm sort of the Lone Ranger out there. At least in the entertainment industry there are more, men and women. That's why it was so great at k.d.'s concert in New York. If someone wants to take a picture of us, I don't have to hide about it. She's out, and it felt so relaxing to just be out and not pretending.

It's hard to ask somebody to [come out]. You're exposing yourself not just to your friends and family, but to the whole world. There are gay football players out there, but they're not going to come out for all the tea in China, because of the public and peer pressure they'd feel. It's much different for someone in the public eye, because you always have to do interviews. Even if you say you won't talk about it, you're going to have to expend the energy, and then it's going to be "the gay football player." That's what my speech was about in Washington. You don't read about "the heterosexual tennis player." I'm just speaking as a human being, not as a gay human being—just a human being. But it just overtakes all the other tags, and it's disconcerting. Like Barbra Streisand said at the Oscars, it will be great when they don't say, "the first female director," but just "director." Hopefully one day those tags won't be there.

You've certainly been speaking out lately. I hear that on "Good Morning America" you said Clinton "wussed out" on gays in the military.

Well, he did! But I didn't know it was going to be such a big deal when I said it. It went over the wires and everything.

How do you feel about the Clinton administration so far?

I think he's trying his hardest. I think he didn't know what he got himself into. I think he didn't know how the machinery works, how you have to oil it and how you have to compromise all the time. I still think he should have just said, "Screw it, I'm [lifting the ban] because I promised," and let Congress override it. Don't try to please everybody. As a result, he makes everybody mad.

Have you met Hillary?

Yes. I met both of them just to say "Hello, good luck," at a fundraiser in L.A. last September. I liked both of them very much. They look you right in the eye, and you get their undivided attention for that sixty seconds. I think they're really good people, they're bright, they're trying to do the right thing. He just didn't stick to his guns. He knows it's the right thing to do. He can't compromise with human rights. You can compromise with the budget—cuts here, taxes there, that's all compromisable. But human rights are not. What's astonishing to me is when people think they have a *right* to *choose* to give other human beings a right—or take it away! That's what blows my mind!

Since you've been out, how have people in your former homeland, the Czech Republic, responded to you?

I don't think they care. They just like me for me. They like the way I stuck it to the system and said, "Up yours, I'm out of here and I'm going to do my thing." So I was a hero to them in that way; I don't think they care about the other too much.

You've been increasingly outspoken about political issues—do you see yourself pursuing politics or activism in the post-tennis future?

Not politics; activism, yes. I think I can make more difference as an activist than a politician. Besides, I can't run for President anyway, so why bother?

And you don't mind being a lesbian spokeswoman?

It's not something I've strived for, but I'm not going to run away from it either. If I can make a difference, then I accept that responsibility with great pride. I'm just astonished I *can* make a difference. I always try to right wrongs, and if I can right this wrong, it's important to me.

To tennis for a moment: you're ranked number four, doing well, but you haven't won a Grand Slam singles title since 1990. As you get older, do you lose more of the mental edge or the physical one?

It's both. You don't recover from a sore body so quickly. It's harder to get out of the bed every morning. If I did a hard work-out when I was twenty-five, the next morning I'd be a little tired but I could get back into it. If I do a hard work-out now, I'm sluggish the whole next day. But it's mental also—"Oh, I've got to run for that ball, and I don't feel like it."

When your autobiography Martina *came out, Rita Mae Brown*

*wrote a rather scathing review in which I think she said something
to the effect that all the energy you put into being number one in
tennis took away from the energy you put into yourself as a person. Do you think that was fair, and is it still true?*

It's fair. You have to sacrifice, and athletes, generally speaking, are very immature human beings. At thirty they're not where
normal thirty-year-olds are, because all their effort goes into the
sport and they don't work on the mental growth, the personal
growth.

But I've been working on that a lot the last couple of years.
After Judy, I went to a therapist—I mean, she threw me for a loop,
and I really had to deal with that. I've done major personal growth
the last two-and-a-half years, especially this year, because I've been
single for the first time and I've really spent time on my own, by
myself. I had a blast! Wish I had done it sooner. It's given me
much better balance as a human being *and* as an athlete, but
maybe it's taken that edge off the tennis, because it's not the only
thing in my life. And it shouldn't be.

Still single, eh?

Yeah. Well . . . I'm seeing somebody, but I'm taking things
slowly. In the past it was, "Let's get married tomorrow." I've
learned. . . .

*When Judy's name comes up in a lesbian gathering, there's both
applause and boos.*

If people knew the real story, there would only be boos. If she
can look herself in the mirror and be happy with what she sees, I
can't be the judge of that. All I know is that if I had done what
she had done I couldn't look myself in the mirror.

Why?

In terms of setting me up, in terms of having me sign that agreement in the first place, and then going after it. In terms of believ-
ing—and she honestly believes—that she should have gotten half
the money I earned. Would I have not have made the same amount
of money had we never met? How much did she contribute to the
fact that I was the number one tennis player in the world? I was
already number one when I met her. I was already making that
kind of money. She didn't contribute. I mean, I worked for twenty
years to be in that position, and then she comes and tries to take
it off the top. Where was she for those twenty years?

The funny thing is, we had these discussions when we were

together, and she absolutely agreed that if somebody had a job and then gets together with someone else, that person should not be entitled to the other person's money. Whether it was heterosexual or homosexual, didn't matter—it was a matter of principle. I mean, when Nancy Liebermann and I split up, and I paid her some money, Judy said, "Oh, you gave her too much money, she doesn't deserve any of it." Nancy did a whole lot more for me than Judy ever did. When Judy and I split up I said, "Judy, what about Nancy?—you said she shouldn't have gotten all that money!" And she said, "This is different." It's not different. But it's different because it's *her.*

Do you think she tried to get the money partly out of spite because you ended the relationship?

No, she really truly believes she deserves half of that money, period. She somehow convinced herself of that.

How do you feel about two of your ex's, Judy and Rita Mae Brown, getting together?

Well, it was strange. That's never happened to me before. But I think those two deserve each other.

We've all watched your public coming out now, but what about the private side of coming out? You were a little coy about it in your autobiography—did you start coming out when you were still in Czechoslovakia?

I left Czechoslovakia about three months after I realized I was gay.

Had you been with someone there?

No . . . I don't want to get into that. But I knew I was going to be gay for the rest of my life. That was it. Looking back now, I realize that may have had something to do with my decision to leave, because I knew I couldn't be gay in Czechoslovakia, because that country is so repressive. *Was* so repressive. They used to put gay people in institutions there. That may have been in the back of my mind, though I really didn't realize it until I thought about it just recently.

So when you came here, was it hard for you dealing with your personal coming out?

I realized that morning [after first being with a woman] that my life would just be a whole lot more difficult, but I knew that that's where my heart was. I thought, "OK, so *that's* what I've been feeling all these years."

If you redid your autobiography now, would it be much different?

Oh yeah. I don't think I would be as revealing on some levels. I said some things I can't believe I talked about.

Like?

Like about getting my period!

Would you be more revealing about other things?

I don't know. It would be a different book; it's almost ten years later. I probably would be more philosophical. I'm sure I'll do another one some day, I don't know when.

How do you envision your life when you hang up the rackets?

First, I'll have unscheduled time. Because I've never had that. Even a month off. I'd like to just be unscheduled for a while. I'm sure I'll be doing political stuff. There are so many good causes out there—recycling, environmental stuff, animals, kids, old people, AIDS, gay rights, women's rights.

Were you always so concerned about issues?

I always had this great urge for fair play, always. Unfairness drove me *nuts*. If I saw a bigger kid beating up on a little kid, I would go help out. That was just inborn in me. I would help old people across the street, carry their bags. And I still do. Or give up my seat for an old woman or man, without thinking. I couldn't believe when other people didn't do it. I guess I'm just doing it on a bigger level, but I always had that sense in me. If I cut up an orange, I'd give my friend the bigger half. I'd feel guilty if I took the bigger half.

These days, that would be called codependence.

If that's what it is, I don't care.

Part 5

FICTIONS

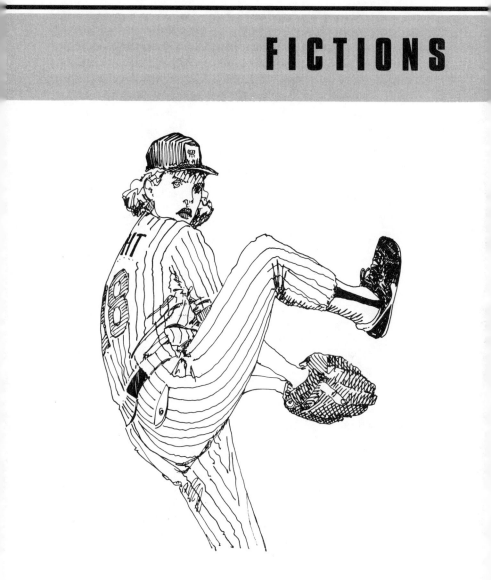

I was drunk sick, I was bleeding. Not the kind that comes from somebody smashing your face in, but the bleeding inside when you're hurt, when you're down, and this whole damn city's like a bunch of sharks smelling something wounded, circling you to bite, swimming around. Stare in the mirror and you say to yourself: Baby, you look like shit. Which I did. Hell, it was true. Like some piece of worm shit crawled out from under a log, squirming around all white, all stripped of the natural color God gave her, crawling in the sunlight. I brushed my teeth. I put lipstick on. Said to myself: Girlfriend, you still got about a ounce of pride left, maybe, so get your ass downstairs and over to the Walgreen's and get some of that stomach-settle shit before you puke all over.

The kid was sleeping. So was Needa and her fucking friends from the grocery shift, snoring, burping beer dreams in a chair, on the sofa, I mean every which place. I tiptoed over bodies. Wrapped keys in a hanky, didn't want to wake them. Then I went down the three flights into autumn, cold sunlight, Sunday.

Usually up here on Sundays you could roll an old empty down First Avenue and it wouldn't touch nothing. Only this day was different. Stepping out of the building was like being wrapped in a big screaming people-circus of arms and shouts. They stayed on the sidewalk, jammed in like fish so you couldn't shove through them to cross the street, you could not hardly move, and some guy's got a radio, and around me every once in a while they're saying, really hushed: "He's coming."

"He's coming."

"He's coming."

There was sirens, red and yellow-white flashes, shadows of light on the empty paved street vivisected by a yellow line, by a pale blue line, and this buzz got loud everywhere around and through me and then, like a Band-Aid, stopped the bleeding.

"Who?" I whispered. "Who's coming?"

"The first man."

"Who?"

"The first runner."

Still, a big sick was in my belly, threatening to lurch out, and there was a part of me thinking: I gotta cross the street, get to Walgreen's. So I started to push, try to make it through the crowd. Some dyke turned to me looking nasty and says, *Mira*, bitch, stay where you are, did your mother raise you in a cave? I mean have some respect! This is the Marathon.

Any other day I would have clawed out her fucking eyeballs. But the sirens, the tires, got closer. Bringing with them the whirling, spattering lights, bright motorcade chrome, October wind, silent feet. And a scream rose up from the whole shark city, from its garbage tins and sidewalk cement, from the sweat and love and hope of human bodies, from my own insides.

Then I saw him.

No, I didn't see him, I caught him with my eyes. But he escaped.

He was tall, and dark, with dark eyebrows and burning black eyes and a fierce young face, and he ran like some great hot flame on the breath of the wind. When he breathed he breathed in the air of the world so that, in that second, there was nothing left for us. His feet were fast, a blur, a howl. He ran like God. Chango, I said silently, here he is, your son. In that second all the air of the world was gone. I choked. I thought I would die. Tears came to my eyes.

"Salazar!" someone yelled.

"It's Salazar!"

"Salazar!"

"Bravo!"

"*Viv!*"

"*Viv*, Salazar!"

He passed, spattering pavement with his sweat.

The sun blew cold, sirens and screams twisted around, wrapped me up into them. Until I fell down into the center of the storm. It blinked up at me, one-eyed, black and fierce.

Woman, it said, you must burn thus. Light a candle. Save your life.

"Help me!" I sobbed. And bit through my lip.

When I opened my eyes the sun had stopped moving. People yelled, cheered, pressed in against me, radios blared, my tears were dry so I yelled and cheered too, and wind whipped leaves down the street as more runners came by, more and more, thousands, until it seemed that they filled the whole city, and that all of us, all of us, were running.

I stayed there screaming for hours. Until the sun started to fade a little, and I lost my voice. Then I stayed there still, way past the time when this guy with the radio said, Okay oye everybody, he won, Salazar won, didn't nobody come close, plus he set a world record.

But here, on our side of town, were still most of the rest of the runners. Fifteen, twenty thousand, someone said. And they all had plenty more to go, more than ten miles, the radio guy said, before they got to the finish.

There were people skinnier than toothpicks running, and a guy wearing pink rabbit ears. Men and girls, both, wearing those mesh shirts so light you can see right through, and men and girls both wearing T-shirts with their names magic-markered on front and back: HELENA, says one; BERNIE'S BOY, says another; and as they went past everyone yells out, "Go, Helena!" and "Attaway, Bernie's Boy!" There were old people running, too, and daughters, and mothers, black and white and every shade in between, from every one of these United States and from plenty of other countries, France and Mexico and Belgium and Trinidad, you had better believe it, so many people, and not all of them real fast, nor all of them skinny—some even looked like me.

I waited screaming with no sound until the crowd began to disappear, lights went on in windows all around, and the sun was going down. There weren't so many runners now but still lots of people walking. Some limping. In the shadows you could see how some had these half-dead, half-crazy expressions. All right, honey, I croaked out about every two minutes to another one, all right, honey, keep going, you're gonna finish. Pretty soon I realized I was shivering and went upstairs.

The kid was watching TV, eating Fritos, most of Needa's scumbag friends were gone, and Needa was pissed. Where you been? she said. You look like something the tide washed in, and how come you didn't get no more beer?

I told her shut up, have some respect, today is the Marathon. The what? she says. The Marathon, I said, the Marathon, and if you didn't spend your weekends being mean and bossing me around like some man, you coulda seen Salazar run. What the fuck, she grumbled. But then she shrugged. We didn't fight after all—even though, truth be told, I was feeling pretty sick of her just then and I wouldn't have minded. I mean, we never even *did* it anymore.

I picked the kid up and danced him around the room a little until he laughed. I thought about how handsome he was—bright smile and big black eyes the girls would all fight and die over some day—and how he was doing okay with the alphabet in kindergarten, too, and the teachers said real nice things about him, and other kids wanted to be his friend. Then I thought, squeezing him close, what a fucking miracle it was, maybe, that such a great kid had come out of a loser like me. Fact of the matter being that neither me nor his father is all that great in the looks department; neither one of us remembered, really, why we ever did that boy-girl shit in the first place—I always did like the ladies better, maybe just got curious. Then first thing I know I'm about to pop, mister father there blows, and, later, there's Needa and me. She came on so sweet to me at first, so butch and pretty. Now life was more or less her working and me working, paying rent, keeping things clean, getting the kid back and forth to school, on weekends some videos, arguments, TV, beer. And neither one of us with a nice word or touch for the other. Nights, I'd get filled with a sudden big darkness when all the lights went out. Filled with a power so black and brown and green, Oggun, Yemaya, iron, water, a big washing-over foaming waving ocean sadness. Then plain exhaustion that pressed my eyelids down. Needa would already be snoring. I'd turn my back, start to dream. In the morning, would not remember.

Stop dancing your son around the room, snapped Needa, you'll turn him into a fucking fairy. Come here, kid. We're gonna get a couple movies.

Fine, I told her, look who's talking. Biggest bull I ever knew. Go on, both of you. Get a couple of Real Man movies. Get a couple of Let's-Kill-Everyone-in-Sight things, why don't you. Fill his head with a bunch of real machitos getting their guts blown out.

When they left, I cleaned up Fritos and beer cans. Got some frozen chicken out. Then halfway through soaking it in a pot of warm water, I wiped my hands with a fresh white cloth, lit a couple candles, offered up a plate of half-thawed gizzards. I stay away from the powers, mostly, but that night felt different. Kneeling in front of the plate for at least a little proper respect, red candles, white candles dripping, watching thin pieces of ice melt off the gizzards and the thawing organs swim in remains of their own dark blood, I thought again about Salazar. I wondered if he ran so hard and so fast that, when he won, his feet were crusted with blood. I remembered things my grandma told me, long ago, when I'd walk out laughing into the sun of a hot sweet summer morning. About the happiness of the air filled with voices and smells, joy of loving, the ferocity of vengeance and of hate, how to heal what you care for, how to ruin an enemy. The holiness of sacrifice.

Not that I even did it right.

When they want live roosters, they don't mean half-thawed chicken gizzards. But it was all for the fire, hungry holy fire that doesn't die, even when the world tries to kill it, that stays alive, eating, eating—I offered it truly in my heart—and God sees everything.

The next morning Needa groaned and stuck her head under a pillow when the alarm clock rang early. I tiptoed around, stuck on a pair of sweatpants, socks, old tennis sneakers, one of her used-up sweatshirts. It was cold out, wind coming off the river. Sun wasn't even up yet. I held keys in the space between fingers and balled up my hand like a fist, like a metal-bristling weapon, and when I started to run could feel the fat bobbling around my stomach and arms and hips and thighs, heavy and disgusting, bringing me a little bit closer to the ground each time the skin folds flopped up and down. After a couple minutes I thought I was gonna die. I had to stop and gasp and walk. Then when I could breathe okay I'd run as fast as I could another half a minute or so, stop and gasp and walk awhile, then run again. I did this about fifteen, twenty minutes. Until snot dripped to my lip, and my face was running wet in the cold, blotching Needa's sweatshirt in chilly clinging puddles. I started to cry. Then I told myself, Shut up you. It worked, the tears stopped. I went back inside, climbed stairs with legs that were already numb and hurting, and made everybody breakfast. Needa growled her way through a shower and padded around with a coffee cup making wet footprints everywhere, watching "Good Morning America."

There he is, she grumbled, there's your *man,* your Salazar.

I ignored her sarcasm.

But I was stuck there in the kitchen, making sure the kid's toast didn't burn. I told Needa tell me what they're saying.

They're saying about how he won yesterday. You know, the race. Guy set a fucking world record or something.

I wanted to run and see, but couldn't.

That's how the weeks went: me getting up early in the dark, going to bash my fat brains out trying to run, getting breakfast for everyone, showering when they were all finished with the bathroom, getting Needa to work and the kid to school and then getting myself to work too. My eyes started hurting bad from being open extra long. My legs were sore, thighs feeling like they were all bruised and bloodied on the inside, calves with pinpricks of pain searing through them. Needa noticed me limping around all the time, and laughed. What's with you, girl? You think you gonna be in the Olympics or something? You think you gonna run that marathon?

Finally, one Saturday, I went to see Madrita.

She took out the cards and beads and shells, there in her little place in the basement, pulled all the curtains closed so everything was cozy and safe like your mother's womb. Outside, it rained. She was trained the old way, did everything absolutely right, took her time. After a while I asked her, Well, how does it look?

"Sweetheart, you gotta lotta obstacles."

Hey, I told her, that ain't exactly news.

She sighed. "You gotta stop worrying about the home. Home's gonna take care of themselves, you be surprised. Lots of rage and pain but lots of love too. See, sweetheart, you can do what you want, only it's difficult. First, purify yourself."

"Purify? Myself?"

"What I said."

She wrote down all the stuff I had to get, white and red roses and violet water and rose water, mint, coconut, a bunch of sunflowers and herbs and things, and made me memorize how to do the bath right. Then she told me go up to the little shop the Jew man has, here's the address, he's one of them from Spain and he knows the right things, even *babalaus* goes there for supplies. And while you're there get a couple pieces of camphor, sweetheart, and some fresh mint leaves. Put them in a little bag, pin it inside your bra, it'll keep you healthier. You got a cold coming on.

Needa wasn't too happy about the bathwater sitting all night, reeking herbs and flower petals, before I got into it—first!—the next morning. Yaaah, she grumped, you and that devil shit. Ever since the Marathon. Makes me feel like I'm living with some fucking boogy. But listen, woman: Don't you go casting no spells on me.

I was stripping sweaty sweats and socks to bathe. Caught her staring, out of the corner of my eye, and bared my teeth. Then she rubbed my naked butt, friendly like, and the both of us laughed.

The mornings got darker, closer to winter, but every once in a while I'd wake up easier when the alarm hit, sometimes even with a feel of burning red excitement in my chest and throat, like the running was something pleasurable, good, a gift. Truth is that it did feel good some mornings. I'd breathe splendidly. Thighs move like water, arms pump rhythm. The feet did not want to stop. Those days I'd stay out longer—half an hour or more—with happy buzzing like music in my head.

Celia, one of the girls at work said, just before New Year's, I been meaning to tell you, you are looking really terrific these days.

It was true.

I circled around the file cabinets all afternoon, putting things away, singing.

That night, after picking the kid up and dropping him and his cousin off with his grandma for a couple hours, I skipped grocery shopping and just went home, changed into some sweaty old things, and I went outside into the wind and dark and I ran again, very sweet and happy and like music, the way I had that morning, running off and onto curbs, twisting around cars and garbage cans and people, I didn't care. I hummed and sang going back upstairs. Needa opened the door for me, mad.

"Where the fuck you been? I feel like I ain't got a lover these days."

"Oh you got one, honey. Whether you want one or not."

"What's that supposed to mean?"

"Whatever you want it to, girlfriend."

She moped around the rest of the evening, drank about a six-pack of Ballantine and fell asleep on the sofa. Later I went to pick up the kid. Walking home he said how big he was getting, how he was gonna be in first grade next year and could take gym, and run at the school track meet next spring.

That's good, I told him, it's good to have a plan.

We ordered pizza, watched TV and drank Coca-Cola while Needa snored away on the sofa. I was feeling different, lighter, happy-headed and full of fresh cold air from running again, but at the same time dark and warm inside. I put the kid to bed and left a kitchen light on for Needa, then turned in myself, breathing full and deep, sniffing camphor, mint, letting some calm, clean-burning soft red feeling wash over me, droop my eyelids shut, wrap me up all safe and bright, and soon I dreamed.

In the dream I was running on dirt and grass through trees near the Reservoir in Central Park—quick, effortless, light, my toes and ankles bouncing and strong—and next to me a man was running, and we breathed in perfect rhythm. I looked over. It was Salazar.

Alberto, I said, I want to run the Marathon.

Listen to me, Celia, he said, you're not ready yet. You gotta do some shorter races first.

Okay, I said.

Then we stopped running.

He faced me, hands on hips, fierce dark flame face, slender and serious and young. I noticed he wore a collar of beads, scarlet-wine red and white. Oh, I laughed, I thought so, you really are a child of Chango. So am I.

It's fire Celia, he said. But everyone has a power. Use it for running. Use it for loving. Use it for God.

I woke up smelling rotten beer breath. Needa was sitting slumped over, head in hands on my side of the bed, crying.

"What is it, honey?"

"Lost," she sobbed, "I got lost."

I put my arms around her. Her cheeks were all soft and smelly, but there was that nice odor to her too, one it seemed like I remembered from long, long ago, woman smell, soap smell, a crumply warm feel of her hair and clothes.

Lost, she sobbed.

No, honey, I told her, holding her, rocking the both of us back and forth. No, honey, no, sweet woman, my Needa, don't you cry. You didn't get lost, you been found.

Help me, Celia, she said. Help me, God. Gotta work harder, keep up with you. I am so ashamed of my life.

I remembered the dream. I pulled her down alongside me on the bed, held her, rocking, whispering true things to the back of her neck. Telling how I was proud of her, and of our child, and our home. How hard we had worked. How far we had come. How, before taking on the whole rest of our lives, we had to do the small, obvious, necessary tasks, one step at a time.

"Like how I'm not gonna just jump in and run the Marathon right off, honey. I gotta do some shorter races first."

"Huh," she sniffed, "get you, the expert. Who you think you been talking to, the angels?"

But she pulled my arms tighter around her when she said that, and I didn't want to fight, or let her go.

It happened like this: no more booze. No more videos. No more shit food.

I shifted the force of the power to purifying myself, for real. And, like magic, once I did that, Needa and the kid came around. Maybe one or both of them would make barf sounds whenever I dished up some brown rice shit for dinner. But Needa's belly flab was littler, and she even started going after work a couple days each week to pump iron with her buddies at some smelly old gym. Those nights she came back fresh from the shower, cold air in her face, smelling of powder with a warm skin glow. Have to keep up with the little lady, she said, but in my own way, love, understand? I mean, running, racing, turning into some skinny fag, that is *not* your Needa's style.

End of May, I was going to run the Women's Mini-Marathon in Central Park, a little more than six miles. I laid down the law at home. No fucking up and no messing up between now and then. Cold weather, warm, and warmer, rains and damp hot sunlight and hazy mist of all the city seasons started floating past, through us, like we were nothing but thin vessels that for a moment could catch a whiff of the breeze and the universe, then lose it, let it go. I kept running, every day. The kid did okay in school. Needa and I started making love again some nights, oh so nice, rubbing back and forth. Oh, so nice, to feel her touch around inside me again. And then, late spring.

How it was, the night before: I'm sitting around, we had some of them buckwheat noodles with vegetables for dinner, everybody's quiet, no TV, thinking about how I'm gonna run the race tomorrow with about nine thousand other women and how they, the family, they have got to cheer us and watch, and I look at Needa and the kid and see how slender they are now, and healthy, how beautiful and handsome and slender, and start thinking how much they are mine—just that, they are mine. And I look down at my own bare feet and see that they are skinny, too. Bumpy with callouses and with veins. Bashed a little bloody around the big-toe edges. The littlest toenail on my left foot is dead and black. All from running through the mornings and the nights. From running in my dreams. We got changed, poof. Just like that. Thought we were gonna change ourselves, maybe even the world. But, poof. The world changed us. Through work, love, sacrifice.

Holy, I thought. This is holy.

I chewed cinnamon sticks for dessert the way Madrita recommended, went to sleep with a hint of fire inside. Morning I got up scared, scared. Too scared to notice how Needa was being so sweet, feeding the kid, making sure I drank water because it was looking to be a hot, hot day, pinning my racing number on my T-shirt straight with safety pins, #6489-F-OPEN. Too scared to notice we were leaving—leaving our home, taking the subway, walking, silent, through the heat and the morning.

There we made it, finally, to the West Side, into the park. To hear music play over loudspeakers. Announcements blaring, half-heard. Reminders about some awards ceremony later. On a lawn. The lawn. Some lawn. To hot bright light crystallized through the trees, sunlight, damp blazing air, water stacked in paper cups on tables, and tables, and the laughing, crying voices like in my childhood, so many people. A banner, a big blinking magic electronic clock, zeroed out, waiting. And runners, waiting—women, all shapes and sizes and ages and colors, thousands of them, of us, just thousands.

Baby, says Needa, I'm proud of you.

The kid'd made friends already. Some other woman's twin sons, about his age. I catch sight of him, out of the corner of an eye, his half-smiling, half-serious little handsome face, glowing under the rim of a baseball cap. Yeah, he's telling them, my mom's fast, too. My mom's gonna run the race. Me and my other mom's gonna watch.

Some things are forever inside us. Some things cannot get said.

That's why, when the gun went off, it was like this piece of me fell deep, deep down inside, into the big dark well of myself—this was the piece of me that recorded, in absolute detail, every moment of the race—and lodged there, safe but never recoverable, at least not in words. I can say that the different-colored crowd of thousands moved in a big shuffle at first, all together; then, little by little, began to unwind into space, like it was some light-stitched vast fabric coming apart at the seams—so that first, we were all the same, then some of us swayed forward, some back, some to one side or another, and the tarred hot surface of the road melted uphill into trees, green, brown, into a hot misty blasting summer air running blue and gray and yellow under sunlight. I can say that my heart popped right into the base of my throat and stayed there for the first mile or so that I staggered along, sweating after the first few yards, gasping to breathe; then something inside me let up—or gave up, yes—and my heart settled down into my chest where it belonged, I was sweating and suffering but could breathe again, and the elbows and bouncing breasts and shoulders and hair and flesh of women was all around me, smells of bodies and of the city and the trees and sun, and I drank water from somebody's paper cup, kept running, tossed it like a leaf to the cup-littered ground. I can say that in the second mile, once in a while, sweating and running, avoiding veering hips and limbs, I saw some girl run by with a Sony Walkman, wearing sunglasses with mirrored lenses, closed off to the world; once in a while, too, conversation filtered into the sponging soaking deep-down fallen-off piece of me, women's voices in English and in Spanish and in other languages, too, trying to laugh, muttering encouragement; but by the third mile, fact is, there was not anyone chatting.

What there was, was the breathing. Hard and uneven, or measured, controlled. I kept the feet moving, slow, steady, like the pace I did each morning, the pace I did some nights—but never as fast and light and easy as my dreams. Still, it moved me forward. Clumsy. Slow. With a little fat bobbling, yet, around hips and belly and thighs. Around me, all shapes. Like crazy soldiers in some war. The sweat gushed down me. It was hotter than I'd thought. At each mile, you heard them, calling out the time. Time? Time? I never thought of it before. How much it took to do one mile, or one block, or twenty—each morning, some evenings, even in my dreams, I ran by the minutes. Thirty-five, thirty-six minutes. Into the fourth mile. Now it was feeling like forever. Now it was feeling like one more hill would be the last. My fat, bouncing thighs and sweating, gushing body would never be things of beauty, like maybe in foolish moments I'd imagined; and maybe in my stupid dreams I talked about marathons—but here, here was a little stupid miniature marathon, and it hurt so bad I could not ever imagine doing this again, much less running anything longer. But more water, more flesh around me, slipping on paper cups in my flopping old tennis shoes with this number safety-pinned right under my tits, over flabbing belly, every slight upgrade of road sending sunlight searing through me, stabbing thighs and ankles, making me gasp and hurt and, without killing myself, I ran as fast as I could. Clumsy. Fat. Slow. But the heart settled back down, pounding with breaths, with mint and cinnamon and camphor. Sunlight shot through the leaves of trees. Hose spray cooled our skin, drenched our socks. More sunlight shot through, blinded me. Fire, I thought. For your husband, your child, your God. To hell with that, Celia. For your own living self. Okay, man, fuck everything. Fuck the whole sunlit sweat-smelling cinnamon-smelling fucking shark-circling world. Whiff of Chango. Fire in the belly. Fuck even your world of dreams. Because this, sweetheart—this, here, is real.

Then, for a mile, I knew what was real. All this, steeped in the miserable sweat and sacrifice. I knew it without knowledge of the mind, only the sure unlying knowledge of the body that can run and love, give birth, sob, suffer. And knowing what was real, and that this, this, was it, now, only this, and it was enough, and that I lived now, really lived, and knew now what it was to breathe— knowing this, blind with pain, sweating and gasping and almost dead, I stared down and saw that there was a little hole in the tip of my right tennis shoe, near the little toe; it had rubbed the toe raw and, around the little hole, the dirty white fabric was soaking through with blood. Then I felt all the dried-up pieces of me come to life and, suffering, I ran on the breath of the wind. Until, after a while, the wind deserted me. Just before six miles. Left me, one faulty woman, in a mob of suffering moving flesh, to finish the last few hundred yards alone. It was all uphill, there were people watching and I was ashamed, people screaming around me, I was running so slow, nearly dead of exhaustion and of shame, stomach in spasms, drenched with sweat, crying. Until I heard someone yell out *Mom* with a voice, among all the other little voices, meant only for me. And I heard Needa, laughing, crying, yelling, and heard that her voice was hoarse, a croak, almost gone: Attagirl, baby! My baby! My lady! You can do it youcandoityoucando-

ityoucandoit! Break an hour breakanhourbreakanhourbreakan-
hour!

Fifty-nine minutes and fifty-nine seconds. But I was not lost, and
I was not last.

Girlfriend, I said, get some pride.

I did.

Then I staggered under the big heartless blinking clock, the yellow sun, dripping water, my shoe spraying blood.

I got a medal. They gave everyone medals. Slipped around your
neck, in the finishing chutes crowded with beaten, grinning
women, a silvery goldlike medal on a red and blue ribbon, like a
necklace, just for finishing. Then they gave you a carton of Gatorade. A free Mars bar. And a plastic egg-shaped container full of
mesh tan pantyhose.

Needa hugged me. So did the kid.

They were all over me, screaming, proud and happy.

Runners were still finishing, running, staggering, walking. I
moved through the crowds. I lay on the grass. Closed my eyes,
with Needa sitting on one side and the kid on the other, each
holding a hand, and I fell down into the deepest, blasted-off piece
of me that had come apart and wedged down inside with the explosion of the starting gun, that would never, ever be the same. It
was so dark, falling deep down there, full of iron and of water,
musty brown and wet wet green and the still malignant air; but
also, it was red like blood, and bright, and filled with a bubbling,
smouldering, surprising color. It was filled with this work and this
imperfect love, and with chicken gizzards, sacrifice, camphor oil,
rainbow light.

Something blared over a loudspeaker.

"—And now, a special treat for all you ladies! To present the
awards, we have with us here—"

I fell into a place of half-dream, half-sleep.

Needa poked my ribs.

There he is, Celia. There.

Who?

Your Salazar.

I turned my head in the grass. Salt was full in my sweat, salt on
my lips, I licked it with the air and it tasted real, good, sweet.
Opened my eyes to see the young, slender, serious man standing

above me, body and clcthes of a runner, his eyes in shadow, fierce face gazing down.

He nodded. Saying softly, politely, Good for you, Celia.

Alberto, I said, can I stop now?

No, Celia. He said it gently. Then he smiled. Not until you die. And even then—who knows?

I opened my eyes.

There was an awards podium, in the sun on the grass. Women, slender and beautiful, gifted young magnificent runners, walking up, intermittently, when their names were called over fuzzy loud-speakers, accepting the bright gold and silver statues they gave for awards. And there, with famous men and women athletes and politicians behind the podium on the stage in the sun and the park, there he was, handing out each statue, shaking each woman's hand. Salazar. There was no collar around his neck, no red and white of gods or saints of fire, as in my dream. Not running, he seemed different. Quiet. Humbly human. Pale and young, and far away.

I started to cry.

Needa held me in her arms.

The kid crawled into my lap, laid his soft little cheek against my drenched, floppy chest.

"What is it, sweet?"

"It don't stop, Needa."

"No, my love."

"I gotta do some more of these."

"Okay, baby."

"And then, in a few years I think, I gotta do the Marathon."

Yes! Alberto muttered, through a microphone, and shook some woman's hand. I squeezed the hand of Needa, and of our child. The fire poured down. It kissed me. It moved in to stay.

I wrote this story for Julie DeLaurier.

All events herein are fictional, except for the New York City Marathon and the Women's Mini-Marathon (once sponsored by L'Eggs, now spon-sored by Advil, under the auspices of the New York City Road Runners Club). I have used these events here solely in a fictional context.

All characters herein are fictional, too, with the exception of the great

American marathon runner Alberto Salazar. I use him here in an imaginary way, as a dream figment or a sort of divinity—and with all due respect. I have never met Mr. Salazar, and do not know if he is a child of Chango. . . .

EINBAHNSTRASSE

Donna Allegra

She's simply late, as usual, right? Maybe doing devotions in the hallway to one more cigarette—that'd be okay. She wasn't in either morning class last weekend. Please don't let her have gone back to Germany or Switzerland or wherever the hell she's from.

I deliberately wore the yellow leotard with the open back to display the web of muscles under my shoulders. After warm-up, I'll take off the sweatpants which presently hide the cutoff tights. That'll take me down to bare legs. This unveiling is aimed at Anneliesce.

Rafaella declared me "the hairless wonder" the first time she saw me wear shorts, so please Anneliesce, come to class. My plan is to show off thigh and calf muscles for you. I'm even flubbing the warm-up isolations, so busy looking to see if you're going to slip into Kaya's class late. It's almost ten after six, girl, where are you?

At least Rafaella's here: such a small woman, a hellified dancer, too. I'm sure she was a ballet-trained baby. I wish I had five to ten years of ballet behind me, but when I mourned my lack, Rafaella responded, "Well, you can have five to ten years of ballet ahead of you." She's right, but how can I get a ballet class into my schedule? Monday, Wednesday and Friday I do African. I've got to have that dance time with the sisters. Tuesday–Thursday evenings and Saturday–Sunday mornings, Kaya has me at her beck and call for jazz.

Rafaella. It's striking how naked someone seems if she doesn't wear socks or leg-warmers with cut-off tights. Her legs, bare from mid-thigh to foot, seem like brazen nudity. And when that little woman takes off her sweatshirt, I could lick her back like a cat lapping milk and just leave class behind.

Ah, there is a Goddess: Anneliesce finally arrives at fourteen after six o'clock. Her hair looks as if she's just gotten out of bed. It's sandy blonde—sunlight and lemon juice would put her in a higher caste among the white folks. She's wearing black today—

tights, leotard, sweatshirt and shorts. The other two colors I see her put on are red and blue. The red works for her skin and the blue heightens her eyes.

The eyes aren't high-noon or midnight blue. They're like twilight. This black outfit gives her another cast. Maybe it just emphasizes that whatever the girl puts on, my eyes look for that dusk.

She and Kaya are buddies. I've seen them laughing together after class. I like it that Anneliesce is friends with our jazz teacher, but I felt my face tighten and close when I saw her joking with that doofey kid who walks with her feet in turn-out. Frustration stung me half mad when Anneliesce and Cassandra were talking as they each smoked in the hallway during the ten-minute break after the warm-up that same Saturday morning.

I ignore Cassandra these days. At first I used to acknowledge her as one Black woman to another, and she'd give me this vacant smile that was from hunger. I went along with her jive-ass "tee hee hee," but I'd be feeling: "Look: don't do me any favors. You aren't even halfway cute."

One day she cut me off from her shit-stupid grin so she could nod up in some white man's face. That did it. She had the nerve to turn her attention away from me to smile at this puffed-up guy acting important. That put her on my permanent shit list. There I was giving her a serious Black sister-to-sister nod and she has to titter while he drones on and on about jazz music.

Why is it white people expect us to get excited about styles Black people got tired of forty years ago, and this same white person can't stand what we do in music today? I still can't get over the fact that she turned to him over me. I've refused to even look at her ever since.

To see Anneliesce talk to Cassandra made me feel even more left out. Even if all they had was cigarette smoke between them, it gave them connection. I don't have anything to bridge Anneliesce to me. Maybe if I got the chance, I could acknowledge her as one of Kaya's regular core of students. A conversation could start on that basis, that is, if I were Rafaella, it could.

I wish the fuck I could talk to women as if it weren't any big thing. Rafaella likes to console me with, "Well, if you could talk, you wouldn't be such a dancer. And you'd interrupt my monologues; you know I wouldn't like that."

Last week, Anneliesce stood on my side of the room during warm-up. I usually stand to the left of Kaya as she directs the class, and Anneliesce would place herself at the far right side of the room. She switches up sometimes; that's unusual. Most dancers choose a spot on the studio floor and want to camp out there forever.

When Anneliesce was on my turf, I felt like we were partners during the technique work. Each time Kaya had us rotate our lines so that the back row gradually made its way up to become the front row, I edged a little closer to where Anneliesce stood. As I spied on her in the mirror, I saw how carefully she works with her body.

Kaya was on me about hyperextending that day. "Soften your knees, Imani." When we went from working the demi-pliés in parallel first position to doing demis in turn-out, Kaya peered at me with an appraising frown. I sent a question to her with my eyes, but she shook her head and smiled. "You've found your turn-out placement. That's good." I grew two inches behind that praise. The least little attention from a dance teacher impacts like a cannon.

I like how I sense in Kaya a special interest in the few sisters who come to her classes, taking this more modern-based jazz style of dance, rather than African folklore or something more obviously Black, like hip hop. Even when she addresses Cassandra, I feel included.

Whenever the class would have to roll down from a standing stretch, as if the body were a caterpillar going down a tree, trying to place the top of our heads on the floor while our hips reached for the ceiling, I'd look at Anneliesce from between my legs. I could see her fingernails—short and manicured—and the veins climbing up from her hands into her forearms, like wisteria vines hugging a tree. She looks dykely, but who can tell with these foreigners? Maybe they just grow the girls butch in Germany.

As the class did the standing floor work, which I know by heart at this point, I'd watch her in the mirror. Handsome bitch. I don't know what I'd do with her if I had her in my arms, but sometimes I feel such a yearning. I long to speak to her about more than dance.

Seven o'clock and we're at the adagio already. I hope it's not obvious why I've been focused to the right side of the room during the tendus and the developés.

What is this? Well, thank you Kaya. No, I don't mind going to the front line on the other side of the room so that the new people can have me and Anneliesce to follow for the adagio portion of our work.

I guess now is as good a time as any to take off my T-shirt and expose my back. If I'm lucky, a shoulder strap will slip down and reveal a moment of extra honey-brown skin before I tastefully put it back in place.

Kaya puts Sarah Vaughan's "My Funny Valentine" on the record player and we wait for the intro to end before we begin the adagio. I should concentrate on my body's placement during this segment of class. The adagio is designed for you to work on technique, but I want more to know what Anneliesce is up to.

Did she just wink at me? Yes, I see the smile in her eyes. Now why'd she do that? I mean, like, is the girl flirting? It's best to be cautious when I take a liking to a woman. Ordinarily I run to the other side of the room when I'm this attracted. Maybe Anneliesce is just being friendly. Perhaps she admires my style as a dancer and wants to catch a whiff by being nice to me. Maybe because she's a foreigner, she wants any ally she can get.

She could be one of those butch het girls. They look like dykes, vibe like dykes, go with boys. I saw one yesterday at the checkout counter in the vegetable market. I thought the woman to be lesbian: short hair, strong-looking, an independent air to her. I gave her a nod and vibed energy toward her with some eye contact. She looked back at me and I caught a smile. Then I backed off to let her be.

As the guy behind the register was weighing my carrots, a man stepped up to her and stuffed some apples and scallions into her arms. He complained, "I don't see why you don't just use onions." She cooed and soothed his whining. Had me fooled. Once again I was imploring the heavens, "Why? why? why?"

Kaya is having us do the damn adagio three times today, not the usual two, which is fine with me. I look good in this mini-combination. My alignment has improved and I've sewn the different parts of the choreography together to make it appear like a seamless fabric. Anneliesce looks good too. She works deeply and is sensitive to the subtleties of technique. The crease down the center of her back has me riveted. Damn, she's hot. She'd probably burn in the sunlight, but it'd be no skin off my nose.

Okay. Group two is on deck for their turn at the adagio. I decide to rest leaning against the back wall near the radiator. I prop one leg against the wall and stand like a stork. This pose shows me off at a good angle for all who care to see. I tune my entertainment channel to Rafaella, with the clean movements that I love on her. I tend to add flourishes with my upper body and while I revel in the shoulder styling I do, I also like it when people are square and neat with the positions, without the ruffles I throw on.

I must admit Cassandra is admirably calm and fluid in the adagio. I won't deny she is a decent dancer. And I always liked the blacker berries on our family tree. It's just, why does she have to be such a dingdong?

I don't notice Anneliesce coming my way and I jump when she taps my shoulder. "I think Kaya will be giving us a new adagio soon. We've been with this one for almost two months." She poses this as a question.

"Could be," I reply. "But Kaya may keep us on it for a while longer. Not everyone really has it into her body. Kaya likes to know we've mastered enough lessons of the technique before she'll teach us more. You know how Kaya can be. She won't even give all the counts in the combination until we get the ones she's handed us, correctly."

I try to keep my whisper low, but I'm excited. I want to make sure Anneliesce understands what I'm saying. Her English is excellent, but I fear she may do English the way I do French. I speak far better than I comprehend. Anneliesce seems to be doing just fine, however. She always gets Kaya's jokes. I don't have the feeling that she laughs just because everyone else is chuckling when Kaya goes, "I have the combination down pat. I don't need to do it again. Which is a lot more than I can say about the rest of you."

Kaya would then stalk off from the center floor, swishing her butt as she'd approach the stereo to start the music. We'd then be expected to take in the corrections she'd just given us to improve on the dancing we'd done.

Group two is finished with their adagio. I take a position on the floor for sit-ups next to Anneliesce. As Kaya explains the abdominal exercises we're about to do for the benefit of the newer people, I prop myself up on my elbows and watch her. I notice her dimples and the process-straightened hair, now come undone from its carved-wood clip. She sometimes threatens us in class with her intention to cut it all off. Black women and their hair. I keep my 'fro, about as long as a finger snap.

I wait until the last minute to get into position. Kaya inclines her head toward me and says to the class, "Imani is looking at me like, 'Okay, get on with it already.' " I smile as if we're on the same wave length, even though that isn't a true reading of me. I enjoy watching Kaya be herself. Because she's so sharp and serious about her dance, she keeps us on our toes. I admire her command of the class and the pleasure she takes in being its main attraction. I could never talk to more than a couple of people at one time.

This smart and funny woman is also a Nazi slave driver when she conducts the warm-up from hell. I get into position to take my medicine: abominables—a hundred sit-ups in a variety of poses.

After abs, we sit in second position to stretch the sides of our bodies and then do leg stretches on our backs. We finally stand to do the battements. I kick high to be in synch with Anneliesce. I fear I'll tear a ligament in my competitiveness. She has legs like a giraffe has neck.

Class intermission for a five-minute break. I don't do my usual sprint for the door so that I can beat out the thundering herd to the bathroom. I linger to see if Anneliesce will say anything more to me. When she doesn't, I trot down the hallway to pee. Some things never lose their urgency.

When I return through the corridor toward the studio, Anneliesce is in the hallway, smoking with Kaya and a couple of others, Cassandra included. I could almost like her when she's quiet and not talking like some perky television ninny. She has an appealing sweetness, the way a ripe melon can allure. But because Cassandra is there, I decide to go inside the studio rather than hang out.

Anneliesce looks up when I come into eye range and smiles like a sphinx expecting company. I smile too, hurrying on my way, delirious with that little bit of connection. Then I'm seized with inspiration from on high.

I turn around and ask, "Where are you from?"

"Germany."

"What city or town?"

"Do you know Munich?"

"Oh, yeah. With the river and the zoo. I saw flamingoes there."
I watch her face as we speak. Her eyes are water-clear, her skin too, as if buffed for Sunday dinner guests.

"You've been to Germany?" Kaya asks, interested.

"Yes, I was on tour in Europe with an African dance group. We got a lot of bookings in German cities."

"That sounds exciting," Kaya says, waving off strands of smoke.

"Truth to tell, I was thrilled. Whenever we'd arrive in a new place, I'd explore as soon as we landed. I'll never forget my first city in Germany, Cologne. My habit was to leave the hotel and walk around as soon as we dropped our bags. My usual routine was to take the hotel business card to be sure of the address. I'd write the cross street on it so I wouldn't get lost. This place was all out of cards at the time, so I just made a note to myself of the street names.

"In Germany, the street signs aren't on posts, they're attached to the buildings." I say this to Kaya; Anneliesce nods.

"It took me a minute to figure out that 'str' was short for '*strasse,*' which means 'street.' After a while, I got tired from my walk and started back. A lot of Germans speak English and I speak French, so I knew I'd be able to ask for directions. I went up to a flower vendor, 'Excuse me, could you tell me where thirty-eight Einbahnstrasse is? It crosses Vogl.' "

Anneliesce laughs and starts hitting her thigh. Kaya looks up quizzically and Cassandra too shows her puzzlement.

I aim my words at Anneliesce and say, "He laughed too. I didn't think it was a kindly way to treat a foreigner."

"Einbahnstrasse?" Kaya asks.

"It means 'one-way street,' " Anneliesce answers.

Back in class, Kaya is giving us difficult movements and complex steps. In the not-too-far-away past, I'd have been whimpering inside myself, "Please don't give us any more, Kaya. This is more than enough to contend with." But tonight I am ready to take on anything she can dish out.

While learning the steps, I watch only Kaya. No one else in the room matters. Oh, I have to check myself in the mirror, to see how my body is translating her movements. I also take note when people leave. This is a long, hard dance combination, with unex-

pected changes of direction and moves that call for inner strength
to hold a position.

Kaya is elegant as she unfurls her labyrinth of steps. She stalks,
leaps, pounces, then hangs suspended. She next strikes like lightning and explodes in a series of tiny, sharp biting strokes. She ends
by wrapping herself in a cloak of flutters. None of us is smiling
as we strain to pick up what she's set before us.

Finally, Kaya sashays across the room in triumph, her dance all
out. Her point has also been made about using the technique work
we do in the warm-up and from the adagio. She is in her glory
and I'd crown her queen of the universe. It is for this as much as
anything else that I adore her. But eight more counts of that stressful eloquence and I would hate that hussy.

She divides us into two groups to mark the choreography with
music. She's chosen Aretha's "Natural Woman." Years ago, it had
been my coming-out anthem. The song still lifts me into an ecstasy
of longing and desire. And that was bad news. When I get caught
and drawn through the music, it's hard to concentrate on dancing.

After Kaya had us mark a couple times to music, she counted
heads to divide us into smaller groups to dance. More people had
slunk out of the studio by this point.

"Okay. Four groups. Who wants to go in the first?" I raise my
hand tentatively, a couple others do also, with a similar reluctance.
"Is your hand raised Imani, yes or no?" I nod yes. She keeps
choosing, "Rafaella, Gail, Leah . . . one more person." No one else
is lifting her arm to be chosen so Kaya takes her pick. "Anneliesce,
thank you for volunteering."

Kaya has us space ourselves into two rows across the studio
floor. I am in the first row, Rafaella stands next to me, Anneliesce
is in the second row behind her.

I have the basic sequence, but Anneliesce doesn't. It helps that
I know this song. Aretha's waltz courses through my blood and I
can draw out a step or hold back from giving in to the movement
until the last minute and then quickly release into the next one.
That's where my body's styling kicks in and I make Kaya's dance
phrases my own.

When group two goes front and center, I move off to the side
to practice and drill the counts so that I can hold on to the sequence. I am loving the song, the dance combination, the erotic
vibe tingling through me like whiffs of baking bread. The room is

steamy from all the women sweating with effort. I catch a scent of something heady in the updraft and feel I can do more than dance.

I glimpse Anneliesce in the back, trying to follow group two for the center section where she isn't getting the soul of Kaya's choreography. She has the outline, but the funks on the movements, the transitions from satin to steel in the phrasing aren't there. She keeps at it, still striving with groups three and four on deck. Again I feel how strongly I like that woman, so piercing in her efforts. She is working hard. Something in her struggle shows me I don't have to be a shrinking violet anymore.

After all the groups have gone, Kaya has us gather together so she can give corrections. She says, "I want you to stretch the hip roll. When you hold back on the step, it doesn't play right. And stay in plié. You all look like the jack-in-the-box going up and down like a hobby horse. Staying low will help you move quickly."

I concentrate on her directions to get more clear about the choreographic patterns. She puts us back on board again, each group to dance it twice. I come back with my movements more clean and strong. Anneliesce still lags behind. I know what I would do were I in her shoes. When I'm in a class that's above my head, I grab somebody on the side and say, "Hey listen; what are the first two sets of eight?"

After our group has gone, I skip to the side to dance with group two, then move to the back of the room where Anneliesce is following group three. I catch her eye in the mirror and slow down the part that is giving her a hard time, demonstrating the steps in bite-sized pieces. Her eyes lock on my body and follow my lead.

Kaya calls all groups front and center for another round of corrections. "Well, there's some great foot work, but a lot of torso missing. You children seem to be having some coordination problems. I see many versions of my choreography. Look kids, match this picture. Each group, let's do it again."

Group one goes to our places on the floor. The six of us listen with our attention, waiting for Kaya to find a point in the music to which she'd clap her hands: "and four, five, six," our cue to begin. On count five, I look for and catch Anneliesce's eyes in the mirror. This time, I am the one to wink.

I aim my dance for her benefit and she tracks me like radar. My torso moves like an electric eel and my arms an eagle's wings. I feel so free, I want to stretch my limbs right out of their sockets. This is one of those times when I feel like a dance animal, drunk on the music, delicious to my bones. I look to Anneliesce as our group makes room for group two. I feel a hot wave in my stomach—part excitement, part triumph, part like anything was possible. I want class never to end.

After group four has gone, Kaya brings us all back front and center for a last round of corrections, then she sets us loose to do with the combination what we can. For the last call, she has everyone dance en masse. Cassandra stands near me on the floor line-up. In dance, it seems, even our discordant spirits match in the kind of harmony that Black people often weave into our music.

When the final go-round is over, we all face the stereo where Kaya is taking the record off the turntable. The applause rises like an earthquake from the ground, showers like thunder.

The music and feeling still flood through my bones, pooling to a glow around my face. I hold the smile my heart has seized upon as we fade our ovation for Kaya.

I savor the moment's sweetness. I look for Anneliesce to catch her eye, but she's left the studio. Now I feel loss, though I don't know what I could say to her. Too bad there are no manuals to consult for how to chat up someone you're interested in. I'm at a dead end, having played out my repertoire of tricks for connecting.

I drape my sweatshirt over my shoulders and pick up my knapsack from the studio floor, nearly hitting Cassandra in the swing of its arc. "Oh, pardon," I say quickly, wanting to get away from her. Her own gear cradled in her arms, she says, "No problem, sis," and I see a for-real live smile on her face. It gives me pause. It'd be nice not to hate her, to embrace her as one of my dance class familiars. She gives her "tee hee hee" and I realize this is a nervous giggle. I'm struck by the revelation. This woman I'd thought a nitwit is shy. And she likes me. I forgive her everything.

I walk out of the studio chastened on the thought of this mended rift with Cassandra and don't even notice Anneliesce standing in the hallway on my path. I stumble into her. She catches me from falling, keeps an arm around my waist after I am steady on my feet and holds me with her gaze. Cassandra, kidding me in our new friendliness, says, "You better watch where you're going, Imani. There's two-way traffic moving through here." I look at Anneliesce smiling, her eyes speaking to me about more than dance steps between us. I am no longer so sure of my direction. More than a little off balance, I give Cassandra all the smile that's in me.

FIRST LOVE, SECOND LOVE

Susan Fox Rogers

I heard about Kim before I met her. Tom came home from his climbing trip out West raving about her. Her footwork was perfection, her balance unmatched, and she was incredibly strong. For Tom, these were the three things one could love a person for. But I knew there was more to her than just her rock-climbing abilities. She was special in other ways. I knew because Tom was half in love with her, and Tom is one of these men who always falls in love with strong, independent women who sooner or later come out. He's done it over and over again. I find it amazing this lack of perception on his part, but it's also sort of sad: he is surprised and hurt every time.

Marsha had just broken up with him when he introduced her to me. He never seemed to mind that we dated for the next three years. Tom has always been good to me. In fact, it was his idea that I take a climbing trip. He lent me money, and gave me Kim's phone number. "Sarah, you have to climb with her. You'll love her," he promised. Fact was, I was already in love with the idea of her: a hard, rock-climbing dyke. It was exactly what I thought I wanted.

I loaded up my VW GTI one Saturday, called Tom to say good-bye, and left. It seemed odd to leave everything, but the dance classes I had been teaching were over for the summer; someone was moving into my apartment the next day; and Marsha didn't care, or even know I was leaving. She didn't want to see me ever again, she said.

As I pulled out of New Paltz and onto the New York State Thruway, I wasn't looking back. I picked up speed, and began to feel free and independent: there was new rock ahead of me. And new love.

What went wrong with Marsha is complex, as these things always are. But I think it can all be blamed on climbing. I wanted a climbing partner who was also my lover. Marsha was my lover and I was trying to make her into my climbing partner. At first she was enthusiastic to get up and do a few routes on a Saturday morning and then leave me to do some harder climbs with Tom. Then one day she became tired of sitting and waiting for me, so she joined us first on MF, then the Yellow Wall. She fell and fell and cursed me and the rock. I think it was when she found herself dangling from No Existence that she called it quits. The climbing and me. I didn't try to fight it until she was gone. Then I made a lot of phone calls, pleaded, cried, and even drove down to the city to see her. She wasn't nice, I made a fool of myself. Marsha said she would stay if I gave up climbing, but she could see it plain enough that climbing was my first love. She was second.

So I spent the last few months single, and climbing like mad. I did a lot of routes and felt in great shape. Whenever I began to feel that my streamlined life was not as fun as I was pretending, I quashed those thoughts and focused. I knew I would eventually give in, but before I found myself with yet another girlfriend who hated the outdoors, I wanted to find one who loved climbing as much as I did. I wanted to share my passion with someone.

I spent three days driving through Ohio, Illinois, and Kansas. I love long-distance driving: the sense of infinite space, the truck stops full of people I only read about, and especially the endless monotonous hours that lend themselves to fantasizing, which is what I did, to the voices of Melissa Etheridge and k.d. lang. It was Saturday, late morning, when I drove into Eldorado Canyon. I felt dizzy from the driving, from excitement, so I drove slowly, savoring my approach. When I spied the steep, mottled walls of the canyon rising up so abruptly from the river I slowed, almost came to a stop. I could see and hear the river as it roared through the canyon and I felt a sense of speed and urgency that made me wildly happy. I parked the car and stood, breathing in the clear air that felt like a silk blanket, light and smooth. The sky reflected my mood: open, hopeful, clear.

I grabbed my pack with my shoes, chalk bag, and rope and headed to the cliffs. There were a lot of people hanging out under the Bastille bouldering, spotting, picking up partners. I joined a group that was watching a couple on Wide Country. The person leading was wearing loose white pants and a small tank top. Her nimble moves, and her tanned arms stretching high for holds, were a wondrous dance, strong and smooth, right through the crux. Everyone was focused on her. In fact, she seemed to have a regular fan club going.

"Who is that?" I asked.

"Kim Smith," some guy answered, not turning to look at me. I nodded and smiled to myself. I figured it had to be her.

"And her husband," he added.

"Her husband?" How could Tom have forgotten to tell me she was married. And to a guy.

"She got married last month."

"Amazing," I let slip.

"That's what everyone thought." My informant finally turned to look at me. "She broke over a dozen hearts." It looked like maybe one of them was his. I felt like one of them was almost mine, and I didn't even know her.

I moved over to the wall, ran my fingers across the hard granite rock, tasting the ridges, knobs that would soon become friends. I propped a leg up, flexed my thigh muscles to be sure they still worked, and leaned over, stretching. I was enjoying the pull in the back of my thighs when I spotted Kim appear from the back side of the Bastille.

She was small and looked energy-packed, ready to spring. Her hair was blond, bleached from the sun, and her smooth skin was a dark brown. I smiled at her and she smiled back, then started to walk toward me. I was sure she had mistaken me for someone else, but she stopped right beside me.

"Hi," she said.

I nodded, feeling curiously mute in front of this woman who I felt I already knew intimately. "Looked good," I offered.

She looked down, rearranging pieces of her lead rack.

"It's a great route." She looked up and smiled. All of her teeth were white, even. I suddenly wondered if maybe she was too perfect. "My name's Kim," she said.

I nodded and we shook hands. "Sarah," I said. "I've heard about you."

She laughed.

"I just got here last night," I explained. I was aware I was staring. Her face was fascinating: round, but angular, with light blue eyes that dropped slightly at the corner, perhaps from sadness. "I'm from the Gunks, I'm friends with Tom." I was suddenly afraid that he didn't really know her, that he was one of her many unknown admirers, one of the broken hearts.

She smiled, her eyes closing slightly. "Tom Haas? So you're Sarah."

"He told you about me?"

"He told you about me."

I laughed. "Fair." But I wondered what Tom had told her.

Kim turned as her partner walked up. "Bill, Sarah, Sarah, Bill. She's Tom's friend from the Gunks," she explained.

Bill nodded. "Ready?" he asked.

"I want to get her phone number so we can climb."

"I don't have a place yet. I'll call you," I offered.

"You can stay with us," she said spontaneously. "Our couch folds out." She bent down to rummage for pen and paper in the top of her pack while Bill walked away. She wrote her address on the paper and began to explain how to find their apartment.

"It's really OK," I said. "I can camp until I find a place."

"That would be stupid," she said. She handed me the address.

"Are you sure?" I nodded toward Bill who was standing with some friends.

She smiled. "Of course. Just ignore him."

Who was he? I wanted to ask.

The next morning I woke with Kim handing me coffee in bed.

"Milk? Sugar?" she asked, nudging the mug toward me.

I sat up and took the mug. "Milk."

"Good," she said. She sat down on the floor next to the bed. "If we hurry we can do a route before I go to work at one."

We did a short route called King's X on the first buttress. It was wonderful watching Kim climb. There was something electric about the way she moved on the rock. She was elastic, able to fold her body, effortlessly matching hand and footholds, then she would unfold, stretching as if she were seven feet tall and no hold was out of her reach. Power and precision.

It was chilly in the canyon when we first got there but by the time I landed on the ledge next to Kim I was sweating.

"This is what climbing is all about," she said. She wasn't talking to me, but was facing the sky, her eyes closed.

I understood what she was talking about. Kim could climb routes a lot harder than this, but it was moving, playing, feeling free and strong as we did that climbing was really about.

We didn't linger with that feeling or over the climb and I soon came to learn Kim didn't linger over anything. She would plan one-hundred things in a day and do one-hundred things because she just kept moving. It was inspiring and a little nerve-racking at the same time.

Once we were down on the ground, we ran back to the car and as I drove down Colorado Boulevard, she changed into a nice pair of blue cotton pants and a white T-shirt. She worked as a waitress at the Cozy Shack. If I came by later, she said she would give me a drink and some food. She stepped out of the car exactly at one.

I spent the afternoon sort of lost. I didn't want to try and find someone else to climb with and I didn't know where to go or what to do. So I drove up to the Flatirons and took a long hike. I thought about Kim all afternoon. It seemed wild we would meet so soon and that she would invite me to stay with her. It was more than a dream come true. And then there was Bill.

The next couple of weeks I virtually moved into their apartment. Kim and I spent our mornings climbing together and in the afternoons I would hike or go bouldering. Once or twice I picked up a partner, or climbed with a friend of Kim's. It was always warm and sunny and I was tanned and feeling strong. I was also completely in love with Kim.

We got along in an intuitive, instinctive manner. As we hiked into climbs we talked about everything from religion to having children to AIDS. But mostly we talked about climbing, affirming each other's conviction that climbing was life.

The one topic we skimmed over was relationships. I did tell her a few details about life with Marsha, just to be sure she was clued in, and to try and get her to talk. But a definite silence would come over her just when she should have been picking up the storyline, so I still couldn't figure out how Bill fit into the picture, though it was true they were married.

We were affectionate together, leaning against each other on belay ledges, hugging each other for courage before a hard lead, or after a tough route, massaging each other in front of the television set in the evenings. It was flirtatious, in a distanced way. And it completely confused me. I know straight women who like to play with lesbians, thinking it's daring and chic. But that's not what Kim was doing. She liked me. And in some ways I don't think she was aware what she was doing, what she was feeling.

In any case, I wasn't taking that sudden bold step beyond flirting. And that wasn't like me.

And then one day as we sat on a belay ledge, two-hundred feet up on the Yellow Spur, the sun just beginning to heat the rock, she leaned over and kissed me on the lips. I was so startled, I didn't respond to her kiss. Instead, I leaned back on my arms, sighed, and giggled. She giggled too. It was almost embarrassing to be acting so adolescent.

We sat for a moment in silence, our shoulders touching lightly as we looked into the valley.

"Want to lead this pitch?" she asked, breaking the silence.

"What?" I asked. I had heard her but I guess I expected her to say something else, ask a different question.

I looked up at the steep red rock. "No," I said flatly. I knew I was far too distracted to focus on leading. She got up and in her sure manner waltzed up the rock, leaving me giddy and puzzled.

Soon she was off belay, tugging on the rope as if she wanted me to join her as quickly as possible.

The rock was steep with sharp solid face holds, the climbing I like best. As I climbed, I felt dizzy, light, like a dancer on point, sustaining an unnatural but powerfully centered pose, and knowing that soon I would return to a flat-footed, more solid position. For a moment I was enjoying that strong sense of flying, of doing the impossible.

"That was wonderful," I said as I pulled onto the ledge.

Kim kissed me quickly. "My favorite climb," she said. She looked at her watch. "I hate work."

I put an arm around her waist and she hugged me back.

"You should have led this pitch," she said. "It's well protected, your kind of climbing."

I laughed. "I was thinking of something else. Other things."

I leaned over and kissed her again, this time lingering over the kiss, playing with her tongue and lips. Her lips were thin, dry from the sun, which made them feel fragile. Kissing those lips made me want to protect her from herself.

For the next week, every ledge meant a kiss and a hug. I lived for those kisses, moved up the rock knowing one was at the end of every pitch. I found myself moving aggressively on unbelievably hard stuff. And our climbing was marvelously in synch. But I wanted more: I wanted to make love to her; I wanted her to be mine all of the time, not just when we climbed.

Then one day, several pitches in the sky, she said quietly and seriously, "Don't fall in love with me."

"OK," I said, letting go, as if it could be that simple.

"I just don't have room. With climbing," she added.

"And Bill?" I asked.

"Bill's not a problem. We agree to love climbing together. If our love meets on the rock, fine, if not, that's fine too. We climb well together."

It sounded very neat, very matter-of-fact. Had that been written into their marriage ceremony? I wondered.

"So do we. But I think there's more to it than that." I thought of our conversations as we hiked in, of our evening runs on the flatirons, of our playful nights making dinner when Bill was working.

"There can't be," she said.

"There already is," I said. I felt a little foolish pushing her. I'm not used to pushing.

"Then why did you kiss me?"

She shrugged and kissed me lightly. "I like you." She leaned back and looked serious and sad. Her eyes were pulling down at the sides and I felt I knew what made her sad. "I've had girlfriends before," she said. "I fall in love. I hate falling in love. I lose control." She looked at me and smiled quickly. "Like barndooring twenty feet out."

I visualized Kim, hands and arms clutching a hinge of rock, her body slowly but inevitably flapping open, out, away from the rock, driven by wind or gravity. I smiled slightly to myself: this was one more climbing-as-life metaphor to add to our growing collection. To Kim I nodded slowly, staring at her, wanting to remind her that just a few days ago on Great Expectations, she hadn't barndoored. And everyone does.

After our talk I needed to be away from Kim before I fell painfully in love. She didn't ask why I was leaving, but she did want to know what the address was, if I had a phone, and if I wanted to climb the next morning.

I couldn't believe she would suggest we climb, as if she hadn't heard anything that we had said.

"How about next Friday?" I figured that eight days were enough for me to cool off.

I found an apartment I could rent on a weekly basis and two other people to climb with: Louise, who was daring and willing to lead desperates, and James, who was funny and eager. During that week I yearned for a storm, or better yet, an overcast gray day, humid and heavy, like we have so regularly on the East Coast: I wanted the weather to match my mood, the weight of my soul. But everything continued shining and blue, relentlessly cheerful, and I found that, despite myself, I would lose myself in the beauty of the area, in the joy of spending so much time moving, playing, and being outside. I thought I could get over Kim, given a few more days. Love had never slowed me down before.

But by Friday I was completely worked up, as if I was going on a first date.

My stomach butterflied when she stepped out of her blue pickup. She was wearing her light green muscle shirt and short black shorts. She looked carefree and animated, in the way I had always known her. I knew my feelings for her hadn't worn off.

We talked haltingly as we walked in to our climb. But once on the rock, we fell into our flow and dance together. The day seemed so perfect in every way that I couldn't believe anyone wouldn't want to be in love, just to extend and amplify the blue in the sky, the green and red tints of the rock, the subtle roll of adrenaline through their body.

At the end of our last climb she leaned over and kissed me.

"Please don't," I said.

She looked away.

"I just can't deal with not really being with you."

She nodded and looked down. "Me too."

"What?"

She shrugged and then began to cry silently. Her determined front melted away as she leaned over, half-slumped so the tears rolled out of her eyes and dropped to the ground. I leaned over and hugged her. We sat there, four hundred feet up, swaying in each others arms.

"It's OK," I kept saying, wondering what was OK, and not completely certain it was OK.

"I'm not happy," she said gently.

I waited for her to go on.

Instead, she started kissing me. Her hands wandered over my body, reaching under my T-shirt and resting softly and definitely on my breasts. We lay naked under the Colorado sun, caressing each other, gently, cautiously. As I had imagined so many times

before, Kim's body was smooth as water on a still summer day, but when I touched her I was caressing the boulders on the bottom of the river, hard, round, supportive. It was bliss. I made love to her and when she came she called out, "I love you."

I lay on top of her, hoping it might be true.

I spent the next few days elated. I thought of our lovemaking, recalling in technicolor every touch and kiss. The more I thought of us together, the more I wanted of her: her body, her heart, her secrets and lies. After four days of sustained fantasies, I also wanted to see her again. Or at least hear from her. I called the apartment and talked to Bill. I drove past the house in the morning when she should have been leaving to climb, but the truck was already gone. I sat by the phone, waiting for it to ring. The silence almost killed me.

When the phone finally rang I jumped.

"Hi," she said quietly.

"Hello," I said when there were a dozen other things I wanted to say.

"We can't go on."

I wanted to hang up.

"Because of climbing."

Why can't I replace Bill? I wanted to ask, though I knew he wasn't the problem.

"I just can't." She didn't finish her sentence.

I wanted to see her, I wanted to talk.

"Can we climb?" she asked through my silence.

"No," I said. "At least not for a while."

"You're like all the others."

"What are you talking about?"

"All or nothing."

"Hardly. But I do want something." So that my heart doesn't break, I wanted to add.

"I'm sorry," she said.

"I'm fine," I said and hung up.

I sat in my living room and thought about Kim. I had finally met someone more fanatic about climbing than I was and it wasn't so nice. "You're like all the others" ran through my head. I was like them and I was like all the women who had loved me. I thought of Marsha, Sheila, Betty, and Joan, wondering if they might forgive me. Not take me back, just forgive me.

I called Tom to tell him my woes, to tell him I was going to pack my bags and head west, perhaps to the Valley. If I ever had a lover again, she would not be a climber, not even want to be a climber. Tom listened when he could have been laughing and said he was sorry, he never intended things to turn out this way. He offered to call Kim, ask her what she was doing, tell her not to torture me, but I told him it wasn't worth it.

I ached in a terrible way when I went to bed that night. I half-slept until four, then decided to leave, make an alpine departure. I burned some toast, brewed a cup of strong coffee and locked the door behind me. When I tossed my bags into the trunk of the car I saw something move in the backseat. I peered in through the window and saw Kim, half-sitting up, wrapped in her sleeping bag, a duffle bag for her pillow. I opened my door and peered in.

"Can I go to the Valley with you?" she asked.

I climbed in, started the engine, then turned and smiled at her before slowly pulling out of the driveway.

THE PASS

Lucy Jane Bledsoe

aby! Baby! Oh, baby!" my coach shouted, gripping my shoulders. Johnny practically yanked me off my bike, seconds after I'd crossed the finish line.

"Easy, man, hey, easy," I protested as he crushed me against his chest in his version of a hug. Johnny slopped a big wet one right on my mouth.

"Johnny . . ." I muttered, shaking his mania off me. Sure, I could understand his ecstasy. His team just took first place in the Rocky Mountain Classic, a fifty-mile road race in Wyoming. I mean, we weren't racing for bigshot teams like Kahlua or TGIF. No one expected a team from an obscure bike shop in Berkeley to take first place. But the finish line meant little to me right then. I was still savoring what had happened up on Snow Pass.

I watched Johnny tackle Julie and Danielle, my teammates as well as my lover of five years and affair of six months, respectively. After Johnny galloped off to greet our fourth teammate Kelly, Danielle turned on me. "What happened?"

"What do you mean?" I knew exactly what she meant. I'd blocked in the final sprint for Kelly, rather than Danielle, to take first place.

"The finish line?" Danielle swung her long black ponytail back and forth across her shoulders in that way she had of trying to look oh-so-relaxed. She fingered the two gold chains glinting at her neck. I think my fascination with her centered on the fact that she was even more femme than I.

"We took first place," Julie defended me to Danielle. "It doesn't matter who she blocked for." Julie stood with her fists on her hips, looking short and sturdy next to wispy Danielle. I used to love the way Julie's face, framed by that short blond hair, looked blunt with sincerity as she argued a point. But now Julie's earnestness put me off. It was overdone, an accessory, like Danielle's gold chains. In fact, it was a lie. Julie was just as angry as

Danielle at what had happened between me and Kelly in this race.

"We had a strategy," Danielle argued. "You had no idea if Kelly could sprint. This was her first race with us. The whole purpose of strategies . . ."

"Yeah," I muttered and stopped listening. I watched Kelly over by the finish line as some guys pressed an obscenely gaudy trophy into her arms. Johnny stood close by hiccuping his wolfish laughter. Kelly looked as if she was searching for someone in the crowd. I caught her eye. She didn't smile, but she got that focused look of hers, as if she was filled with intent. I could tell that she too felt something much bigger than that trophy in her arms. She'd taken off her helmet and her hair was slick with sweat. Her big legs glistened with sweat as well. Though she was a good twenty yards away, I felt Kelly's presence as powerfully as if she were occupying every cavity in my body. I forced myself to turn my back. I didn't need to posture or rush. I had all afternoon and evening. More, if it took more.

"See you in a bit," I told Danielle and Julie and walked off, pushing my bike. Most of the racers and spectators were heading for the barbecue, but I wanted a moment alone. A good distance away from the food tables I found a small grove of aspens. I propped my bike against a tree and lay down on my back in the spotted sunlight. The leaves above me were an iridescent yellow with auras of orange and red. Beyond the leaves I could see the steel-gray mountains and the sky so dense with blue you could stab it with a fork. I felt the sweat on my body drying into a sandy film. I licked the corner of my mouth and tasted it, gritty and salty. Every muscle in my body felt like liquid bliss. If just thinking about that woman made me feel like this, what would touching her be like? I closed my eyes, praying that Johnny, Danielle, and Julie would leave me alone for at least five minutes.

Until about three hours ago, at the beginning of the hill leading up to Snow Pass, I'd barely acknowledged that Kelly had joined the team a few weeks ago. I guess I was too enmeshed in the sticky triangle with Julie and Danielle. It shouldn't have been sticky. Julie, who called herself a socialist, always said that, and I quote, "Jealousy is simply a residual emotion left over from the corruption of capitalism." We'd both had affairs and jealousy had never played a part. Something about Danielle, though, really set Julie off. I think it was her corporate job. She was a buyer for Macy's.

Danielle liked to tell Julie, "Competition is everything." To me, when Julie wasn't around, she would add that Julie would only be a good bike racer, never great, because she always compromised the spirit of competition. I was tired of being in the crossfire of their ideologies. And I wondered if either of them could ever understand what had happened on Snow Pass.

As the pack approached the bottom of the hill, I was a lot more tired than I should have been. Sweat drenched my jersey. Sharp pains traveled from my neck across my right shoulder. That hill was eight miles long and the pack was already moving pretty fast. Yet, as the strongest hill climber on the team, in spite of my being the oldest at thirty-eight, I was supposed to lead an attack at the start of the hill.

Trying to ignore my fatigue and pain, I rose out of the saddle and pumped to the front of the pack and then out in front. At first I thought the whole pack was coming with me, but I guess most of the riders figured an attack so early in the climb was foolish. We made a strong break with Julie, Danielle, Kelly, two riders from a Denver team, as well as an independent rider, coming along.

"Excellent," Kelly growled after climbing for a mile. "Perfect breakaway." She pulled in front of me so I could draft her for a while.

I needed the encouragement. The breakaway effort nearly killed me and I wasn't recovering quickly. It *was* pretty spectacular that all four of us on the Berkeley team broke away together, no one stranded back in the pack.

As we continued up the mountain pass in a paceline of seven riders, I realized that one thing I liked about bike racing was how cooperating with your competition is an essential part of the strategy. This was a good group. Everyone, except for Danielle who was saving herself for the sprint at the finish line, was willing to work, taking her turn pulling at the front, then falling back to draft and "rest."

Despite our successful escape from the pack and the smooth work of my teammates, I felt weaker and weaker. I couldn't get enough oxygen into my lungs. My legs felt like they were going to burst apart. When it was my turn at the front, I just couldn't keep the pace. I knew I was hitting the wall in a very serious way.

The girls from Denver and the independent rider took advantage of my failing strength and worked together to break away from us.

"We've got to go with them," Danielle ordered. I watched their three behinds swinging from side to side as they moved up the hill ahead of us. Danielle snarled, "Come on, *jam.*"

"You can do it," Julie urged me. "We can bridge up if you try."

"I can't," I gasped. I knew this was not a phrase that athletes use. Ever. But it was the truest thing I could say.

"I don't mean you," Danielle said to me. Which made me think immediately of how she was twenty-five next to my thirty-eight.

"Then who *do* you mean?" Kelly, who was taking a pull at the front with me right behind her, asked. I felt a surge of emotion for her. It was as if I noticed her, really noticed her, for the first time.

Danielle, knowing that she couldn't bridge up to the other riders alone and probably not wanting to ask Julie to go with her, muttered, "There goes the race."

"They're not going to be able to hold that pace," Kelly shouted from the front of the paceline to Danielle at the back. "Don't worry about them." In a lower voice, just to me, she said, "How come Danielle never takes a pull at the front?"

Julie, who rode right behind me, heard the question and smirked, "Because she's a prima donna."

"Don't start," I found the breath to say.

"What?" Danielle yelled from the back of the paceline.

Luckily, I couldn't answer. The wall felt grayer and thicker and harder than it ever had before. My gut was heaving up into my throat with every revolution. I felt as if a massive steel weight rested on my shoulders.

"Danielle!" Kelly called back. "Take your turn at the front."

"Since when is she calling the shots?" Danielle called up and I knew she was asking me.

"Take a pull," I told Danielle. "We need help."

"It's about time," Julie mumbled as Danielle rode past us on her way to the front of the paceline.

I was surprised that Danielle complied. She espoused "team play" all the time, whether she was talking about selling clothes or having sex, but in cycling, team play meant our catering to her role as finish-line sprinter. She threatened me as she went by, "I just hope I have it in me to sprint at the end."

"You're climbing up to Snow Pass now," Kelly said, sliding in behind Danielle. "Think about sprinting to the finish line in twenty miles. If you get there."

Kelly's voice felt good. I couldn't tell what it was, but it had to do with massaging the wall instead of beating it, like Julie and Danielle's voices seemed to do. Watching her ride helped me, too. I'd never seen a smoother cyclist. Her muscles flowed with each pedal stroke. She could tell how badly I was struggling and counseled me in a low voice, "Let go of your mind. You don't need it. Don't think. Your legs will do all the work."

That's when the wall in front of me metamorphosed and I realized it was my whole life in my face, like a blockade. Two girlfriends, two part-time jobs, the eternal mess of my apartment . . . The whole shebang felt like a badly written short story meandering through piles of extraneous material. Everything was overstated, boring in its drama, too careful in its detail. If I was going to make it up this hill, something had to go. I drew a few lines through Danielle as if she were a couple of bad paragraphs. Maybe this one-minute manager routine worked on the job, but applied to me it was a drag. Julie was right: Danielle's oh-so-femme corporate number was definitely expendable.

I breathed deeply and heard Kelly say, "That a girl. A few more miles."

"Sure," I said. Deleting one girlfriend helped, but was only a beginning.

"We've got to pick up the pace," Danielle prodded. She'd slipped rather quickly back into the fold and Julie now led us up the hill.

No one answered her. Something cruel in me enjoyed knowing that I'd broken up with her and she didn't even know about it.

Kelly said, just to me, "I don't know, but I think this might be the ideal pace. I have a hunch that we'll bridge up to those others without trying. And we'll be fresher."

I didn't have the strength to tell her that fresh, fresher, and freshest were relative terms, none of which applied to me.

To take my mind off the hill, I concentrated on each muscle in Kelly's legs, one at a time. She reminded me of an elk I'd seen once running in a Canadian forest. The elk had the most magnificent set of antlers which it negotiated through the tree branches and even under fallen logs with complete grace and precision, clearing obstacles by half an inch but never knocking its antlers.

Kelly's legs, and the memory of that elk, made me consider editing Julie out of my life along with Danielle. The thought felt razor-sharp and clear. As I thought it, the structure of the wall shimmered as if it were deconstructing. Then I wavered, feeling the loss, of Julie or the wall, I wasn't sure. My breathing became ragged and my shoulders suddenly ached even worse. Again I thought of that elk and how Kelly reminded me of it and how *that* made me think about how there had never been passion, real passion, between Julie and me, in all our five years. We used to believe that neither of us ever got jealous of the other's affairs because of our superior ability to deal with nonmonogamy. In truth, our lack of jealousy was probably more a sign that our love wasn't the kind you can cut yourself on.

I felt something like an explosion in my head. The wall melted away in its heat. I reached a blank place, but blank in the sense of remembering, not forgetting. Blank and utterly peaceful. I realized how badly I had been missing myself.

A fluid strength took residence in my body. I pulled to the front of the paceline to haul us the last mile to the top of the pass. Now Kelly drafted me and I could hear her breathing, even, full, and deep. I could feel her front wheel inches behind my back wheel. She hadn't said more than a few sentences to me in all the time I'd known her, but the way her body worked told me plenty.

As we drew near the top of the pass, I shifted up a gear to push our pace. My legs and mind were free now. I could do anything. I jammed up that hill with Kelly breathing on my back, and I knew that all that mattered was the taste and texture of this blue sky. The flow of sweat off my head. The rolling muscles in my back. I gulped the Rocky Mountain air as if it had nourishment.

As we crested the top of the pass, I sat up in my saddle for a moment and whooped, "Yeah, *baby!*"

Julie warned, "Take it easy," and I knew she meant to check the joy in me as if it were decadent.

"Take it easy?" Danielle snarled. "Now's the time to *hit it.*"

Kelly shifted into her biggest gear and pulled in front of me. We soared over the top of the pass and began down the other side. Like hers, my chin nearly rested on my handlebars and we moved as one machine flying down the hill. I didn't care anymore what Julie or Danielle had to say. I didn't care anything about the race or the finish line. All I cared about was the relief I felt in having one focus, to ride with Kelly.

On either side of us, the late-afternoon sun painted angular shapes onto the rocky cliffs. We flew into patches of shade where I thrilled on riding nearly blind and then sped out into the bright sunshine again.

"There's a hairpin turn at the bottom of the hill!" Julie screamed and I was surprised that she and Danielle had kept up with Kelly and me. "Slow down," she yelled.

Her words were lost in the rush of wind in our ears. I'm sure I was the only one who heard her and I didn't answer.

A moment later, the independent and two Denver riders came into sight ahead of us.

"Attack on the turn," Kelly shouted back to me just moments before we bridged up to them. But we were already upon the turn before we had time to even settle into the small pack and Kelly sailed right through them.

It was then, as we screamed into that hairpin turn, that I grasped the one hard knot of truth I'd been missing. I was a wild animal then, the bicycle was my set of antlers, and I knew down to a fraction of an inch how to maneuver through that turn at this wild speed.

I also knew, right there at the apex of the turn, that I had to have Kelly. I wanted her because I knew that when I touched her I would relive screaming through this hairpin turn, because I knew that she would feel excruciatingly necessary, like the hard knot itself.

I heard Johnny shout, "There she is!"

Cracking open an eye, I saw him corraling Julie and Danielle over to my place under the aspens. He held up a paper plate piled high with chicken, fruit and pasta salad. "I got ya some eats!" Poor Johnny, I thought. He knew everything there was to know about cycling and nothing about the dyke subtext, the very soul of competition, that drove every race.

Danielle's cleats tapped along on the cement pathway just as I imagined her high heels did in the management hallways of Macy's. Julie looked a little confused and I figured that she was constructing her case against me.

I had an awful lot of explaining to do. I wished I could have stood up and said, "Look, I decided during the race that I want to break up with both of you. And the reason I blocked for Kelly,

rather than you, Danielle, at the finish line was because, well, I
wanted to."

A thread of courtesy kept me from giving that speech. Instead,
I pretended to doze.

"We're having a team meeting. Do you think you could regain
consciousness for a few minutes?" Danielle wanted to know.

"Sure." I rolled over on my side and propped myself up on an
elbow. Johnny placed the plate of food on the ground in front of
me.

Then I saw both Julie and Danielle glaring at something behind
me. I looked over my shoulder and saw Kelly approaching with a
plate of food in one hand. She cradled the enormous trophy with
her other arm.

"Hi," I said, my voice full of her. That thread of courtesy
snapped and I caressed Kelly with my eyes right there in front of
everyone.

Not that I was in a hurry. *Au contraire.* But I wasn't about to
waste another moment of my life, either.

"Hi," Kelly answered after a long pause. Then she smiled, her
whole face crunching up in a look of complete happiness. I think
I moaned a little.

"So Johnny wants to know," Julie said flatly, "how Kelly got
into the sprinter's position."

Everyone looked at me.

"I mean, I have no problem with it!" Johnny bellowed, still
grinning widely. "First place is first place. I just want to know
how you all rode the race."

I sat up suddenly, feeling delirious. "Hey! I've had an insight."
I said, "When you think about it, it's pretty strange we have these
big knobs, called heads, bobbing around on the tops of our bodies.
I mean, heads are just very densely packed masses of nerve cells.
No wonder we all get so twisted up mentally. I know we have
nerve cells all over, but the great majority of them are way up in
our heads. Wouldn't it make a lot more sense if those nerve cells—
our intelligence—were spread evenly throughout our whole bodies? Julie, in your terms, it would be a kind of distribution of the
wealth. In yours, Danielle, let's just call it diversification."

I let that sink in and then said more quietly, "What happened
in the crucial moments of this race is that Kelly and I managed to
psychically spread our nerve cells throughout our bodies. So that

our bodies were able to make all the decisions. Does that make sense?"

I looked at Kelly. She looked as if she were about to kiss me and I was flooded with unbearably intense desire.

"No, it doesn't," Danielle said. When I looked over at her, she was smirking at Julie. Julie's face relaxed and she smiled at Danielle. Ah, the subtle beginning of an alliance. It was inevitable, really. In the course of one race, I'd transformed a triangle, with all its stagnant tension, into a square. Triangles can stay in place forever, but squares break off into pairs quickly.

"The problem with you two," I said to Julie and Danielle, "is that you both live too much in your heads."

I enjoyed the silence I'd shocked them into. I glanced at Johnny and he looked thoroughly confused. Kelly remained quiet and still.

I picked up a chicken leg and teethed off the meat. When the bone was clean, I cracked it in two and began sucking out the marrow. I wasn't sure if this would impress or disgust Kelly, but I didn't feel very cautious today. I needed a woman who could handle a marrow-sucking, hill-jamming, hard-cycling femme. Take it or leave it. I put down the hollowed-out chicken bone, wiped my mouth on a napkin, and smiled at Kelly. She cracked the chicken bone on her own plate, put it to her mouth, and started sucking out the marrow.

"I can't believe this," Danielle said. She got to her feet. "Let's go."

Johnny looked downright spooked. Maybe I was acting even more deranged than I felt. Usually I'm a nice person. You know, considerate of other people's feelings. He said, "Yeah, well, maybe we all need to rest a little before rehashing the race."

He, Danielle, and Julie were all standing now, ready to leave. The light was beginning to fail. The leaves of the aspens deepened to a rich mustard color. It began to get a little chilly and still I didn't want to move. I was afraid that if I did, the nerve cells would all rush back into my head.

Johnny and Danielle began walking back to the van. Julie waited.

She looked hurt and I felt a spasm of guilt. She said, "What's wrong with you? Come *on*."

I answered, "I think I'll ride my bike back to the motel."

"In the dark," she snapped. "Twenty miles."

"Yeah," I said. "In the dark. Twenty miles."

Julie didn't bother asking if Kelly was coming. I watched her turn her back and head for the van. Briefly I wondered why I felt so detached, so careless with her feelings. My worries only lasted a millisecond. The earthy smell of the ground beneath me and the papery rustle of the alder leaves above returned me to the present. I turned to Kelly. Her face looked like a racer's, intent and specific.

"That was only the beginning," she said, and I knew she was talking about what happened on both sides of the pass. She leaned forward and untied the laces of my cleats. Her fingers brushed my ankles, searing the skin as hotly as if she'd touched my most sensitive places.

Then someone shouted her name. She laughed and looked over her shoulder at the couple dozen racers, spectators, and reporters gathered around the food tables.

"Your public is waiting for you," I said.

She retied my cleats and then ran her hands up my leg. "Then maybe I'd better leave your clothes on until I finish talking to the reporters."

"I'm in no rush," I told her. "I'll be right here."

I watched her walk toward the crowd. There was no swagger to her movement, no butch announcements, though she was as beautifully butch as my dreams could hope for. I closed my eyes, listening to the alder leaves and thinking that the fourth dimension had dropped out altogether up there on Snow Pass. I could wait a lifetime for this woman and feel as if I hadn't missed a thing.

DIAMONDS, DYKES, AND DOUBLE PLAYS

Pat Griffin

I've known I was queer since I was about twelve years old. I'm twenty-eight now. I've had my share of relationships in that time and I read somewhere that they were "serial monogamous" relationships. Whatever you call them, some were good and some were pretty horrible. Right now I'm coming off of one of the latter: a real tantrum-throwing, kick and screamer of a thing that left me exhausted and looking for a fresh start. So, I left Maryland, my job as a high school gym teacher, my sparring partner, and moved north.

I'd heard that Northampton, Massachusetts, was a great place to be queer, so I packed up my Toyota and took off. Despite all the good things I'd heard about being queer in Northampton, I was one lonely dyke for a long time after I got here in late August. I did get a job right away. I was a long-term sub teaching high school PE and coaching a girl's basketball team, but I could not seem to break into this great lesbian community everyone talked about. I went to the women's bookstore, women's music concerts, college field hockey games, the bars, but I couldn't seem to find a way in.

I was surrounded by dykes, but I felt like a stranger in a strange land, a real alien from outer space. You don't have to go out of the country to experience culture shock. What I mean is, the women and the "women's community" in Northampton are nothing like what I was used to in Maryland. Basically, back there we had our crowd who played softball in the summer, basketball in the winter, drank beer all year round, and tried to keep track of who was with who, or not speaking, or putting the moves on who. It may have been crazy, but at least I had some sense of the rules, and I had friends who I could count on in a pinch (most of the time). I felt like a beggar at a banquet in Northampton. All these women and, somehow, I didn't speak their language.

I spent the fall and winter reading about (but not attending)

potlucks advertised in *The Labrys,* a local lesbian monthly. You
wouldn't believe the options: potlucks for left-handed working-
class lesbians who won the state lottery; lesbian children of adults
who pick their noses; lesbians who occasionally sleep with men;
lesbians against nuclear war, famine, and plastic shrink wrap; you
name it, there's a potluck for you. Somehow, I knew that these
were not the kind of women who wanted to talk about the Washington Redskins or the New England Patriots. What I needed was
to find the jocks. Where were the beer-drinking, sports-minded
dykes who were into competition, not contemplation, who were
into personal relationships, not political action. I thought about
submitting my own potluck notice for lesbians who like to play
sports, drink beer, and have serial monogamy with teammates, but
I was too shy.

When Susan, the woman I was sharing an apartment with,
asked if I wanted to play on her softball team I jumped at the
chance. At last, the long drought would be over. I circled April
15, the date of the first team meeting, on my calendar and started
oiling up my softball glove in February. I couldn't wait to meet
women who slid into second with spikes high, who knew how to
stand in at the plate against a fast pitcher, who turned double plays
with cool assurance: my kind of dyke. The softball team's first
meeting was, you guessed it, a potluck. This was my first clue that
even softball in Northampton was to be a new cultural experience.

I found out quickly (and the hard way) that there is an ironclad
etiquette surrounding these potluck gatherings. Here's a tip: never
(and I mean never) bring, as your contribution to the meal, anything that used to breathe. I found out about this faux pas when
my dish of hamburger casserole sat untouched by lesbian hands
for the entire evening. Women circled that sucker as if they
thought a hoof was going to shoot out of the bowl and beat them
senseless next to the table. I learned from overhearing a conversation that lesbians here do not eat "land-walking animals." Being
the adaptable dyke that I am (and lonely), I made a mental note
never to eat land-walking animal meals in public. In my own
home, under the cover of night, well, I figure that's another story.

Anyway, I filled my plate with shit called "tempay" and "toe
foo," which I had never seen before. I bypassed my own dish,
wrinkling my nose in proper disgust, as if the thought of a big
juicy land-walking animal burger was repellent to my politically

pure palate. I realized that if I wanted to make friends here, it was going to cost me one casserole dish. I knew I'd have to leave it. I could never admit I had brought that, that abomination, to the potluck. I tried to remember who had seen me come in with it. What would I say if someone asked which dish was mine? What if I claimed one that belonged to the asker? Bullshit! This was getting too complicated. I backtracked and, with a grand, politically incorrect flourish, dug deep into my ground beef casserole. I heaped it on my plate and grabbed a beer out of the cooler. Hey, this is who I am: a burger-eating, beer-drinking kind of dyke. Take it or leave it.

The rest of the evening, introducing new players (there were three of us rookies) and reviewing the league rules, was too bizarre for words. I sat in shocked silence as I learned that in this league 1) we basically play fast-pitch rules, but if the batter thinks the pitcher is too fast, she has to slow it down; 2) it is totally unacceptable to ride the other team. We are to treat them as sisters (Hell, I yell at my sister all the time); 3) everyone will play equal amounts of time regardless of skill; 4) we will take turns being coach; 5) no men are allowed to umpire games; and, the one I was most intrigued by, 6) we all must wear clothes to play. Not to worry, the thought of sliding into home bare-assed held no allure for me.

I also learned that after games we will sit in a circle and do something everyone called "processing the experience" where we'd give each other "feedback" and "share our feelings" about how we "interacted" with each other and the other team. Now, this is something I knew about, only in Maryland we just called it "going out for a beer" after the game.

The name of our team is, get this, "Amazon Vision." In fact, I learned that all the teams in this league have names like "The Vegetarians," "Womynpower," "Circle of Peace," "The Raging Hormones," "Revolting Hags," and "I Am Womon." When I asked who won the championship last summer, everyone acted like I'd farted. Uh-oh, another mistake.

A woman wearing a lavender T-shirt with female genitals printed on it finally broke the silence and said:

"This is a noncompetitive league. We don't keep track of our wins and losses. The obsession with winning is a vestige of the patriarchy."

I nodded my head like this was not new information for me.
What could I do? I love competition, and the best part of it is
winning. I knew to admit this, however, would make me a "male-
identified tool of the patriarchy," not a good way to start the
season with my strange new teammates.

Little did I know that this was only the beginning of my education about what they kept calling "noncompetitive feminist softball." I left the potluck with lots of doubts about all this, but I
was lonely and I wanted to play softball. Maybe it wouldn't be as
weird as it sounded once we got out on the field and started whip-
ping that baby around the infield.

Our first practice demolished that illusion. Now, I don't want
to sound elitist in any way. I mean, as a gym teacher, coach, and
former college athlete, I guess you could think that of me for saying this, but this was one sorry collection of dyke jocks. Since we
don't have a coach, like in the traditional sense, we decided what
to do by consensus. After tossing the ball around in pairs to warm
up, it took us twenty minutes to decide to do infield practice and
even at that two women, Moonwolf and Morningdew, had to go
off and "process" something before they could "join our energy"
on the field.

Finally, I trotted out to third base, my regular position, and
spent some time checking the area for little rocks and stuff. Joan,
the woman playing first base, sidearmed a ground ball to me, I
scooped it up, stepped and threw it back to her. The ball thwacked
deliciously into her glove. At last, we were playing softball. At last
something felt familiar. Joan aimed the next grounder at Micki,
the shortstop. She fielded the ball with her left boob, retrieved it,
and threw it over the fence behind first base. Joan was prepared
for this: she had a whole pile of balls beside her in foul territory.
This did not look good.

Apparently the woman playing second base, Marie, took her
responsibility literally: she was standing on top of the bag waiting
for her grounder from Joan. I couldn't stand it, so I said as gently
as I could:

"Marie, the second baseman usually plays off the bag about five
to ten steps toward first."

Well, by the way she looked at me I knew I had blundered into
another social miscue. I just couldn't figure out what it was. Did
they have a rule that whoever played second was supposed to
stand on the base? Finally, Micki said:

"In this league, we call it second basewomon."

I could tell there was no "man" in this word by the way she emphasized the "mon."

"Great idea," I said, and then to Marie: "The second basewomon," I smiled at Micki, "plays off the bag, Marie."

With this translation, Marie moved toward first and looked at me questioningly. "Here?"

"That's great." I smiled back.

Things actually went OK for a while. Janice, our leftfielder, was pretty good at hitting infield practice and we spent about thirty minutes fielding grounders and pop-ups and throwing them to different bases. This was more like it. Then we took a water break. After that, we decided to do outfield practice. Moonwolf asked if anyone could "throw up and hit the ball" to the outfield this year. I had this image of someone alternately retching beside home plate and then hitting fungoes. Apparently, no one else thought this particular image was odd. Moonwolf filled the new players in.

"Last year no one could throw up and hit the ball to the outfield, so we never got to practice outfield."

"I can throw up and hit," I volunteered, blending in with the native culture.

"Great," Moonwolf smiled, and all the outfielders turned to jog out to their positions.

I've always loved hitting fungoes. The challenge of hitting to every field, putting the flies just within the range of the fielders, and occasionally, just for fun, going for the fence. I found myself just naturally kicking into my coach mode.

"Nice try, Morningdew." I wanted to call her Dewey or something, anything but Morningdew, but I knew she wouldn't appreciate a nickname and we'd probably have to process the experience if I tried to give her one without her permission.

"Call it, Janice, that was yours." "Throw it to the cut-off, Gerry." "Call it, Moonwolf," I yelled.

They were a silent bunch, working independently. I started hitting the ball randomly to each fielder so they had to decide whose it was. I hit a high fly to right center. Moonwolf and Morningdew both ran toward it, gloves up. At the last minute, they both stepped aside, parting like the Red Sea, and the ball thudded to the grass and rolled behind them.

"Call it, you have to call it," I yelled for the millionth time.

I started to hit another ball, but caught it instead. I walked out to second base waving all the outfielders in to meet me. They trotted in.

"Look, you have to call the ball. If you're going to catch it, yell 'mine' or 'I have it' or something so other fielders know to back off, OK?"

This information was greeted with silence. "Do you understand what I mean?" I checked.

Morningdew looked troubled. "That's such a commitment. I've always had trouble with commitments. I mean, to yell out 'I have it,' what if I drop it, what if I don't have it?"

Could this really be happening to me? I wondered. I looked at the rest of the outfield for confirmation that this was nutty. They were all looking intently at Morningdew and nodding in agreement.

"I feel the same way," Moonwolf solemnly confessed. "Plus, for me, it seems so, so territorial, so capitalistic, so male."

Gerry and Janice moved over to put their arms around Morningdew who looked like she was going to cry.

"Look," I said, trying to make the commitment seem more manageable, "It's not like you're promising to catch it every time you call it. You're really just saying that you're going to try to catch it, see?" I didn't have a clue how to deal with the capitalistic shit Moonwolf had brought up.

I could see that they were thinking this over. Finally, Morningdew smiled and said:

"That really helps me. In fact, you could say, that even if you miss it, it helps another womon since we are all sisters on both teams."

I just knew I could hear that music from the "Twilight Zone"— do, do, do, do. This was so weird, but I knew by now not to laugh.

"Well, yes, I guess that's true, but it's OK to want to help our team first, isn't it?" I asked gently, "Then, of course, if you drop the ball it helps the women from the other team." This seemed to make sense to everyone. I exhaled a sigh of relief.

"Water break," Micki, who had been doing tai chi along the first base line, called. Everyone walked over to the benches on the third base line.

The rest of practice went pretty well. We did some batting practice and talked about our first game the next week with "I Am

Womon." I was given my team T-shirt: lavender with a picture of a fierce-looking womon in full armor on the front of it. Behind her was a rainbow or sunrise, I couldn't tell which. Across the back in big letters was "Amazon Vision." For a dyke used to more traditional uniforms and sponsors like "The Hideaway Lounge" or the "Tick Tock Club," this was quite a change.

On game night everyone on our team arrived early. Moonwolf was coach for this game so she was hard at work trying to identify a starting lineup and batting order. Janice and Sandy were gathered around second base trying to hammer the base spike in with a large rock. The rest of the "Amazon Visions" were spread out around the infield in pairs throwing balls back and forth and chatting about the fate of the local women's center since the coordinator came out as a bisexual in last month's newsletter. The requisite woman umpire was pacing off the distance between homeplate and the pitcher's rubber, only we didn't have a rubber so she dragged her toe through the dirt to make a line.

"I Am Womon" had dropped their equipment on the third base side with our team's stuff. The benches along first base were deserted. This seemed odd to me. I was used to the two teams in a softball game sitting on opposite sides of the infield. As I stretched out my hamstrings, I asked Micki about this.

"Some teams feel that sitting on separate sides presents a false division between teams and leads to objectifying the women on the other team. This way we are reminded that we are all one united sisterhood," Micki explained in her solemn way.

"But don't each team's bats and balls and stuff get mixed up too? Is there room for everyone to sit down?" I asked. This sitting together with the other team felt wrong to me. I'd been able to roll with a lot of strange stuff to play softball here, but this was too much.

"Well, new players sometimes take awhile to root out the ways male-identified sports have conditioned us to view the other team as an enemy. This is a more collaborative way," Micki replied.

I shook my head. I'd have to think this one over. I put on my glove and trotted out to take infield practice.

Finally, we were about to begin the game. Since we were the home team, we took the field and Joan, with her pile of balls beside her, threw grounders to the infield. Then the first batter for "I Am Womon" came to the plate. Our pitcher, Tina, was accurate, consistent, and really slow. On a humid night when the air is heavy, I didn't think the ball would make it to the plate. As it was, her pitches spun toward the catcher's glove barely reaching home plate before dropping in the dirt like they had rolled off a table. No worries here about being asked to slow down. The result was pretty interesting. The batter, the catcher, and the umpire all seemed to lean toward the incoming ball on each pitch willing it to stay in the air long enough to be hittable.

As it turned out Tina's pitching was pretty difficult for "I Am Womon" to hit . . . for most of the game. We were ahead 2–0 going into the seventh. Now, this game wasn't anything pretty, but we were having fun and, though I knew they wouldn't admit it, our team of "noncompetitive" players wanted to win . . . badly. Apparently they hadn't won many games in seasons past, so the experience of being ahead was new and a little dizzying. They could smell a victory.

When "I Am Womon" scored two runs in the top of the seventh to tie it up, Moonwolf gathered us together as we got ready to go to bat for the final time. We all stood huddled in our lavender T-shirts looking expectantly at our coach.

She said, "Come on, Amazons, let's get some hits!"

I looked around the circle. Everyone looked flushed, eyes blazing. I smiled. This was starting to feel like the kind of softball I was familiar with. We all put our hands in the center in a pile and shouted, "Hits and runs" three times.

Micki was up first. She hit the first pitch, a short chopper to the shortstop who snagged it and threw the ball to first. One out. Micki looked back at our team with an apology on her face. We all shouted stuff like, "Nice try, Mick," and "No problem, team."

Morningdew was up next. I don't mean to be unsisterly, but, take my word, Morningdew was not the woman you wanted to see at the plate in this situation. She walked to the plate and took her position in the box. Then she reached down with her bat and tapped home plate three times. She waited for the pitch in an awkward-looking crouch, the bat resting on her shoulder. Well, here comes the second out, I predicted to myself. Morningdew watched the first pitch.

"Strike one!" called the ump.

Morningdew took two practice swings and settled in at the plate again. Both teams were yelling appropriately supportive cheers to teammates. The ump and catcher crouched for the pitch. Morningdew spun in a circle as she aimed her bat at the ball. Unfortunately, there was a foot of air between the ball and bat. "Strike two!" called the ump.

The catcher threw the ball back to the pitcher and everyone regrouped for the next pitch. It came toward Morningdew—she swung and made partial contact. The ball skittered lazily down the third base line. The third basewoman, the pitcher, and the catcher converged on the ball, hovering over it as they willed it to roll foul. At first, Morningdew stood rooted in the batter's box, looking at her bat in surprise.

"Amazon Vision" erupted from the bench, "Run, run, Morningdew!" She jumped toward first as if we'd goosed her.

Meanwhile the catcher, realizing that the ball was going to die in fair territory, snatched it up and threw it toward the first basewoman's outstretched glove. Sensing the approaching ball, Morningdew ran the last few feet to the bag bent over with her arms wrapped over her head for protection. She reached for the bag with her foot and, forgetting that she could overrun first, fought the momentum of her body to maintain her position. The first basewoman caught the ball. Morningdew was safe. We yelled and cheered. Morningdew looked somewhat dazed as she realized that she was actually a base runner. We had the winning run on first and Gerry coming to the plate.

Gerry was a pretty good hitter, so things were looking good. The evening air was thick with tension. Both teams shouted encouragement to themselves. Anything was possible here.

Gerry worked the pitcher to a full count, then hit a fly ball to short leftfield. The leftfielder moved under the ball and made the catch. Two outs. Suddenly our whole team realized with horror that Morningdew was standing on second base looking very pleased with herself.

"Go back, go back to first!" we yelled.

Our whole team was on our feet, pointing at first base. Morningdew looked puzzled now. She took a step back toward first and looked at us questioningly.

We all nodded and screamed, "Yes, yes, go back!"

Morningdew shrugged and took off toward first. Meanwhile, the leftfielder was so surprised to see the ball in her glove that she had spent these few minutes jumping up and down in celebration until she realized that her team was yelling at her to throw the ball back to first. She hurriedly made the throw.

Morningdew staggered into first and cowered on the bag with her arms wrapped around her head again. The ball whistled over the first basewoman's outstretched glove. There was a beat of silence and then we began jumping up and down screaming at Morningdew.

"Run, run, go back to second!" We all pointed at second and waved our arms.

Morningdew, looking thoroughly confused, covered her head, and ran back toward second. Morningdew reached the bag and looked to the bench as if to ask, "Is this right?" We nodded and cheered. She smiled and pumped her fist in the air like Arsenio Hall.

OK, two out, bottom of the seventh, score tied, and Tina coming up. Tina can pound the ball, if she can make contact. She strikes out a lot, though. Both teams were quiet. Everyone was concentrating. We all had butterflies. I thought to myself: it doesn't matter what you call it or even how well everyone can play, softball doesn't get much better than this. Two teams down to the final out with the game on the line.

With the count 2–1, Tina unloaded on the next pitch. It was a long fly to left center. Morningdew took off toward third. We all were jumping up and down, winding our arms in circles to signal that she should go home.

"Go home, run, Morningdew!"

The leftfielder took the ball on the hop and fired it immediately toward the plate. The ball and Morningdew were on two different trajectories heading for the same point. I covered my eyes: this was going to be close.

The catcher stood over the plate reaching for the ball. The umpire stood to the side, her eyes glued on the catcher. The shouting of both teams echoed around the field. Then an amazing thing happened. Morningdew slid into homeplate. It wasn't pretty, but she did it just as the ball arrived and the catcher swept her glove down for the tag. Homeplate was a cloud of dust. The sudden silence of both teams fell over the field like a blanket. Eighteen pairs of eyes looked to the umpire.

She stood motionless blinking into the clearing dust. Morningdew lay on her back looking up, her face hopeful. The catcher, having fallen back on her fanny after the tag, sat with the ball in her glove, her eyes riveted on the umpire's face. Finally, the umpire looked up from the tangle of bodies at her feet and shrugged her shoulders.

"Who knows? I couldn't see with all the dust."

At first, there was a lot of yelling as our team tried to convince the umpire that Morningdew was safe and the other team tried to convince her that Morningdew was out. To be honest, I don't think anyone really knew for sure, even the catcher and Morningdew. Finally, someone suggested that we just leave it a tie and go have a beer together. So we did.

After I got home that night, I realized what a good time I'd had. Everything was still a little odd and I knew there was still a lot I didn't understand about playing softball in Northampton. The rest of the team wanted to pick hand signals, though, and start putting coaches on first and third when we were up at bat. This was hopeful.

Also, I had to hand it to Morningdew—she was tougher than I'd thought to slide into home like that. And Moonwolf turned out to be the biggest surprise of all. We all went to her place later to process the experience. When I went into her kitchen to get another beer, I saw our game schedule stuck to her fridge with a woman symbol magnet. She had filled in the score for our game with "I Am Womon." It read 3–2, us.

Part 6

SEX AND
OTHER GAMES

THE EX-GIRLFRIENDS

Kris Kovick

IT'S HOW YOU PLAY THE GAME

Roxxie

Some people in gay leagues go to check out other players as much as the sport itself," says Tommy Windsor, a bowler in Atlanta. Small wonder. On lesbian and gay teams nationwide, every teammate is a potential lover. In fact, in some sports, so much happens off court, it's amazing the games ever get played. How much sex do athletes have with their teammates? Is teammate dating a high-risk sport? If your New Year's resolution involves taking up athletics, consider some sporting side effects.

Teammates give a whole new meaning to the term *togetherness*. They practice many times a week, sweat, share equipment, slap each other's butts, compare bruises and aching muscles, shower, and eat together. Frequently they even know what color underwear other players wear. Some players spend so much time together, fellow team members are often the only people they get to know.

Yet secrecy cloaks many of the sexual relationships among team members. Dede Ketover, of the Boston lesbian softball team No Sweat, recalls that "the center fielder and the third base player were having a secret affair. They told us after the season was over. Our feelings were hurt because they hadn't told us sooner."

Members of the San Francisco Bay Area's SheHawks, a mostly lesbian rugby team, have created a "cone of silence" ritual to keep secrets when they travel to tournaments. A special gesture (players clasp their hands together in a triangular shape and hold them above their heads) invokes the cone of silence. "It gives players carte blanche to be a slut, asshole, philanderer, or flirt," explains team player Lisa Leal.

Revealing any secret from the cone of silence is taboo and just cause for a disciplinary trip to the SheHawks Infamous Touring Side (SHITS) court. SHITS punishment is often humorous but seldom humiliating. "One player who revealed a cone-of-silence secret to another player's girlfriend was banned from talking to any

206

teammate's girlfriend for a season," explains Leal. "We really look forward to the cone of silence. Mostly it covers stuff we don't want people at home—like our girlfriends—to know about."

"Athletes like to have affairs with other athletes," confirms Robin Stevens, a women's sports appreciator and former managing editor of *Out/Look,* a San Francisco-based lesbian and gay publication. "Sex becomes another athletic event: There's the element of understanding that comes from pushing bodies to the limits, working out together, being into your own body, and liking other bodies."

"There is a tremendous amount of cruising the rookies," notes Art Quick, a member and organizer of the New Orleans volleyball team the Tired Queens. "It promotes a lot of . . . um . . . camaraderie. On tournaments, there is more serious cruising. The lovers who don't play volleyball know that's not a good thing, so often they come along too. It keeps our players more focused on the sport. But many people play better after a first-time sexual encounter. I think it's because of the high, the conquest, the thrill of the 'success' sitting on the side of the court watching you."

For some athletes, the actual playing of the sport is a sexual fantasy come true. Boston touch football devotee Tony Watson says, "Football is erotic and laced with homosexuality. The boys are cute, and they are out there sweating! Everybody fights over who gets to play center."

Watson was brought up by a strict Southern Baptist grandmother who wouldn't allow him to play football. "My grandmother thought football was sinful," he explains. "I grew up with sexual fantasies of playing football and taking the Lord's name in vain. Playing on a Sunday afternoon makes it even worse."

Robert Weaver, a Honolulu-based board member of the Federation of Gay Games and an organizer for the Organization of Hawaiian Amateur Neighboring Athletes, says, "Libido and adrenaline are very similar chemicals. Naturally, there will be some cruising because of higher sex drives. It is well-known throughout the professional sports world that pro athletes are very active sexually. I think there is a strong connection, but it isn't unique to gay and lesbian sports. I know that in the straight community, where I played sports for years before I came out, there was just as much screwing."

The downside of such close team interaction comes when players' love relationships don't work out, but they are still stuck together on the team. There are horror stories of teams falling apart because of too many breakups among players in which other teammates take sides. There have been cases in which ex-lovers decide who gets what night of practice or, in a messy divorce, who leaves the team.

"Up to 40 percent of gays and lesbians live in rural areas," notes Jeff Pintor, a member of the Madison Dairy Queens, a Madison, Wisconsin, volleyball team. "And sports may be their only outlet. You hear about ex-lovers in Chicago or Milwaukee dividing up teams in the divorce. But in a small town, there may not be a different team to play on if things don't work out."

The Oakland Follies, a largely lesbian soccer team in Northern California, created rules to counteract the negative effect of lovers' quarrels on the playing field. Says Follies member Lyanne Miller: "The first rule is, Don't sleep with anyone on the team. The second is, If you are sleeping with anyone on the team, don't break up. But we still break all the rules. And the question often comes up, Who has slept with the most women on the team?"

"In any sport you must be aware that when you cross *that* line, it can affect the whole team's play," says Sara Lewinstein, a San Francisco-based board member of the Federation of Gay Games. "Because sports is how so many people meet each other, you can't put rules on it. Everyone has his or her own opinion."

Canadian John Goodwin, a former world-class rower profiled in Brian Pronger's book *The Arena of Masculinity,* found that at world-level competitions, he was focused exclusively on the sport. He explains, "You have to be really crazy and fanatical to win. It puts you on a one-track course. When you really go for it, everything else falls to the side."

"When we were young," says No Sweat's Ketover, "all the wildness, recklessness, and carelessness hardly affected our playing. We were all nuts and in the bars every night. As we've gotten older, we're more focused on stretching the muscles and getting them to play ball. Will she still catch the ball? is the big question for us old fogies, not, Who's sleeping with whom?"

On the other hand, Alison Pappe, a Berkeley, California, rugby player, volleys, "Go with your feelings and emotions. If you have a crush on a team member, go for it!"

FROM THE SIDELINES

Robbi Sommers

Sports Enthusiastic? Me? Well . . . I suppose so. No, I don't play soccer. Baseball, volleyball, basketball? No. So what *do* I play? I play rough. I play hardball. I play with the best. Sport erotics, that's my game.

Oh yeah, act like you don't know what I'm talking about. Act like you go to those games to watch a ball be smacked by a stick or tossed over a net. Nothing like that kind of excitement? Yeah, right.

I tell the truth about athletic events. A sport is a sport, wherever it's played. Doesn't make much difference to me. Whether on a field or in a gym—tie a bandana around a woman's head, show off her thighs in a pair of shorts, tease me with her biceps in a short-sleeved shirt and that's what I call a good game.

Take baseball. Tough-faced, with a jock swagger that could knock me from the bleachers, the batter approaches the plate. Shoulders back, attitude seeping like thick honey, the woman means business. Damn. If she's got that much intensity on the field, imagine what she'd be like in bed.

I watch her tap the bat against her cleats. Her weight shifts from foot to foot and her hips rock slightly. Nice ass, great ass, she bends slightly and does a warm-up swing. She's serious, all right. It's written all over her face. I like a woman with a one-track mind; a woman who can focus on the subject at hand.

I visualize myself across from her with a pitcher's mitt. High heels, garter belt, a bright red baseball hat—sure, I know about uniforms. She looks me straight in the eye with fierce, butch concentration. I toss her a pouty little smile. *You ready for a curve ball?*

Her eyes drop from mine and skim my tight, thin tank top. Strike one. I'm looking good, I'm looking fine.

Nervous, caught off-guard, she shoots me a lucky-break smirk. I spread my legs slightly. My high heels pierce the dirt, the tank top rides high on my midriff. Strike two.

Yeah baby, oh baby. I'm hot now. A harsh edge replaces the batter's smirk. She doesn't like my sassy attitude? I don't care. Let her come to the pitcher's mound if she's got a problem with me. Let her come right up and show me what she wants, show me exactly how she'd like me to do it for her.

Last inning, last chance. The score is tied. A tense silence blankets the crowd. Women in the stands, women on the sidelines— they all have their eyes on me. Can I do it again? Can I bring her to her knees?

The sweet scent of desire swirls from the batter and surrounds me in a sudden heat. Unbridled power spills from her strong arms, her thick hands, her muscular thighs. Our eyes lock. She's ready for it. She's hungry for it.

I caress the baseball against my smooth fingers and consider her firm breasts. An immediate compulsion to drop the ball, rush to home plate and press my desperate hands against her overwhelms me.

Breaking rules, playing dirty, she looks at me with fire in her eyes. It's clear she could take me. It's clear she could suck me dry. Dizzy, disoriented, I hold the ball close to my face. I focus, zero in on the imaginary line between us. Sparks dart from her eyes, her mouth, her fingertips.

She has me. She has me good. I throw the ball. It slices the air and the crowd begins to roar. Let her run. Let her go wherever she wants. I drop the mitt, I head toward first base. If she slides, let her ram into me. I can take it hard. I can take it as hard as she can give it.

The ball soars across the field and she leaps, as though in slow motion, to first base, second, then third. Her thighs are tight with power, her arms grab through the hot, summer air.

C'mon. C'mon. C'mon.

An explosion of pleasure races through me. Her ass is taut. Her eyes, determined. Into home she slides. I want her more than anything. I'd do anything to have her. I snap from my fantasy and hurry toward the field.

Yes! Yes! Yes! That's it, baby. That's it!

Dust on her shirt, sweat on her face, she sees me, dressed to kill, on the sidelines.

"Need something cool?" I ask sweetly as I offer her a soft drink.

She nods her head and smiles.

Home run, for both of us.

And therein lies the concept of sport erotics. From start to finish, you'll find me at all the games. After all, I play hardball. I play with the best. I play to win.

Sure, I go to the gym. Sure, I work out. On the weight bench, wet with sweat—that's where you'll find me. Lift free weights? Leg curls and extensions? Not quite. After all, I'm a true sport's woman, I know the score.

Lie down, press hard and then get pumped. That *is* the idea, isn't it? Who needs three sets of twenty reps to accomplish that? Not me, not since Ace.

Ace works Thursday evenings. She trains the novices. Yeah, I'm a beginner—looking for a work-out, looking to get wet. I walk in and sign up. My hot pink spandex outfit clings to my full curves and I can see a glimmer of approval in Ace's eyes.

Oh please, tell me you don't understand what I'm talking about. *Sure . . . we all wear spandex for maximum workout ease.* Yeah, right.

Only thinking of work-out ease, I strut in skin-tight hot-pink to the barbells. What a *big* surprise . . . Ace, most probably thinking how easy a work-out I'll be, is there in less than a spandex-snap second.

"So, how much experience you got?" she says, her voice as sultry as the summer night.

What do you say when a rock-hard butch asks a question like that? I glance at her bulging biceps, her thick thighs, her firm hands. *Plenty, baby.*

"Not much," I answer coyly.

She looks me up and down. "You lookin' to tighten up or build?"

I focus on her bodybuilding fingers and murmur, "I guess I want to be tight."

"Gettin' women tight, that's my specialty," Ace says, attitude seeping from every pore.

That's when I start wondering why I had wasted so much goddamn time hanging around the baseball field the last month or so. Shit, when it comes to athletics, a smart sports enthusiast has to have her priorities straight.

"Got to warm you up first." Ace points to an exercycle. "Ten minutes."

I climb on the bike and start to pedal. Ace loses no time picking up a barbell and doing some reps. Standing before the full-length mirror, her muscles are firm, her stance steady, she looks good.

Beads of sweat tickle on my brow. One minute on the bike and I'm already sweating.

Ace tosses me a quick look. "You gettin' warm?"

"Yeah," I pant. I try to look nonchalant, like this goddamn bike is no big deal. Sweat starts seeping from under my arms. Perspiration on my brand-new outfit, son of a bitch.

"This is a leg press," Ace says as she straddles a machine bench.

She's faceup, legs bent in the air. From where I sit, I can almost see up her baggy gym shorts . . . and I thought spandex was the only way to go!

Was this bike set on uphill, or what? I'm drenched with sweat, pushing harder on the pedals and Ace lies, legs up and out, across from me.

"Works the thighs," she grunts as she extends her legs.

My sudden view up her shorts disappears. I lean forward and pedal faster, as if somehow, if I hurry, I'd get a better peek.

Ace's legs resume their original, out and spread position. I'm whirling on the bike. Racing on the bike. Closer and closer. Yeah, if I look just right, if I angle just so, I'll see up those shorts—those deliciously loose shorts.

My feet fly on the pedals. Sweat drips from my face. I'm so close I can almost see everything Ace has to offer. Her nipples stand erect beneath her thin white T-shirt. Her dark hair is plush under her panty-free gym shorts.

I make a sudden commitment to work out three, no four, no five, times a week. Ace spreads her legs wider and I, leaning over the handlebars, zoom toward heaven. Oh shit, I can see everything. Faster, faster, I race alongside her.

C'mon, Ace. Keep them spread, Ace.

I grip the handle bars. I'll shoot through space if I let go.

Yeah, Ace. Yeah, Ace. Let me see it all.

I'm soaking wet. I'm sliding back and forth on the thick bicycle seat. *I'll work out everyday, two times a day, three times a day— just don't move your legs, Ace.*

Out of nowhere a tiny bell rings. Ace climbs from the leg press and clicks off the exercycle timer.

"Good warm up, huh?" She runs her fingertip across the sweat on my face then down my neck to my breast.

Yeah, I think I'm going to like getting pumped.

They dragged me to their impromptu soccer game last Sunday morning. What I told them—before they forced me out of the warmth of my bed and into their car—is that I couldn't understand what a group of women were doing, up at the crack of dawn, out in the cold, kicking a ball across a wet field. Like I'm the only one who went out Saturday nights? Like I'm the only one who wants to sleep in one lousy day a week?

I said no way. I work out at the gym three times a week, I get my exercise there. But my buddies, playing on my well-known weakness for sporting events—*okay, they hinted that Evelyn Anderson was known to ref these games*—talked me into it.

Evelyn "the butch" Anderson? . . . Shit, I figured I could sacrifice one Sunday morning for the good of the team. I said okay, one game, and one game only.

My damn alarm went on the blink Sunday and they showed up, pulling me out of bed at eight-fifteen. I barely had time to pull my hair into a ponytail.

"What point is there in playing when you don't look your best?" I complained dismally, thinking that perhaps a minor femme tantrum would buy me enough time to dampen and blow-dry my hair.

Ginger tossed me shorts and a sweatshirt from my drawer as Kim pulled me away from the mirror. No one seemed interested in my perspective. Am I the only woman who understands the value of sexual distraction as a game strategy? Perplexed, I shook my head.

Within minutes, we were out of my apartment and piling into the car. As we raced over the bumpy back roads, I did my best to apply mascara and gloss. Things were going progressively downhill—hair in a ponytail, poor makeup lighting. I traced my lips with liner as best as I could and blotted them on Kim's matchbook cover.

I glanced one last time into the mirror. Eyes okay, lips looked full. All things considered, I could hold my own. Contemplating game strategy and the fact that a very hot Evelyn Anderson was calling the shots, I added a touch more blush. Well, if nothing else, at least *I* was looking out for the team.

We got to the field and stood around in the damp cold twenty minutes waiting for everyone to show. And worse than that, Evelyn Anderson was nowhere to be seen. Early Sunday morning and I'm standing in grass, out in the middle of nowhere, like I'm waiting for a goddamn bus.

Hell, I hadn't even had a chance to pee before they had hauled me out of bed and tossed me in the car. I headed toward the rest rooms. Not paying much attention, I stepped in an unlocked stall, only to find myself face to face with none other than Evelyn Anderson.

"Oh, god, I'm sorry," I mumbled, embarrassed. "The door was unlocked . . . I thought it was . . ." I turned to exit the small booth.

From behind, Evelyn grabbed me by the sweatshirt and pulled me close. "Playing soccer today?" Her voice was a seductive whisper.

"Wha . . . well, yes," I stammered, caught off guard. My back was against her breasts. I didn't move.

"Wanna win?" She purred like a hungry cat. Her cold hand pushed beneath my sweatshirt.

I considered the team—the joy of winning, the agony of defeat. *Of course we wanted to win. What kind of question was that for a sports-minded woman like myself?* Evelyn's breath was hot on my neck, her hand only inches from my tingling nipples.

She tugged my ponytail. "Well, Ms. Soccer girl?"

Her hand slid toward my breasts and my heart began to pound.

"Yes," I muttered. "Yes, yes, yes."

Evelyn pushed her fingers beneath my lace bra. My nipples hardened to tight points. She jammed her hands in my shorts and I was suddenly soaked with desire.

"C'mon," she urged. "All the way. All the way to goal."

She rooted me onward. Eyes closed, I raced, I flew, down the field—the ball was mine, the shot was mine, the glory was all mine. And her hand was relentless; her fingers nonstop.

"C'mon," she panted. "C'mon."

"Yeah," I moaned. And her fingers went on and on. She had me now. She had me good. "Yeah, yeah, yeah."

Whistles blew, the crowd roared. I was on my own—sweating, out of breath, faster, faster, faster. With the ref behind me all the way, I let it go with everything I had.

*   *   *

We won Sunday's game. Ginger and Kim were pretty impressed with my enthusiasm. In fact, they asked if I'd be interested in signing on this season with the bookstore team. I shook my head. After all, I could see Evelyn Saturday nights.

TOUCHING GOYA:
THUNDER VS. BOMBERS 1992

Kimberly Miller

Any time Thunder plays the Bombers I pray to the Goddess that Goya doesn't hit the ball to me. This is my game and I'm good at it, but since Goya joined the league three years ago my knees go weak whenever she strides to the plate.

She's tall, young, sexy and as cool as a mango in the refrigerator. She doesn't seem to want anything to do with a boring white chick like me, but I foam over her anyway. Last year she said hi to me once and I recorded the moment by taking a mental photo of her standing there in the park, ivory teeth gleaming against her smooth terra-cotta skin. She was warming up before a Bomber game against Las Fuertes, gracefully playing catch with a teammate, her long, slender fingers delicately gripping and releasing the ball. I remember wishing Goya were her glove and I was her softball, leather fitting snugly inside leather.

I must have been drooling when I said hi and smiled back because Goya has not looked at me since. Not one glance when her team beat mine in the final regular-season meeting between us last August. Not one word when Thunder went on to victory over the Bombers in the championship game last September. Nothing but chilly silence despite all the usual camaraderie, and even the occasional torrid love affair, between the members of our two teams.

So the Bombers were winning by a few runs in the middle of our game last Wednesday night. They had a runner at first and a runner at second. There was one out. Ann was pitching well and I was confident Thunder would pull together to turn the game around.

On any other night I'd be out in center field, breathing nervously and trying to concentrate, remembering with each pitch what I would do if the ball came to me. But tonight was special. I had inserted myself at first base because Laura, our regular first base

216

player, was at school, acing her final exam. When Goya stepped up to bat, I was playing behind the runner and close to the line, a position I would take up against any decent lefty.

Ann looked around and reminded the infielders that the play was to third. She inspired us to be calm and play with poise, assuring us all that we could get an out and quell this Bomber threat.

In an attempt to focus my mind on absolutely nothing but softball, softball, softball, I squinted my eyes just slightly and tried to relax. My gaze settled casually upon that magical space above home plate, between the batter's knees and sweaty armpits, extending out toward the pitcher's mound to define the area where all the action in a game originates. It is the zone of emptiness that shimmers and shifts the most on hot, hazy, sweltering days. It is a column of air untouched, unbothered until a twentysomething-ounce aluminum shaft slices through it to meet or miss the offered pitch. It is the area I carefully patrol with my vision in the hopes of getting a good jump on any batted ball.

When batters hit the first pitch they do the opposing team a huge favor. There's less time to think, less time to worry, less time to overstrategize and fewer times crouching into the ready position. Goya dug in and ran the count to three and two.

The sixth pitch hit her level swing and bounced right toward me. In a flash the runners headed for second and third, the ball disappearing for a moment behind a cleated shoe of the woman vacating my base. When I caught sight of it again it was visibly slowing due to Parks Department neglect. The infield grass had not been cut in perhaps ten days.

I moved in and to my right and backhanded the weakening grounder, thinking that a good throw would catch the lead runner at third. But a quick glance there confirmed my fears that it would be too late. Our only hope for an out rested in my glove. I could step on first base and be clinical about it. Goya would be dead before she even got two thirds of the way there.

Or I could run in and touch Goya.

Run in and actually unite a part of me with a part of her. Create a brief moment when our actions would merge, would blend. Force her to acknowledge my ability.

My confidence.

My existence.

The decision was simple. Her lithe and muscular body raced

gracefully toward me and for an instant we were both in a slow-motion perfume commercial. An orchestra was playing Ravel and poppies were gently swaying in a balmy southern breeze. I squeezed the ball tightly and brushed my glove against her left hip, a current of sexual energy instantly reverberating between us. Our eyes met and the air temperature in Brooklyn momentarily and undetectedly rose to 98.6°F. No one felt it except Goya and me.

The umpire shouted, "Out at first," bringing the game back into focus. I left Goya in her grinning reverie and ran toward home plate to make sure the runner at third stayed where she was. It was only after I tossed the ball to Ann and asked for time that I was able to enjoy the adrenaline rush to my chest and the creamy, pulsing feeling between my legs.

The next batter popped up to short and the half-inning ended. Eventually, the game ended too. The final score was Bombers 7, Thunder 1. In the postgame line to shake hands I gave Goya a warm smile and a high five. "Good game," I said as a cloud of infield dust erupted from between our meeting palms. But Goya was already cool again. Cool, like a mango in the refrigerator.

Roxxie

They love big hair, women, cool jerseys, and skates. They make things travel at speeds of 80 miles per hour and they wear tons of padding. They believe big hair and big muscles should go together. Their worst fear is a groin pull, so they're always stretching "down there." They define themselves as, "BEE•Hive (be'hiv'), n. lesbian on skates with *Big Hair* and a penchant for black rubber."

With female hockey players making national news by breaking into the men's pro leagues, a new national trend of female interest and participation in ice hockey has taken off. Even women who love big hair are drawn to this helmet-mandatory sport. The Boston Beehives, a lesbian ice hockey team, even sport T-shirts with an ultrafemme icon—a big-haired woman powdering herself in the mirror. Why are so many women of all hair types drawn to this fast-moving, well-padded sport?

This pressing question drove *GirlJock Magazine* to find the behind-the-scenes story about Boston's Beehives, big hair, pads, and lesbian skating action.

GirlJock Reporter Roxxie: What stylistically separates you from other hockey teams?

Beehive Maria Vetrano, Queen Bee: And we're not talking ice dancing, here. We are babes on blades who fire a puck 80 miles an hour. We are women of the blue line. We love ice rinks, hockey sticks, cool jerseys, women, and big hair. I suppose you could say we have a sense of camp, because, unlike your typical team, with names like "Sharks" or "Chargers" or "Barbarians" or whatever, we are the "Beehives," and we want to play hockey and exploit humor at the same time. Why should gay men have the corner on camp?

R: Good question. What does it take to become a Beehive? Do you have special initiation rituals?

M: Well, if a new player were six feet tall with nineteen-inch hair, we'd roll out the red carpet for her. We'd probably be so distracted we couldn't even practice. She wouldn't need an initiation ritual; some of us might even kowtow to her. Now, if a more typical-sized player wanted to join the Beehives, we would ask her about her political affiliations and make sure she wasn't a vegetarian. No really, we'd ask how long she'd played hockey, what her favorite colors are, has she ever wounded anyone with a slapshot . . .

R: *Do you recruit musical players as well?*

M: YES! Beehives love to sing and otherwise carry on. We could always use more Divas. When we were in Montreal last April for the first Gay & Lesbian North American Hockey Challenge, we won the Talent Competition.

R: *What did you perform?*

M: An original spin-off of "Mr. Sandman" and customized version of "It Had to Be You," which we sang to my friend, Al, who was wearing a wig, heels, and one of my mother's dresses. He looked like a very butch Patsy Cline with facial hair.

We sang before and after practices, we sang walking down the street, we sang at the Montreal talent competition—that was actually pretty competitive, what with a men's team from LA being there and all. We even sang at Boston's Gay & Lesbian Pride Parade in June.

R: *So what's the hockey like on your team? How competitive are you?*

M: We have a mixed-level team. Some players will go on to the U.S. Nationals this year, some are moderately competitive and experienced. Almost all of us play every week in one of the Boston women's leagues and one coaches girls' prep ice hockey.

R: *What are the main hockey injuries and how do you avoid them?*

M: Well, the one which I detest the absolute most and can be very limiting, shall we say, is the groin pull. If you're skating a lot, it's important to stretch the groin—or say good-bye to your love life during hockey season. Knee injuries, like ligament strains and pulls, are also fairly common. I've seen some nasty things over the years—broken collarbones and one broken pelvis—but those are few and far between.

R: *Can you cruise the other teams during games or is the play too fast?*

M: It's very hard to cruise someone who's wearing a helmet. It's not like the old NHL days when players skated around *sans* head protection. So, you really can't see anyone's face in great detail. Maybe her skating style and puck handling will drive you crazy, who knows? Cruising is usually reserved for pregame and postgame celebrations. At the postgame party in Montreal, some of our players engaged in mega-adult "Truth or Dare"; more than one of us walked up to the opposition, delivering kisses on mouths and navels.

R: Did drag queens influence the evolution of your "big hair" style, or was it a leftover from childhood?

M: Drag queens, no. Doris Day, yes. The big hair thing flies in the face of how hockey players usually define themselves—macho, virile, all of that. Beehives are a contradiction in terms: we are silly women with a femmy icon who can REALLY play hockey.

R: Of all hair options, why big hair?

M: Because we get sick of cruising cute blond boys on the street, having mistaken them for women. We think big hair AND big muscles go together.

R: Do you keep "big hair" when you play?

M: No, it wouldn't fit under our helmets—and it would look really terrible after a game of hockey. "Big hair" is a way of life—a Beehive mentality. We are "big hair," so we don't always have to wear it. We do have some official wigs, though, and one of our be-wigged players once metamorphosed into a suburban housewife while we weren't looking. It's a sad story. We now call her Louise. Last I know, she was buying a Volvo. Tragic.

R: Do fans wear wigs?

M: Only our male ones, for some reason. I guess our female ones are too concerned with catching our attention. Unlike the other team, they're not wearing helmets. So we can see them quite well. Our fans also perform a Beehive cheer of sorts—it's called the "Beehive Buzz." When a Beehive scores a goal or a Beehive goalie makes a great save, they do this buzzing thing. This happened in Montreal. Unfortunately, some of the Montreal fans caught on and they started spraying our fans with imaginary RAID. It wasn't pretty.

R: Do drag queens get jealous of your wigs or hockey drag?

M: The drag queens again! Are your best friends drag queens? We've never had any protests by drag queens or anything—and I think they have fancier wigs. As for our hockey drag—it's not the most attractive garb in the world, although some women do seem to look hot in it. I don't think a drag queen would be caught dead in a hockey uniform. It doesn't have any sequins.

R: *So, what does your uniform look like?*

M: We aim for classic line and color—we have white jerseys with black line art. The art is of a Beehive woman in uniform on skates. We also have matching socks and some of us wear lipstick under our helmets.

R: *How do you Bees get ready for games?*

M: We usually sing in the locker room in a little pregame psyche-up ritual. Sometimes we also hum the theme from "Mission Impossible." We've only sang on the ice once, but look forward to more opportunities in the future.

R: *Are bigger hockey sticks more macho, or are hockey sticks all the same size?*

M: Some sticks are more macho than others—they're called goalie sticks. I'm one of the Beehives' goalies, but I'm not feeling that macho right now, so I'm learning defense.

Goalie sticks are much larger. They're designed for deflecting shots; forward sticks (used by defense, wings, and centers) are designed for shooting and controlling the puck. Some players are more "macha" than others, but that's got nothing to do with the sticks.

R: *What kind of padding do hockey players wear and where does it go?*

M: Well, I think I'll start with forward equipment; it's easier to explain. Forwards wear pants, knee/shin guards, shoulder/breast pads, pelvic protectors (more important than you know!), elbow pads, gloves, helmets, and skates. Goalies wear all the padding they can get their hands on. Sometimes they look like Michelin Tire Women on skates. Goalies wear special pants, big leg pads that extend from their lower thighs to their skates, pelvic protectors, goalie skates, arm and chest pads, special gloves—a blocker and a catcher, and a helmet with a throat protector. Goalies don't travel as fast as forwards.

R: *While wearing full hockey uniforms, can you tell the difference between a man and a woman? A butch and femme?*

M: You can't always tell the difference between men and women. It's those helmets again. If Mary Stuart Masterson wore one, I wouldn't even recognize her—and that would be terrible.

So, you can't always tell gays and lesbians apart, either. There are some excellent lesbian and gay male (not drag queens) ice hockey players. One of the guys on the Montreal team used to play in the NHL, and he didn't wear a helmet. He also had a mustache. I knew HE wasn't a woman! As for butches and femmes, it's like I said before. We're all butch and we're all femme. Almost all. One of our players, Donna, is really pretty femme. If she lost her Lancôme, all hell would break loose.

R: *What are good ways to stay in shape for hockey?*

M: Biking, stairmaster, racquetball, weight training, jogging (if your knees are okay) are all good. Hockey requires both strength and speed, sprints and endurance. It's flavorful, yet piquant—know what I mean?

R: *Will there ever be women's professional ice hockey?*

M: I don't know. Will there ever be women's professional basketball or softball? Both of those games have more participants nationwide. Even men's hockey isn't as big a sport as baseball or basketball, so I don't think that women's hockey will be one of the first (other than golf, tennis, or beach volleyball), to go professional. Also, one of the sick things about men's professional hockey is the contact—checking and fighting. These things are not (generally) part of the women's game. I think that women will have professional hockey when all the homophobes and most of the men are sent to Idaho to live. When our neo-Amazonian society is in place, then women will have professional hockey. I'm hoping that will be soon.

There's a woman goalie who's playing professionally now, and I think she's the first woman to ever get a real contract with a pro team. Her name is Manon Rheaume, she's only twenty years old, and she's a native of Quebec. On September 23rd of this year, she was the first woman EVER to play in a major league men's professional game. She played one period (that's twenty minutes, not five days) for the Tampa Bay Lightning, an NHL expansion team run by Phil Esposito. After the game, she signed a three-year contract with the Atlanta Knights, the Lightning's International Hockey League affiliate (minor league team).

R: *Do you think she'd like to be a Beehive?*

M: I think she's straight, and a lesbian team wouldn't be the place for her. Besides, she's much more serious than we are. I would love to see her play. Any Beehive in her right mind would.

One of our coaches, S.T., who's an excellent goalie in her own right, ran out and bought Manon Rheaume's rookie card. She was psyched. We all were.

    R: What would you say to Manon Rheaume, if you could?

    M: I'd say (in perfect Canadian French), "It's an honor to meet you. Your accomplishments and your courageousness are awesome. . . . Hey, you're cute. Have you met my friend, Louise?"

BEEHIVE LORE AND HERSTORY

The Beehive Mission: 1) To woo women from the (softball) mounds of their experience and bring them into a cold, but thrilling alternative world; 2) To prove that big hair, lesbian camp, Doris Day, and ice hockey are all inextricably linked; 3) To confuse the hell out of JoAnn Loulan, who would run around us till blurry eyed trying to figure if we're femmy butches, butchy femmes, or in a third, heretofore, undefined class of our very own.

The Birth of the Beehives: The Beehives were conceived in a kitchen by a core group of women who had just spent their last twenty Sunday nights playing against straight men in a dreary Hyde Park league. The motivating factors? A burning desire to design a hockey jersey with some panache (they were too, too tired of wearing things like Sharks, Bears, and Flames emblazoned on their chests and were starving to make a fashion statement) and a deadline to enter the first Montreal North American Gay & Lesbian Hockey Challenge in April of 1992. They also wanted to sing in a foreign land.

Beehive Captains: Paula Stanton, an athletic goddess and former Olympic luger, and Whitney Robbins, a scoring sensation and talented artist/photographer.

Beehive Pastimes: Ice Hockey, singing, stand-up, and girl watching. Also, shopping and politics. Okay, okay, world peace, too.

Beehive Song Selection: The Beehives have sung versions of "I'm Too Sexy" (only two brave ones did that) and "I'm a Beehive" ("I'm a Wanderer"),* but their most famous songs are the following two:

Spoken words are strategically interjected throughout the song; you'd have to hear us in person to get the whole picture.

THE BEEHIVE BUZZ (sung to "Mr. Sandman")

Bum bum bum bum bum bum bum bum bum bum bum bum
bum
Bum bum bum bum bum bum bum bum bum bum bum bum
bum
We all love hockey
Oh, don't you know?
Some of us like it fast
Some like it slow
This is our version of gay romancing
We'd rather score a goal than go ice dancing
Bum bum bum bum bum bum bum bum bum bum bum bum
bum
Bum bum bum bum bum bum bum bum bum bum bum bum
bum

I met this player
I dreamed for weeks
She once played defense
For the Nordiques
Her hair was golden
And it was real high
I almost fainted when she skated by me
Bum bum bum bum bum bum bum bum bum bum bum bum
bum
Bum bum bum bum bum bum bum bum bum bum bum bum
bum

We won't let you score
At least not on the ice
And we'll cross-check you
If you're not nice
We speak your language
Ooo La La, chou chou
We can say French fries and pommes frittes, too
Bum bum bum bum bum bum bum bum bum bum bum bum
bum

Bum bum bum bum bum bum bum bum bum bum bum bum
    bum

That's why you see a smile on our face(s)
We think Quebec is one heck of a place
So now that you all know we're queer
Can we play you ev-e-ry year?
Bum bum bum bum bum bum bum bum bum bum bum bum
    bum

(Originally sung to the French Canadian teams in Montreal.)

IT HAD TO BE YOU*

It had to be you
I tripped over the blue
Stick handled around
And finally found
Someone to pass to

I took a wrist shot
I thought it looked hot
It traveled so fast
It sailed right past
The goalie was blue

Some players I've seen
Might be called obscene
They slash at your head
Don't care if you're dead
They border on mean

But at no other rink
Will you ever find
A gay team like us
We'll blow more than your mind!
It had to be you, hockey player you, it had to be you

Beehive Goals: To have even bigger hair and to "lick" the competition in the 1994 Gay Games in New York, where we dream of playing tall Scandinavian women named Brigitte and Helga. We *do* hope that a Scandinavian team will show up. We also plan to stage some world premiere musical numbers, including a seriously abbreviated Beehive version of "The Sound of Music" (So, we have a thing for nuns—and Julie Andrews!).

MY FITNESS ROUTINE?

Yvonne Zipter

When I was a kid, staying physically active wasn't a problem. Staying physically still was maybe a problem, but staying active—never. Whenever I was not in school, I was outside playing: running, jumping, climbing trees, biking, tumbling, skate-boarding, pogo-sticking. (I don't want to brag, but I jumped a mean pogo stick in my day.) Now, however, when I'm not at work, I'm writing, cleaning the house, doing laundry, attending meetings, defending women's clinics from the so-called pro-life folks, visiting family and friends, and so on. "Playing" just doesn't fit in quite as naturally as it once did. Then too, I don't have the same love of movement for the sake of movement that I once had. I'm active, and some of my activities could even be described as physical, but I suspect that little of what I do as a matter of course would be described as "exercise"—or else you'd see more vacuum cleaners in the weight room down at the gym.

And exercise has definitely become trendy. It used to be enough to not be fat, but now you have to be svelte and muscular too in order to be "in." Not that I'm all that concerned with being in, mind you. If I were I would hardly have opted to be a lesbian. Although, to look at all the attention Northampton, Massachusetts, has been getting in 1993, you'd think being a lesbian was the hottest new trend since Nehru jackets. But that's another story. Anyway, my concern with exercise is less a matter of wanting to be cool than wanting to avoid ending up like my grandmother who, at age seventy-five, can hardly walk down the hallway without having to stop to rest. But that's what fifteen or twenty years of watching late-night (and late-afternoon and early-evening) TV and a diet of hot dogs will get you. So to guard against such an eventuality, I have chosen to eat a healthy vegetarian diet and to exercise.

However, delay of gratification is not as easy for me as it once was. Knowing that something will be good for me in the long run is not quite enough to make me want to "feel the burn." If something hurts, I want to do whatever I can to make the pain go away—which is usually stopping! So, I have had to resort to trying to trick myself into exercising.

Combining my social needs with my exercise needs—that is, team sports—has historically worked fairly well. The camaraderie usually keeps my mind off of the fact that I'm panting like a dog as I fetch balls of one size or another. Also, knowing that my teammates are depending on me (for what I'm not sure—coffee and doughnuts at Saturday morning practices?) makes me more responsible about keeping my commitment. However, playing first base and maintaining a .100 batting average are not exactly conducive to burning off those calories and honing those muscles.

I once tried taking a jogging class (all right: stop snickering—this was 1978 in *California*), figuring that if I paid money for it, I'd do it. And it worked. As long as the classes continued. My friends who jog always go on and on about how, after you're out there running for a while, you just get into this zone, this meditative state, and it's, like, really beautiful, man. But when I run, the only thing I'm thinking is, When will I be *done?*

So. Having eliminated jogging—along with sports such as football, basketball, and soccer—as a little too aerobic for my clogged bronchioles and schnoz, I have resorted to such less conventional pastimes as the local Y's aqua aerobics class. I tried that for several months, but there was just something a little too frighteningly surreal about slogging through four feet of water with rusty hand weights to the tune of "Pump Up the Jam" with ten middle-aged housewives. And to tell the truth, I sometimes felt a little conspicuous when, arms raised over our heads, we walked in a circle, and I was the only one in the group sporting hairy armpits—except that time when one of the husbands came.

Hailing originally from Milwaukee as I do, I have of course contemplated bowling. But those few mincing steps up to the foul line don't seem very likely to produce a healthy sweat. About the only thing that gets exercised in bowling is your wrist—and not necessarily from releasing the ball. As Anthony once said on an episode of "Designing Women," "Any game where you can eat hot dogs and drink beer while you're playing is not a sport."

My real preference would be to go bicycling, and I do sometimes do that, but not as often as I would like or enough to be truly beneficial. One of my stumbling blocks in this area is that Chicago's streets are terribly inhospitable to cyclists. Not only are there the same hazards as those motorists have to contend with—potholes the size of German shepherds and people who seem to have learned how to drive from playing video games—but there is scant room for vehicles traveling less than 40 mph (and that's on the side streets). So basically, for stress-free riding, one needs to get to a forest preserve, bike path, or park, which isn't a bad thing, if one of those places is nearby. But frankly, I resent having to load one form of transportation onto another before the first is usable. If I wanted to do that, I would have become a trucker, hauling cars in from Detroit. (Which, when you're home nursing a cold under the watchful eye of daytime UHF TV, can start to sound pretty good—"Yeah, now that you mention it, I *am* getting rather tired of sitting at a desk all day. . . .")

Consequently, and being the time-conscious kind of gal that I am, I have arrived at my own safe and efficient exercise routine: I have mounted my bicycle on a stationary trainer and now I ride, ride, ride while watching reruns of Oprah and the sun coming up. But wait: there's more. While a lovely routine in and of itself, I just felt like, darn it, my arms were being neglected. And being the fair-minded woman that I am, I have now taken to storing hand weights on the rack at the back of the bike and, about halfway through my riding, I begin doing bicep curls and the like—all the while continuing to pedal. (It's a little like rubbing your belly and patting your head at the same time.) So yes, it's two—two—two routines in one. I am so taken with this method, in fact, that I've thought about doing a video. . . .

But, realistically, I suppose shots of me in gym shorts and a ratty-looking T with bed-head are just not as appealing, somehow, as, say, Cindy Crawford in a swimsuit. Oh well. So much for fame and fortune. However, I would still maintain that, as goofy as my routine may sound, it way rules over The Thigh Master (which, if you ask me, sounds like something that might have come out of the S & M movement).

Still. . . . There are times—maybe when Oprah's closing theme is playing or after I've seen that annoying commercial for "Full House" one too many times—when I long to have that line drive bouncing off my shins and hear that encouraging cry rise up from my teammates—"Stay with it! Stay with it"—no matter how bruised my shins are or how badly I've misplaced the ball. Something tells me, in fact, that at the end of next summer, when I climb up on that bike again, I'll be doing it with seam marks on my chin. . . .

THE HONEST GOLFER, *or*, WHAT BEGINS WITH A DRIVE AND ENDS WITH A PUTT

Kris Kovick

Once upon a lovely summer afternoon, a woman was teeing up her shot on the first hole of a magnificent green golf course. Before her, eighteen holes of wide fairways, carpets of lawn, and contemplative quiet. She faced the pin boldly and took a long, slow backswing, all the while keeping her eye on the ball between her feet. Back and back the clubhead traveled around her, until she could almost see it in her periphery. She unloaded a twisted swing so savage she sent her golf ball soaring 200 yards off to the right. "Damn slice!" she cursed.

She did not see her ball as she approached her lie in the rough, but after some searching she found it under a rotting branch, and wacked it into the open. "Two," she whispered to herself. Just then she sensed she was not alone. Maybe it was just a chill, for no one appeared in the underbrush. She shivered away the fear, and then she distinctly heard it again, a faint rustling of leaves.

"Hey, ppsst, lady!"

Still she saw no one. It was slightly creepy even though she was armed with a five iron.

"Hey! Down here."

Near the branch where her ball had landed was a sublime vapor that was becoming less ethereal. It was coalescing into a tiny figure, like a genie, although without a lamp.

"Hey! Lady!" the mist roared.

"What can I do for you?" she asked. "Are you lost or do you need help?" And more to the point, "Can I play through you?"

"I am the spirit of the golf course," the apparition began, "but I only appear to the honest golfer."

They both laugh at the oxymoron. As the golf elf transsubstantiated, she saw he had on miniature red and black plaid polyester putees and a houndstooth check sweater. He also wore a matching hat with a knitted puff ball on the top. He looked like a cross between a color blindness test and a Hostess Sno Ball. His clubs were no bigger than match sticks and his balls were BBs. His spikes looked like two shiny black beetles, both terrifying and ridiculous. "Anybody else woulda kicked that ball out from under the bush and never counted it."

"Oh, that," she toyed with the open face of her wedge.

"I am prepared to grant you one wish." The sprite puffed his chest out but it evaporated into a vignette of his ghostly visage.

"Any wish?" the golfer brightened.

"No, you get to choose one of two wishes. You get either perfect sex or perfect golf. You can have anyone, anytime, or the best golf game on earth."

The woman took a step closer to the genie. "You mean just one perfect game or each time I play I shoot championship golf?"

"Each time, or you can fuck anyone you want."

"I'll take the golf," she snapped.

"What!? . . . okay." The homunculus grunted and disappeared into the ether.

Just as promised, her game steadily improved. Soon she was playing par, and shortly after, a couple of strokes below par. Her score after eighteen holes was in the mid-50s. She frequently shot holes-in-one and birdies. She never bogied, shanked, hooked, sliced or cut a divot. She was about to go on the Ladies Pro Golf Circuit, and was practicing for the Dinah Shore Desert Classic, when she was teeing off again on that same hole where she first encountered the golf sprite. Her stance was masterful. Her ball was Maxfly. Her pad was Maxi. She had a future rich in product endorsements, hers for the taking. As she gripped the leather club handle, her sinewy forearms flexed and pulled the chrome shaft back like a rope. She unloosed her backswing with a whip and smashed through the ball with a wicked whack. Her ball lifted high and sailed along the thermal drafts, then plunked down in some trees off to the right.

"Damn slice!" she hissed. She found her ball under the same log in the same rough, and knocked it for a better lie. "Two," she figured. And just as before the spirit of the golf course began to materialize.

"Hey, listen, I'm sorry. Usually I grant the wish and then split forever. But I had to come back," the golf leprechaun said.

"Am I getting my old handicap back?" the golfer wanted to know. "Will I beat Nancy Lopez in Palm Springs?" There was desperation in her voice.

"No, your wish is granted—except that last shot—I'm sorry. But I had to come back because no one's ever wished for a perfect golf game. Everybody wishes for sex." He looked her up and down, more and more closely. "What are you, a lesbian?" As he solidified, he looked like Bob Hope, only less than a foot high. "Is your sex life that great!?"

"Well . . . It is adequate," the lady golfer said.

"What's 'adequate'?" the miniature Bob Hope demanded.

"Two or three times a month," she trailed off.

The gnome started to laugh so hard his vapors condensed into big tears around his crinkled little eyes. "Two or three times a month . . . You *are* a lesbian!" His guffaw was a deep rumbling roto-rooter of a sound, a humiliating hardee-har-har that made the little animals of the forest sniff her disdainfully.

She thought he was an awful troll with a scratch handicap and perhaps a stepladder for schtupping. He kept squealing, "Two or three times a month!"

The lady golfer stiffened and adjusted her blazer, knocked a piece of sod off her cleats and regained her composure. She was after all the world's greatest golfer. "Two or three times a month is pretty good for a parish nun without a car," she said as she reached for her five iron.

Deborah Abbott, when not pursuing her favorite indoor sport, may be found in water, swimming, sea kayaking, or raft guiding. On land, in Santa Cruz, California, she tandem bicycles and works as a psychotherapist. Her poems and stories have appeared in many anthologies including *Lovers, With the Power of Each Breath: A Disabled Women's Anthology, Touching Fire: Erotic Writing by Women*, and in *Common Lives/Lesbian Lives* (Issue 43).

Donna Allegra writes poetry, fiction, and essays. A 1992 cowinner of the Pat Parker Memorial Poetry Prize, she has been published in *Sinister Wisdom, Conditions, Common Lives/Lesbian Lives, Heresies*, and *Aché*. She has been anthologized most recently in *Sister Stranger: Lesbians Loving Across the Lines, Woman in the Window—Tales of Desire, Passion and Love*, and *The Persistant Desire*. Her cultural journalism has appeared in *Gay Community News, Sojourner, Sappho's Isle, Tradeswomen*, and *Colorlife*.

Lucy Jane Bledsoe won a bronze medal for cycling in the 1990 Gay Games. Her fiction has appeared in *New York Newsday* (as a PEN Syndicated Fiction Project winner), *Northwest Literary Forum, Evergreen Chronicles, GirlJock*, and *Conditions*, and in several anthologies, including *Afterglow, Women on Women 2*, and *Tickled Pink*.

Nancy Boutilier has played, coached, and officiated basketball, yet she now maintains that the sportswriter is always right. Her collection of poetry and fiction, *According to Her Contours* (Black Sparrow Press), was a finalist for a 1993 Lambda Literary Award.

Victoria A. Brownworth is a syndicated columnist for the *Philadelphia Daily News*. She also writes a monthly column for *The Advocate*. Her work appears in numerous queer and mainstream publications, including the *Village Voice, Spin, Out*, and others. She is the author of four books, is a former basketball player, and currently lives with her partner, filmmaker Judith M. Redding, in Philadelphia with seven cats, a dog, and many articles of sporting equipment.

Maria Noell Goldberg's short fiction has appeared in the anthologies *Word of Mouth* and *American Fiction*. A recipient of a Henfield Transatlantic Review Award for Fiction and a grant from the New Jersey State Council on the Arts, she is completing a novel.

Pat Griffin is a forty-eight-year-old Associate Professor at the University of Massachusetts in Social Justice Education specializing in education about lesbians and homophobia in women's sports. She played high school and college varsity field hockey, basketball, and swimming during pre–Title IX days. She plays third base in a lesbian softball league in Northampton, Massachusetts.

Betty Hicks has taught, and published numerous articles, books, and scripts on aviation and golf. She has been flying since 1958 and has received many honors for her work in aviation education. It was in a freshman class in Long Beach, California, in 1937 that she began playing golf. Four years later, she won the USGA Women's National Amateur, and in 1944 won the All-American Open. In 1941 she was selected "Woman Athlete of the Year" by the Associated Press and in 1944 she became the first president of the Women's Professional Golfers Association (predecessor to the LPGA).

Joan Hilty was born in Kentucky, grew up in Northern California, and now lives in New York City. She has previously been a crew jock and a soccer jock, and now aspires to volleyball. Her comics have appeared in *The Advocate, GirlJock, Real Girl, Gay Comics, OH,* and *Sojourner.*

Michele Kort is a writer living in Venice, California, who has written about women's sports for the last sixteen years. She competed in basketball at UCLA pre–Title IX, then in a recreational league for many years. She received a Miller Lite Women's Sports Journalism Award in 1993.

Kris Kovick is an adult child of golf enthusiasts, living in San Francisco with a Labrador who retrieves her putts. She is the author of *What I Love About Lesbian Politics Is Arguing with People I Agree With* (Alyson).

Jenifer Levin lives and writes in New York City. She is the author of four novels: *Water Dancer* (Simon & Schuster), *Snow* (Simon & Schuster), *Shimoni's Lover* (Harcourt Brace Jovanovich), and *The Sea of Light* (Dutton). She has written for numerous publications, including *Rolling Stone, The Advocate,* and *The New York Times,* and has taught writing at the University of Michigan. A former U.S. masters swimmer, she has coached women's running and weight training, and is a slow but persistent runner. She is married to actress Julie DeLaurier, a magnificent 3:11 marathoner.

Laurie Ellen Liss was forgotten in the crib while her mother wept over John F. Kennedy. Although her head tells her otherwise, in her heart she subscribes to the "nurture" theory. She works as a literary agent in New York City.

Rachel Lurie is a lifelong butch who regularly beat the boys in all sports until about the seventh grade, when they refused to continue competing with her. A native New Yorker, she now makes her home outside of Burlington, Vermont. She covered the 1990 Gay Games in Vancouver for *The Village Voice* and continues to write on queer and gender-identity issues.

April Martin is a clinical psychologist working in New York City and is the author of *The Lesbian and Gay Parenting Handbook: Creating and Raising Our Families* (HarperCollins). She lives with Susan, her life partner of fifteen years, and their two children, Emily and Jesse. She trains about ten hours a week and belongs to the International Gay Figure Skating Union.

Kimberly Miller has been playing organized softball for twenty-seven years and writing about it for twenty-five. She likes to slide and score a lot.

Bonnie Morris is a Jewish lesbian writer and professor of women's history. In addition to her university teaching and academic work, she travels around the country performing one-woman political theater at colleges, women's music festivals, and feminist conferences. She has published essays and stories and is currently writing a screenplay.

Merril Mushroom lives in rural Tennessee and was a jacks champion as a child.

Mariah Burton Nelson is the author of *The Stronger Women Get, the More Men Love Football* (Harcourt Brace). Her first book, *Are We Winning Yet?: How Women Are Changing Sports and*

Sports Are Changing Women (Random House) won the Amateur Athletic Foundation's 1992 Book Award. She also ghost-wrote JoAnn Loulan's *Lesbian Passion*. At the first Gay Games she won two gold and two silver medals in swimming.

Lesléa Newman is a writer and editor with sixteen books to her credit including *Heather Has Two Mommies* (Alyson), *A Letter to Harvey Milk* (Firebrand), *In Every Laugh a Tear* (New Victoria), and *Writing from the Heart: Inspiration and Exercises for Women Who Want to Write* (Crossing Press). She has never played a team sport in her life, though she was one of the official scorekeepers for LaMix, one of sixteen teams of the Mary V. Womyn's Softball League in Northampton, Massachusetts. "Less Ugly" is taken from her latest short story collection, *Every Woman's Dream* (New Victoria Publishers).

Susan Fox Rogers has written on rock climbing for the *Village Voice*, *Climbing*, and the anthologies *Leading Out: Women Climbers Reaching for the Top* and *Sisters and Brothers*. She is the editor of *Another Wilderness: New Outdoor Writing by Women* (Seal Press).

Roxxie the sleepless is a devoted soccer player and editrix of *GirlJock*, the sporting magazine for the perpetual tomboy.

Harriet L. Schwartz lives in Pittsburgh, Pennsylvania, and has been playing hoops for fourteen years. She is also an up-and-coming rock drummer but will keep her day job in higher education until the right gig comes along. She has worked as a sports writer and has written on student leadership, student affairs, and ethics.

Louise Sloan is a native of Richmond, Virginia, and the black sheep of an athletic family. Her journalistic writing has appeared in *The Sacramento Bee*, *The Boston Phoenix*, *The Providence Phoenix*, *Frighten the Horses*, and *The San Francisco Bay Guardian*, where, as far as she knows, she was San Francisco's first openly lesbian columnist for a nongay newspaper. She now lives in Manhattan with cartoonist Joan Hilty, her partner of six years, and their dog, Ripley.

Alisa Solomon is a staff writer at the *Village Voice* where she writes news analysis, commentary, reportage, and criticism on such topics as the Middle East, feminist issues, city and national politics, gay and lesbian issues, and contemporary theater. The winner of journalism awards from the National Women's Political Caucus and the Women's Sports Foundation, she has also written for *The New York Times, New York Newsday, Glamour, Mirabella, Theater, American Theater,* and other publications. She is also an Assistant Professor of English/Journalism at Baruch College–City University of New York.

Robbi Sommers is the author of the bestselling erotica *Pleasures, Players, Kiss and Tell, Uncertain Companions, Behind Closed Doors,* and *Personal Ads*—all published by Naiad Press. Currently thigh-high in research for her next book, she often asks herself, "Is it hot in here or is it me?"

Jaye Zimet is a certified couch potato who designs books in her spare time. She has short hair and lives in Manhattan with her cats, Nora and Spooky.

Yvonne Zipter is the author of *Diamonds Are a Dyke's Best Friend* (Firebrand), and *The Patience of Metal* (Hutchinson House). She writes a syndicated column, "Inside Out." Currently, she and her girlfriend Kathy are "on leave" from softball. In the meantime, Yvonne continues to search for the perfect exercise routine.

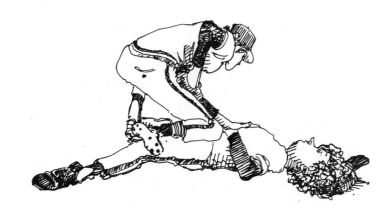